NETWORK+™
CERTIFICATION
FOR
DUMMIES®

by Ron Gilster

IDG BOOKS WORLDWIDE

IDG Books Worldwide, Inc.
An International Data Group Company

Foster City, CA ◆ Chicago, IL ◆ Indianapolis, IN ◆ New York, NY

Network+™ Certification For Dummies®

Published by
IDG Books Worldwide, Inc.
An International Data Group Company
919 E. Hillsdale Blvd.
Suite 400
Foster City, CA 94404
www.idgbooks.com (IDG Books Worldwide Web site)
www.dummies.com (Dummies Press Web site)

Library of Congress Catalog Card No.: 99-63207

ISBN: 0-7645-0545-9

Printed in the United States of America

10 9 8 7 6 5 4 3 2 1

1B/TQ/QX/ZZ/IN

Distributed in the United States by IDG Books Worldwide, Inc.

Distributed by CDG Books Canada Inc. for Canada; by Transworld Publishers Limited in the United Kingdom; by IDG Norge Books for Norway; by IDG Sweden Books for Sweden; by IDG Books Australia Publishing Corporation Pty. Ltd. for Australia and New Zealand; by TransQuest Publishers Pte Ltd. for Singapore, Malaysia, Thailand, Indonesia, and Hong Kong; by Gotop Information Inc. for Taiwan; by ICG Muse, Inc. for Japan; by Norma Comunicaciones S.A. for Colombia; by Intersoft for South Africa; by Eyrolles for France; by International Thomson Publishing for Germany, Austria and Switzerland; by Distribuidora Cuspide for Argentina; by Livraria Cultura for Brazil; by Ediciones ZETA S.C.R. Ltda. for Peru; by WS Computer Publishing Corporation, Inc., for the Philippines; by Contemporanea de Ediciones for Venezuela; by Express Computer Distributors for the Caribbean and West Indies; by Micronesia Media Distributor, Inc. for Micronesia; by Grupo Editorial Norma S.A. for Guatemala; by Chips Computadoras S.A. de C.V. for Mexico; by Editorial Norma de Panama S.A. for Panama; by American Bookshops for Finland. Authorized Sales Agent: Anthony Rudkin Associates for the Middle East and North Africa.

For general information on IDG Books Worldwide's books in the U.S., please call our Consumer Customer Service department at 800-762-2974. For reseller information, including discounts and premium sales, please call our Reseller Customer Service department at 800-434-3422.

For information on where to purchase IDG Books Worldwide's books outside the U.S., please contact our International Sales department at 317-596-5530 or fax 317-596-5692.

For consumer information on foreign language translations, please contact our Customer Service department at 1-800-434-3422, fax 317-596-5692, or e-mail rights@idgbooks.com.

For information on licensing foreign or domestic rights, please phone +1-650-655-3109.

For sales inquiries and special prices for bulk quantities, please contact our Sales department at 650-655-3200 or write to the address above.

For information on using IDG Books Worldwide's books in the classroom or for ordering examination copies, please contact our Educational Sales department at 800-434-2086 or fax 317-596-5499.

For press review copies, author interviews, or other publicity information, please contact our Public Relations department at 650-655-3000 or fax 650-655-3299.

For authorization to photocopy items for corporate, personal, or educational use, please contact Copyright Clearance Center, 222 Rosewood Drive, Danvers, MA 01923, or fax 978-750-4470.

Trademarks: All brand names and product names used in this book are trade names, service marks, trademarks, or registered trademarks of their respective owners. IDG Books Worldwide is not associated with any product or vendor mentioned in this book.

 is a registered trademark or trademark under exclusive license to IDG Books Worldwide, Inc. from International Data Group, Inc. in the United States and/or other countries.

Network+ Certification For Dummies®

Cheat Sheet

The OSI Reference Model

Layer	Name	Primary Activity
1	Physical	Moves data bits to and from the network media
2	Data Link	Manages communications, flow control, error checking, and addressing on a simple network
3	Network	Manages communications, addressing, routing, and delivery of packets on complex internetworks
4	Transport	Ensures delivery of a packet to its destination, performs connection services for the Network layer, and provides communications services for the upper OSI layers
5	Session	Manages simplex, half-duplex, and full-duplex dialogs between computers
6	Presentation	Ensures data passing from the Application or the Session layers are in the appropriate format
7	Application	Provides a consistent and neutral interface to the network and notifies the network of a computer's available resources

Phrases used to remember the OSI layers

Forward: Please Do Not Throw Salami Pizza Away

Backward: All People Seem To Need Data Processing

Common well-known port assignments

Port Number	Assignment
20	FTP data transfer
25	SMTP (Simple Mail Transfer Protocol)
53	DNS (Domain Name System)
80	HTTP (Hypertext Transfer Protocol)
110	POP3 (Post Office Protocol)

Cable media characteristics

Cable Media	Bandwidth	Max. Segment Length	Resistance to Interference
Thin coaxial (10Base2)	10 Mbps	185 meters	Good
Thick coaxial (10Base5)	10 Mbps	500 meters	Better
UTP (10BaseT)	10–100 Mbps	100 meters	Poor
STP	16–1,000 Mbps	100 meters	Fair to Good
Fiber-optic	100–10,000 Mbps	2,000 meters	Best

Network+ Certification For Dummies®

Cheat Sheet

IP address class ranges

Class	Address Range (hhh = host computer)
A	1.hhh.hhh.hhh to 126.hhh.hhh.hhh
B	128.0.hhh.hhh to 191.255.hhh.hhh
C	192.0.0.hhh to 223.255.255.hhh

Special IP addresses

Special IP Address	Usage or Meaning
0.0.0.0	This host
0.0.0.34	Host on this network
10.0.0.0 to 10.255.255.255	Internal networks and Intranets
127.0.0.1	Loopback testing
172.16.0.0 to 172.31.255.255	Internal networks and Intranets
192.168.0.0 to 192.168.255.255	Internal networks and Intranets
255.255.255.255	Broadcast to local network

Common subnet masks

IP Address Class	Subnet Mask
Class A	255.0.0.0
Class B	255.255.0.0
Class C	255.255.255.0

On test day . . .

At the testing workstation, but before the test begins, write down

- ✔ OSI Reference Model layers
- ✔ Cable media, segment lengths, and connectors
- ✔ Diagrams of topologies
- ✔ Class A, B, and C license ranges
- ✔ Default subnet masks

Routable and non-routable protocols

Protocol	Routable/ Nonroutable
AppleTalk	Routable
IP	Routable
IPX	Routable
NetBEUI	Nonroutable
SNA	Routable

RAID disk drive types

RAID 0: Striped disk array without fault tolerance.

RAID 3: Parallel transfer with parity.

RAID 5: Data striping with parity.

OSI Model layers of common network devices

Device Model Layer	OSI Reference
Bridge	Data Link Layer
Brouter	Data Link and Network Layers
Hub	Physical Layer
Repeater	Physical
Router	Network

Universal Naming Convention (UNC)

\\SERVER_NAME\SHARE_NAME or PATH

The IDG Books Worldwide logo is a registered trademark under exclusive license to IDG Books Worldwide, Inc., from International Data Group, Inc. The ...For Dummies logo is a trademark, and For Dummies and ...For Dummies are registered trademarks of IDG Books Worldwide, Inc. All other trademarks are the property of their respective owners.

...For Dummies®: Bestselling Book Series for Beginners

 ™

...For Dummies

BESTSELLING BOOK SERIES

Certification for the Rest of Us! ™

Are you intimidated and confused by computers? Do you find that traditional manuals are overloaded with technical details you'll never use? Do your friends and family always call you to fix simple problems on their PCs? Then the *...For Dummies®* computer book series from IDG Books Worldwide is for you.

...For Dummies books are written for those frustrated computer users who know they aren't really dumb but find that PC hardware, software, and indeed the unique vocabulary of computing make them feel helpless. *...For Dummies* books use a lighthearted approach, a down-to-earth style, and even cartoons and humorous icons to dispel computer novices' fears and build their confidence. Lighthearted but not lightweight, these books are a perfect survival guide for anyone forced to use a computer.

> *"I like my copy so much I told friends; now they bought copies."*
>
> **— Irene C., Orwell, Ohio**

> *"Quick, concise, nontechnical, and humorous."*
>
> **— Jay A., Elburn, Illinois**

> *"Thanks, I needed this book. Now I can sleep at night."*
>
> **— Robin F., British Columbia, Canada**

Already, millions of satisfied readers agree. They have made *...For Dummies* books the #1 introductory level computer book series and have written asking for more. So, if you're looking for the most fun and easy way to learn about computers, look to *...For Dummies* books to give you a helping hand.

IDG BOOKS WORLDWIDE ®

About the Author

Ron Gilster (Network+, A+, MBA, and AAGG) has been operating, programming, and repairing computers for more than 30 years, and networking them for more than 13 years. Ron has extensive experience in training, teaching, and consulting in computer-related areas, having spent more than 10 years as a college-level instructor in A+, CCNA, MCSE, and MOUS programs. His experience includes mainframes, minicomputers, and virtually every type of personal computer and operating system in use. In addition to a wide range of positions that have included systems programming supervisor, customer service manager, data processing manager, management information systems director, and vice president of operations in major corporations, Ron has served as a management consultant with both an international accounting firm and his own consulting firm. Ron is employed by HighSpeed.Com, a leading telecommunications company, where he manages the internal and external information technology and Layer 3 (networking) activities of the company.

He is the author of *A+ Certification For Dummies,* plus several books on computer and information literacy and programming.

ABOUT IDG BOOKS WORLDWIDE

Welcome to the world of IDG Books Worldwide.

IDG Books Worldwide, Inc., is a subsidiary of International Data Group, the world's largest publisher of computer-related information and the leading global provider of information services on information technology. IDG was founded more than 30 years ago by Patrick J. McGovern and now employs more than 9,000 people worldwide. IDG publishes more than 290 computer publications in over 75 countries. More than 90 million people read one or more IDG publications each month.

Launched in 1990, IDG Books Worldwide is today the #1 publisher of best-selling computer books in the United States. We are proud to have received eight awards from the Computer Press Association in recognition of editorial excellence and three from Computer Currents' First Annual Readers' Choice Awards. Our best-selling ...*For Dummies®* series has more than 50 million copies in print with translations in 31 languages. IDG Books Worldwide, through a joint venture with IDG's Hi-Tech Beijing, became the first U.S. publisher to publish a computer book in the People's Republic of China. In record time, IDG Books Worldwide has become the first choice for millions of readers around the world who want to learn how to better manage their businesses.

Our mission is simple: Every one of our books is designed to bring extra value and skill-building instructions to the reader. Our books are written by experts who understand and care about our readers. The knowledge base of our editorial staff comes from years of experience in publishing, education, and journalism — experience we use to produce books to carry us into the new millennium. In short, we care about books, so we attract the best people. We devote special attention to details such as audience, interior design, use of icons, and illustrations. And because we use an efficient process of authoring, editing, and desktop publishing our books electronically, we can spend more time ensuring superior content and less time on the technicalities of making books.

You can count on our commitment to deliver high-quality books at competitive prices on topics you want to read about. At IDG Books Worldwide, we continue in the IDG tradition of delivering quality for more than 30 years. You'll find no better book on a subject than one from IDG Books Worldwide.

John Kilcullen
Chairman and CEO
IDG Books Worldwide, Inc.

Steven Berkowitz
President and Publisher
IDG Books Worldwide, Inc.

Eighth Annual
Computer Press
Awards ≥1992

WINNER

Ninth Annual
Computer Press
Awards ≥1993

WINNER

Tenth Annual
Computer Press
Awards ≥1994

Eleventh Annual
Computer Press
Awards ≥1995

IDG is the world's leading IT media, research and exposition company. Founded in 1964, IDG had 1997 revenues of $2.05 billion and has more than 9,000 employees worldwide. IDG offers the widest range of media options that reach IT buyers in 75 countries representing 95% of worldwide IT spending. IDG's diverse product and services portfolio spans six key areas including print publishing, online publishing, expositions and conferences, market research, education and training, and global marketing services. More than 90 million people read one or more of IDG's 290 magazines and newspapers, including IDG's leading global brands — Computerworld, PC World, Network World, Macworld and the Channel World family of publications. IDG Books Worldwide is one of the fastest-growing computer book publishers in the world, with more than 700 titles in 36 languages. The "...For Dummies®" series alone has more than 50 million copies in print. IDG offers online users the largest network of technology-specific Web sites around the world through IDG.net (http://www.idg.net), which comprises more than 225 targeted Web sites in 55 countries worldwide. International Data Corporation (IDC) is the world's largest provider of information technology data, analysis and consulting, with research centers in over 41 countries and more than 400 research analysts worldwide. IDG World Expo is a leading producer of more than 168 globally branded conferences and expositions in 35 countries including E3 (Electronic Entertainment Expo), Macworld Expo, ComNet, Windows World Expo, ICE (Internet Commerce Expo), Agenda, DEMO, and Spotlight. IDG's training subsidiary, ExecuTrain, is the world's largest computer training company, with more than 230 locations worldwide and 785 training courses. IDG Marketing Services helps industry-leading IT companies build international brand recognition by developing global integrated marketing programs via IDG's print, online and exposition products worldwide. Further information about the company can be found at www.idg.com.   1/24/99

Dedication

To my loving, patient, and understanding family: Diane, Jeana, Rob, Kirstie, and Mimi.

Publisher's Acknowledgments

We're proud of this book; please register your comments through our IDG Books Worldwide Online Registration Form located at http://my2cents.dummies.com.

Some of the people who helped bring this book to market include the following:

Acquisitions, Editorial, and Media Development

Project Editor: Nate Holdread

Acquisitions Editor: Joyce Pepple

Copy Editors: Linda Stark, Kim Darosett

Technical Editor: Sento Training Corporation

Media Development Editor: Joell Smith

Associate Permissions Editor: Carmen Krikorian

Media Development Coordinator: Megan Roney

Editorial Manager: Leah P. Cameron

Media Development Manager: Heather Heath Dismore

Editorial Assistant: Beth Parlon

Production

Project Coordinator: Maridee Ennis

Layout and Graphics: Tom Emrich, Angela F. Hunckler, David McKelvey, Barry Offringa, Brent Savage, Janet Seib, Brian Torwelle, Dan Whetstine

Proofreaders: Rachel Garvey, Nancy Price, Marianne Santy

Indexer: C2 Editorial Services

Special Help

Publication Services, Stephanie Koutek, William Barton, James Russell

---

General and Administrative

IDG Books Worldwide, Inc.: John Kilcullen, CEO; Steven Berkowitz, President and Publisher

IDG Books Technology Publishing Group: Richard Swadley, Senior Vice President and Publisher; Walter Bruce III, Vice President and Associate Publisher; Steven Sayre, Associate Publisher; Joseph Wikert, Associate Publisher; Mary Bednarek, Branded Product Development Director; Mary Corder, Editorial Director

IDG Books Consumer Publishing Group: Roland Elgey, Senior Vice President and Publisher; Kathleen A. Welton, Vice President and Publisher; Kevin Thornton, Acquisitions Manager; Kristin A. Cocks, Editorial Director

IDG Books Internet Publishing Group: Brenda McLaughlin, Senior Vice President and Publisher; Diane Graves Steele, Vice President and Associate Publisher; Sofia Marchant, Online Marketing Manager

IDG Books Production for Dummies Press: Michael R. Britton, Vice President of Production; Debbie Stailey, Associate Director of Production; Cindy L. Phipps, Manager of Project Coordination, Production Proofreading, and Indexing; Shelley Lea, Supervisor of Graphics and Design; Debbie J. Gates, Production Systems Specialist; Robert Springer, Supervisor of Proofreading; Laura Carpenter, Production Control Manager; Tony Augsburger, Supervisor of Reprints and Bluelines

◆

The publisher would like to give special thanks to Patrick J. McGovern, without whom this book would not have been possible.

◆

Author's Acknowledgments

I would like to thank the wonderful folks at IDG Books who helped get this book published, especially Joyce Pepple, Sherri Morningstar, Linda Stark, Kim Darosett, Carmen Krikorian, and a special thanks to Nate Holdread, who once again saved my sanity. I would also like to thank the people at Sento Training Corporation for the excellent technical editing job they provided.

Contents at a Glance

Cartoons at a Glance

By Rich Tennant

page 9

page 37

page 121

page 193

page 253

page 289

page 327

page 375

page 389

Fax: 978-546-7747 • **E-mail:** the5wave@tiac.net

Table of Contents

Introduction

*I*f you have purchased or are considering purchasing this book, you probably fit one of the following categories:

- ✔ You know how very valuable Network+ certification is to a network technician's career and advancement.
- ✔ You're wondering just what Network+ Certification is all about.
- ✔ You think that reading this book may be a fun, entertaining way to learn about computer networks and their components.
- ✔ You love all *...For Dummies* books and wait impatiently for each new one to come out.
- ✔ You're a big fan of mine and can't wait to read my new book.

Well, if you fit any of the first four scenarios, this is the book for you! However, I'm not certified in the appropriate medical areas to help you if you chose the last category!

If you're already aware of the Network+ Certification program and are just looking for excellent study aids, you can skip the next few sections of this introduction in which I do my best to convince you that this is the book you are looking for, because your search is over. However, if you do not have the foggiest idea what Network+ Certification is or how to prepare for it, read on!

Why Use This Book?

Combining networks together to form networks began as simple affairs that allowed users to share resources. Fortunately for computer users (and unfortunately for anyone trying to learn all there is to know about networks), computer networks have become very complex affairs involving many different hardware and software technologies. As a result, even the most knowledgeable network technician needs some help getting ready for the Network+ exam. This book should help you to shorten your preparation time for the Network+ exam.

As with all other ...*For Dummies* books, this book is a no-nonsense reference and study guide. It focuses on the areas likely to be on the exam plus a little background information here and there to help you understand some of the more complex concepts and technologies. It presents the facts, concepts, processes, and applications included on the exams in step-by-step lists, tables, and figures without long explanations. The focus is on preparing you for the Network+ exams, not on my obviously extensive and impressive knowledge of network technology (nor on my modesty, I might add).

In developing this book, I have made two groups of assumptions:

- ✔ You have a working knowledge of electronics, computers, software, networking, and troubleshooting procedures and are looking for a review and study guide for the exam.
- ✔ You have limited knowledge of electronics, computers, software, the OSI model, network protocols, network operating systems, networking devices, and cabling and could use a little refresher on the basics along with a review and study guide for the exams.

If my assumptions in either case suit your needs, then this is the book for you.

Using This Book

This book is organized so that you can study a specific area without wading through stuff you may already know. I recommend that you skim the whole book at least once, noting the points raised at the icons. For your last minute cram before the exam, each part and chapter of the book is independent and can be studied in any order without confusing yourself.

Each chapter also includes a pre-test (Quick Assessment quiz) and post-test (Prep Test questions) to help you determine where your knowledge is weak and where you need to continue studying. The following sections tell you what I've included between the covers of this book.

Part I: About the Network+ Examination

Part I provides you with some general information about taking the exam and an overview of the topic areas you should study for the Network+ test. This includes an overview of the Network+ exam and its objectives and benefits, how to arrange to take the test, and some general tips on what to study and how to get ready for the test.

Part II: The Basics of Networking Technology

Part II provides you with the networking fundamentals and background information you should know to be successful on the Network+ exam. This includes definitions of common network components, media, network operating systems, topologies, protocols, and other terminologies and how each relates to network operation.

Part III: The Layers of the OSI Model

The OSI (Open Systems Interconnection) Reference Model forms the foundation on which nearly all networking is built. After you know everything you need to know about networking basics, you need to know about the layers of the OSI Model and how each relates and supports the process of transferring data across a network or between networks.

Part IV: Working with TCP/IP

Part IV has everything you need to know about the protocols and utilities to use for transferring data to and from local and wide area networks using the TCP/IP (Transmission Control Protocol/Internet Protocol) protocol suite. The Network+ exam can be generally described as measuring a technician's ability to install a TCP/IP client on a network. To prove you know how to do so requires that you know and understand the protocols and utilities of the TCP/IP protocol suite.

Part V: Remote Connectivity and Security

As its name implies, this part of the book covers the protocols, processes, and practices used to set up a computer for remote connectivity as well as setting up a security system that lets the good people in while keeping the bad people out.

Part VI: Networking Management

This part covers the myriad responsibilites, duties, and tasks that must be carried out by the network administrator to keep the network functioning properly. Also included are the steps used to install a network, protect it from the environment (both natural and man-made), and all of the mundane stuff network administrators must do on a regular basis to maintain the integrity and relibablity of the network, such as backups, documentations, and record-keeping.

Part VII: Maintaining and Supporting the Network

Over 16 percent of the Network+ exam is devoted to the practices, procedures, and tools used to maintain, support, and troubleshoot a network. This includes information on backup procedures, antivirus software, installing vendor patches and updates, troubleshooting procedures, and when and how certain troubleshooting tools are used.

Part VIII: The Part of Tens

This section provides additional motivation and study guides to help get you ready for the test, with advice about how to be sure that you're ready to take the test on Test Day and ten great Web sites where you can find study aids.

Part IX: Appendixes

This section gives you even more practice test questions, with ten sample test questions on each domain, as well as information about what's on the CD in the back of this book and how to use the CD.

CD-ROM

The CD-ROM included in this book contains a variety of study aids and practice tests to help you prepare for the Network+ exam. In addition, the QuickLearn game is on the CD-ROM to provide you with an easy, fun way to study. A few links to the Web sites of companies with training sites and sample copies of their wares are also on the CD.

Studying Chapters

Network+ Certification For Dummies is a self-paced method of preparing for the exam. You don't have to guess what to study; every chapter that covers exam objectives guides you with

✔ Preview questions

✔ Detailed coverage

✔ Review questions

This step-by-step structure identifies what you need to study, gives you all the facts, and rechecks what you know. Here's how it works.

First page

Each chapter starts with a preview of what's to come, including

✔ Exam objectives

✔ Study subjects

Not sure that you know all about the objectives and the subjects in a chapter? Keep going.

Quick Assessment questions

At the beginning of each chapter, you find a brief self-assessment test that helps you gauge your current knowledge of the topics that chapter covers. Take this test to determine which areas you already understand, as well as to determine the areas that you need to focus on most.

✔ If you're in a hurry, just study the sections for the questions you answered incorrectly.

✔ If you answered every question correctly, jump to the end of the chapter and try the practice exam questions to double-check your knowledge.

Study subjects

When you're studying a chapter, carefully read through it just like any book. Each subject is introduced — very briefly — and then you discover what you need to know for the exam.

As you study, special features show you how to apply everything in the chapter to the exam.

Labs

Labs are included throughout the book to step you through some of the processes you need to know for the exam, such as installation or configuration of a particular component. Here is an example of a lab included later in the book:

Lab 15-1   Setting Up a Modem Connection

1. **To set up the modem, use the Modem Installation Wizard, which you access from the Windows Control Panel and the Modems icon. The window that opens is the Modems Properties dialog box. To start the Modem Installation Wizard, click the Add button on the Modem Properties window.**

   You have the choice of letting the Wizard detect the new modem (assuming that you've already installed the modem into an expansion slot or connected it to a serial port) or picking the modem from the list of supported modems (my recommendation).

2. **On most newer systems, a modem is standard equipment and already installed and configured. In this case, check its configuration settings by clicking the Properties button on the Modems Properties window.**

3. **Configure a dial-up destination by clicking the Dial-Up Networking icon on the My Computer window. The My Computer window is opened from the My Computer icon on the Windows Desktop.**

   On the Dial-Up Networking window, you should see a New Connection icon and possibly some existing connections.

4. **Click the New Connection icon to open the Make New Connection Wizard, which guides you through the creation of a new dial-up remote connection.**

Tables

Sometimes, you need just the facts. In such cases, tables are a simple way to present everything at a glance, like:

Table 7-1	The Hardware at Each OSI Model Layer
OSI Layer	*Device(s)*
Physical	NIC, cable and transmission media, repeater, and hub
Data Link	Bridge and switch
Network	Router, brouter
Transport	Gateway
Upper Layers	Gateway

Prep Tests

The prep tests at the end of each chapter gauge your understanding of the entire chapter's content. These prep test questions are structured in the same manner as those you may see on your exam, so be sure to try your hand at these sample questions. If you have difficulties with any questions on the prep test, review the corresponding section within the chapter.

Icons Used in This Book

 Time Shaver icons point out tips that can help you manage and save time while studying or taking the exam.

 Instant Answer icons highlight information to help you recognize correct and incorrect exam answers.

 Remember icons point out general information and subjects that you should know and understand for the test. While the information may not appear directly on the exam, it provides you with information you need to identify the correct response.

 Tip icons flag information that can come in extra-handy during the testing process. You may want to take notes on these tidbits!

Feedback

I'd like to hear from you. If an area of the test isn't covered as well as it should be, or if I've provided more coverage than you think is warranted about a particular topic, please let me know. Your feedback is solicited and welcome. You can send e-mail to me at `rgilster@innw.net`.

Part I

About the Network+ Examination

The 5th Wave   By Rich Tennant

BEING NETWORK+ CERTIFIED GAVE PHIL A KNOWLEDGE OF NETWORKING TECHNOLOGY, NETWORKING PRACTICES, AND NETWORKING VOODOO

In this part . . .

You've decided to become Network+ certified and let the world know how much you know about networking. So where do you start? In this part of the book, I give you the particulars about the test, such as how to schedule the test, where to go, and what to do.

The Network+ exam does not include questions on everything there is to know about installing, administering, and maintaining networks, but it does cover most of this. The exam doesn't ask you specifically about bits and bytes, basic electronics, electricity, number systems, or the use of basic tools, such as screwdrivers and other hardware-related tools. The Network+ exam assumes you know this stuff, or you wouldn't be working (or trying to be working) as a network technician, or preparing to take the Network+ exam.

Before you begin preparing for the test, use this part of the book to learn about the tests and to review some of the basic and underlying knowledge you need for the exams.

Chapter 1

The Network+ Certification Examination

CompTIA, the A+ certification outfit, has a new certification program for the hard-working network technician with an excellent general knowledge of networks and internetworking technologies — the Network+ certification.

Unlike A+ certification, which provides you with the official title of CompTIA Certified Computer Technician, the Network+ certification goes by no other name. The exam label was formerly IT (Information Technology) Skills, but the testing program is now officially known as the Network+ Certification. Passing the Network+ exam certifies to the world that a technician possesses the knowledge required to configure and install TCP/IP clients.

Unlike other networking certifications, such as MCSE (Microsoft Certified Systems Engineer), CNE (Certified Novell Engineer), or CCNA (Cisco Certified Networking Associate) certifications, Network+ covers all kinds of general network technology knowledge and practices instead of revolving around just the brand-specific stuff. Microsoft, Novell, Cisco, and other manufacturers and their products are included on the Network+ test, making it the true measure of a networking technician's overall grasp of networking and internetworking technology.

Checking Out What the Network+ Exam Covers

The Network+ exam is the result of an industrywide analysis of a networking technician's storehouse of skills and knowledge after 18 to 24 months of on-the-job experience. The final test, the one published on April 30, 1999, reflects the culmination of over three years of skill set and test development by the IT Skills Project task force.

The Network+ exam consists of 65 questions that cover two general areas of networking technology knowledge: Knowledge of Networking Technology and Knowledge of Networking Practices. These two knowledge areas are broken down into specific knowledge areas, as shown in Table 1-1. Some of these areas are emphasized more than others, and the number of questions in any one area varies with its emphasis.

Table 1-1 lists and describes the two major knowledge areas of the Network+ exam, the topics within each major area, and the percentage (and number of questions) that each area represents on the total test.

Table 1-1		Network+ Knowledge Areas	
Area	*Percentage of Test*	*Number of Questions*	*Content*
Knowledge of Networking Technology	*77%*	*50*	
Basic Knowledge	18%	12	Basic network terminology and knowledge of networking elements, including protocols, media, connectors, structure, fault tolerance, OSI model, topologies, segments, and backbones
Physical Layer	6%	4	Networking hardware at the OSI physical layer including installation, configuration, or troubleshooting of network interface cards (NICs), hubs, switches, transceivers, MAUs, and repeaters

Area	Percentage of Test	Number of Questions	Content
Knowledge of Networking Technology	*77%*	*50*	
Data Link Layer	5%	3	Bridges, IEEE 802 standards, and the use of MAC addresses at the Data Link layer of the OSI Model
Network Layer	5%	3	Routers and routing, brouters, gateways, and subnetworks
Transport Layer	5%	3	Connectionless and connection-based transports and name resolution
TCP/IP Fundamentals	17%	11	Elements of basic TCP/IP operations, including IP default gateways, DHCP, DNS, WINS, TCP/IP protocols, A, B, and C class IP addresses, default subnet mask numbers, port number assignments, the purpose and use of an IP proxy, and workstation client configuration
TCP/IP Utilities	11%	7	Common TCP/IP utilities to test, validate, and troubleshoot IP connectivity
Remote Connectivity	5%	3	Remote connectivity principles and concepts, including PPP, SLIP, PPTP, ISDN, PSTN (POTS), dial-up networking, modem configuration, and the requirements for a remote connection

(continued)

Table 1-1 *(continued)*

Area	Percentage of Test	Number of Questions	Content
Security	6%	4	Security models (user- and share-level), standard password procedures, data encryption, and the use of a firewall
Knowledge of Networking Practices	*23%*	*15*	
Implementing the Installation of the Network	6%	4	Network planning processes, including the identification of network elements and environmental factors that must be identified prior to network implementation
Maintaining and Supporting the Network	6%	4	Network maintenance and support issues, including standard backup procedures and media storage practices, periodic software patches and fixes, and the use of anti-virus software
Troubleshooting the Network	11%	7	The use of a systematic approach to identifying the source and extent of a network problem, and the application of the appropriate procedures, tools, and utilities to troubleshoot, diagnose, and resolve the problem

The format of the Network+ exam is a hybrid of the formats used for the A+ exam and the MCSE-style exams. You can expect to see predominantly multiple-choice questions. The really nice thing about this test is that you don't have to worry about not giving all of the correct answers on multiple right answer questions. There are no "Choose All That Apply" questions. Any question that has more than one correct answer has two tip-offs. The first is that instead of a round button beside each answer choice, there is a square box. The second tip-off is that at the bottom left-corner of the screen, you are told the exact number of answers expected. In fact, when you finish answering the exam questions, any that you have not given enough answers for are highlighted as incomplete. Many of the Required-Objective/Optional-Objective scenario questions common to MCSE exams also show up, and a few questions ask you to mark components and network types on electronic illustrations.

Counting up the questions

The Network+ exam has 65 questions for you to tackle in 90 minutes. If you choose to do the optional test tutorial that can orient you to the various question types you're about to encounter, this time does not count against the one and one-half hour time limit. Your actual testing time does not begin until you click the Start button for the test. You really do have plenty of time for the test and another look at questions you mark for review as you proceed through the test. I recommend that you use the Item Review feature that's built in the test engine, pacing yourself to allow some time at the end of the exam for another look at any questionable answers or unanswered questions (although a guess is better than no response at all, because you may not get a chance to review everything you marked).

To become Network+ certified, you have to score at least a 68 percent on the examination. Like all CompTIA tests, you know immediately how you did. After you completely signoff and exit the test engine, the test center administrator has a printout of your results waiting for you. The Score Report is a standardized format that shows you both a Gantt chart and a section by section breakdown of how you did. The Gantt chart shows your score represented as a bar plotted against a bar of the Required Score to pass the exam. Below that you get a Section Analysis that shows for each section how many questions were on the test and how many you answered correctly. For any sections in which you answered incorrectly, the blueprint summary is printed.

Although the exam blueprint is divided into two distinct sections, the questions on the test are not. Questions from both sections and all topics are intermixed throughout the test.

Picking from multiple choices

The general format of the majority of the questions is multiple choice. Some of the multiple-choice questions ask for a single answer (those with option buttons), and others require two, three, or even more answers (those with check boxes). Before you read a question, look at the lower-left corner of the screen to see how many answers are needed. If a question instructs you to "Choose Two Answers" on a multiple-choice question, you need to choose two (no more, no less) correct choices to get credit for the answer. No partial credit allowed! Be sure you look at the Item Review function at the end of the test and review any marked as Incomplete. With all of the help the exam is giving you, it would be a real shame for you to exit the test with incomplete answers left behind.

Responding to a scenario

A favorite question format on the MCSE (Microsoft Certified Systems Engineer) exams is the scenario-based question. The following is an example of this type of question:

A company has decided to install a network and link every employee's desktop computer to it. The plan is to provide desktop interactive video teleconferencing, e-mail, and client/server applications on the network. The company wants the network to provide adequate bandwidth and to be as fast as possible.

Required Result: The network must support data transmission speeds of 100 Mbps.

Optional Desired Results: The installation of the network, including transmission media, should be as inexpensive as possible. As the network technician and administrator, you want the installation to be as easy as possible.

Proposed Solution: A consultant has recommended that an Ethernet network with Category 5 UTP and hubs used to connect the network's workstations be implemented.

A ◯ The proposed solution delivers the required result only.

B ◯ The proposed solution delivers the required result and only one of the optional results.

C ◯ The proposed solution delivers the required result and all of the optional results.

D ◯ The proposed solution delivers only the optional results.

The correct response for this question is C — the proposed solution delivers the required result and all of the optional results.

You can expect to see one or two scenario-based questions on the Network+ exam, especially when the subject relates to knowledge of networking practices. Carefully read each of these questions and then test each of the required and optional results in a true or false manner. You may even want to jot down a few notes about the situation as you read on the paper or plastic that you are provided by the test administrator to help you gather the facts. Apply these results to the multiple-choice options given. The key to answering these questions, of course, is to know the technology and its applications.

Enjoying just two options — true and false

You can count on a few true or false questions on the test. These questions are straightforward and are not likely to trip you up, if you know the targeted subject well. They are tricky only if you have to guess — you can't uncover any hints in this type of question.

Drawing on your knowledge

You may encounter a question that asks you to mark items on illustrations with a crosshair-looking cursor. You use this icon, which looks something like the one shown in Figure 1-1, to pick which part of a network diagram includes a repeater, or to locate a bus topology, or to hone in on a network segment.

Figure 1-1:
The crosshair icon used to mark answers on illustrated questions.

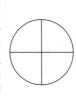

Serving no long sentences

Worry not: You're not going to face long questions. Other than the situational analysis questions, which have some reading involved, nearly all of the questions are short and to the point. Most are one or two sentences with the longer questions having one paragraph of two to four sentences.

CompTIA makes no attempt to trick you or mislead you with unnecessary information. The Network+ exam is designed to give you the best possible chance of passing, provided you know your stuff.

Working a Study Plan

Knowing your stuff is the key to passing the Network+ exam. So, how do you make sure that you're ready and able to give certification your best shot? Use the questions in this book or on a test simulator to determine the parts of the test that you need to study, which is not to say that you can ignore completely any of the topics on the test, but you need to focus on those areas where you need to improve your knowledge.

At the beginning and end of each chapter in this book, you can find a Quick Assessment quiz and a Prep Test, respectively, that cover the topics in the chapter. Many commercially available test simulators are available in the certification marketplace. I include URLs for some of the better ones in Chapters 1 and 24 (some are even free!).

Go through this book and mark the pages that have lists, tables, and diagrams. It's a fact of certification life that certain information requires memorization. The maximum distance for a thinnet cable, the number of bits in a subnet mask, or the address range for a Class B network are typical answers that you cannot figure out from the data in the question. You have to know this stuff inside and out. Begin committing this information to memory as soon as you can — and remember to refresh your quick recall regularly.

Allocate time right before the test for systematic — and calm — review. Look over your notes, lists, tables, and diagrams at least twice. Finish by reviewing all the lists that you memorized. Allow yourself time to focus and remain relaxed. Take as many deep breaths as necessary, but keep cool.

You are not allowed to take any paper, notes, books, computers, virtual reality goggles, or the like into the test area. You will be given a sheet of plastic on a clipboard and a grease pen, or a sheet of paper and a pencil to use during the test. When you take your assigned seat at the testing center, use the plastic or paper you are given to quickly brain-dump all of your memorized lists and acronyms. This creates a legal cheatsheet for reference during the test.

If you haven't taken a Sylvan Prometric or Virtual University exam before, use the pre-test tutorial to acquaint yourself with its operation, but don't dilly-dally, it is likely that your short-term memory is expiring.

Practice makes passing

The best place to begin is right in your hands! Use the quizzes, tests, lists, acronyms, and tables in this book to prepare for the memorized portions of the test, and then read through individual topics to shore up your understanding of concepts and principles. This book is unorganized just enough to allow you to wander through it studying only those areas in which you need help. Of course, you can read it front to back, if you like. There are no set rules here.

Keep yourself focused on the topics that I identify as being on the test and avoid studying any new technologies that debut within the six-month period before the release of the exam. The brand-new, cutting-edge stuff won't be on the test – guaranteed.

You may want to use other resources as well. Sometimes, a slightly different explanation or approach to a subject can bring the material into sharper focus. The CompTIA Web site (www.comptia.org) lists a number of companies offering study aids and practice tests. Practice tests and test simulators can be good measurements of whether you are ready or not. If you can consistently pass the practice exams (with the answers hidden from your view), you're probably well-prepared. Many practice tests are actually much more difficult than the actual test anyway.

The benefits you enjoy from Network+ certification are well worth the time you invest in passing the test. Whatever method you use to prepare for the test, create a plan and then stick to it. Give yourself ample time to truly understand the material, instead of relying purely on memorization. If you can grasp the concepts behind the details, the facts may start to make some sense.

Here are a few tips to consider as you prepare for the test:

- ✔ Focus on the exam blueprint, which lays out the full landscape of test coverage. CompTIA is very good at staying within the boundaries established by the exam objectives; you can access the full blueprint at www.comptia.org/networkplus/html/exam.html.

- ✔ Use the Quick Assessments, Prep Tests, and sample exam questions throughout this book and on the accompanying CD, as well as any other practice tests to which you have access. You can't take too many practice tests.

- ✔ Take occasional short breaks, a day or two, from studying. You can overdo the intensity and burn out. This test is very important, but it is not a life and death thing. Keep your perspective.

How much studying is enough, anyway?

It all depends on you. Gilster's Law of Test Preparation says: You never can tell, and it all depends. You never can tell how much preparation you will need, and it depends on your experience, your education, and so on. Seasoned veterans of the networking wars may need only to catch up on the very latest stuff, and someone just starting out in network technology may have a much greater challenge getting ready for the exam.

You need to find the tools that work best for you. If you have a good deal of experience in networking, you may only need to bone up in certain areas. If you are new to networking, you should seek out as many sample tests as possible and keep taking them until you pass consistently. There are a number of interactive study aids available, some for purchase and some free to download.

Because someone (probably you!) is investing real money for you to take this test, I suggest erring on the side of too much studying, if that is possible. If you are intent on passing, make your goal to pass the first time (unless you can afford to take the test just to find out what you should study). All I can say to that is, "this book is much less expensive than the test, and I tell you what to study." But, then again, it's your money! Any excess funds that are burning a crater in your pocket, kindly send to me in care of IDG Books Worldwide, Inc.

Each chapter of this book contains tables and bulleted lists of the items you need to commit to memory for the test. Use these for general study as well as a last-minute review. Use the questions at the end of each chapter to test your general knowledge of the chapter contents and when necessary, review the section referenced in the answer for additional study. Sample test questions are also available in Appendix A and on the CD. In every case, where you can find more information on an answer in the book is listed.

Scheduling the Test

An important move toward grabbing that golden ring of certification (after repeating right out loud — with feeling — "I think I can, I think I can . . .") involves registration through Sylvan Prometric. To schedule an exam, call Sylvan Prometric at 1-888-895-6116. If your company is a member of CompTIA, you can register for the Network+ test via Internet Registration at www.2test.com. Otherwise, you need to call to register for the test.

Be ready with credit card information or plan to mail a check for the registration fee (not a great option if you're in a hurry). Call as much as six weeks in advance, but at least two days before your desired test date. The friendly and knowledgeable counselor can help you not only set a date and time, but also pick a testing center near your home — or close to the vacation spot where you'll celebrate after the exam. Sylvan has more than 2,000 locations in 105 countries worldwide, so it shouldn't be too hard finding one near you.

I recommend contacting the testing service as soon as you think you are entering the final phases of your preparation for the exam. Some sites are not available every day of the week, and some have only certain hours of the day available. So the earlier you contact them, the better.

Paying the Price

The cost of the Network+ exam is $185 in United States dollars or $135 if you or your company is a member of CompTIA. If you can round up about 50 or so of your friends or co-workers to take the test, the price can be even lower.

Sylvan Prometric welcomes all generally accepted credit cards. You may make other payment arrangements with the testing folks, such as paying by check or money order, but before you can take the test, you must be paid in full.

Seeking Help Via the World Wide Web

Here are some URLs that have either free information, sample tests, or products to help you prepare for the Network+ exam:

AMSI.org: `www.amsi.org/networkplus/`

CompTIA: `www.comptia.org`

CramSession: `www.cramsession.com/cramsession/aplus/network/`

Dali Design: `www.networkpluscertify.com/`

Marcraft International: `www.mic-inc.com/nplus`

Self-Test: `www.selftest.co.uk/networkplus`

Wave Technologies: `www.wavetech.com`

You can find more information about each of these sites, plus a few more sites, in Chapter 24.

Chapter 2

The Network+ Exam and Some Basic Terminology

*A*s I see it, four groups of people are likely candidates for braving the Network+ exam:

- ✔ A+ certified service technicians. (You don't need A+ certification for the Network+ test, although it is a natural next step, and certainly can't hurt.)

- ✔ Experienced network technicians looking to add more letters to their résumés.

- ✔ Experienced network technicians certifying their knowledge to meet an employer's minimum requirements.

- ✔ Technicians fresh out of training programs, schools, or colleges looking for job-seeking credentials.

If you have ten years of internetworking experience and can fieldstrip a router blindfolded in less than one minute, then maybe — just maybe — you have a good chance of passing the Network+ exam without studying. Remember that this test covers networks from soup to nuts, including all the stuff you have never quite got around to learning. On the other hand, if you are coming straight out of school and want to establish your job-seeking credentials, Network+ can put you head and shoulders above the feeding frenzy for entry-level jobs in networking.

This chapter has two distinct parts: an outline of the exam blueprint, and a review of common (meaning commonly used on the test) networking and communications terminology and concepts. The first part is intended to help you plan your studies and the second part is provided to give you a foundation in the essential terms and concepts you find on the exam.

How much you need to study is directly related to the length and breadth of your experience. Whether you're a veteran of the network service or an anxious neophyte, you need to review what's on the test and study the areas in which your experience or knowledge is less than perfect.

Reading the Blueprint

Just like building a house, preparing for the Network+ exam requires a blueprint. CompTIA developed a blueprint for the Network+ exam early in the development stages of the test. Like the technical domains outlined for the A+ exam, the Network+ blueprint is your guide to the areas you need to study for the exam.

Tables 2-1 and 2-2 contain summaries of the networking technology and practices that are included in each emphasis area. These tables also list the chapter in which you can find information on each area to help you plan your studies.

Table 2-1	Knowledge of Networking Technology Emphasis Areas	
Emphasis Area	*Description*	*Chapter(s) for Review*
Basic Knowledge	Basic network terminology and knowledge of networking elements	Chapters 3, 4, 5, 6, and 7
Physical Layer	Networking hardware at the OSI Physical layer	Chapter 8
Data Link Layer	Bridges, IEEE 802 standards, and the use of MAC addresses	Chapter 9
Network Layer	Routers and routing, brouters, gateways, and subnetworks	Chapter 10
Transport Layer	Connectionless and connection-oriented transports and name resolution	Chapter 11
TCP/IP Fundamentals	Elements of basic TCP/IP operations	Chapters 12 and 13

Emphasis Area	Description	Chapter(s) for Review
TCP/IP Utilities	How and when TCP/IP utilities are used	Chapter 14
Remote Connectivity	Remote connectivity principles and concepts	Chapter 15
Security	Security models, password procedures, data encryption, and firewalls	Chapter 16

Table 2-2   Knowledge of Networking Practices Emphasis Areas

Emphasis Area	Description	Chapter(s) for Review
Implementing the Installation of the Network	Network planning and implementation processes	Chapters 4, 17, and 18
Administering the Change Control System	Network administration as affected by changes applied to the network	Chapter 19
Maintaining and Supporting the Network	Network maintenance and support issues	Chapter 20
Identifying, Assessing, and Responding to Problems	The appropriate priority, type, and action for network problems	Chapters 20 and 21
Troubleshooting the Network	Identifying a network problem and using the application of the appropriate procedures, tools, and utilities in troubleshooting, diagnosing, and resolving the problem	Chapters 21 and 22

I organized this book to match the sequence and content of the Network+ blueprint — hey, I want to make it easy for you to plan your studies. You may also want to use the blueprint as a checklist right before you take the test.

The following sections provide you with a little more detail on each of the emphasis areas listed. For the sake of space, I offer you a whole bunch of acronyms and mnemonics with this list. Fear not: I define and explain each of these abbreviations and techno-names later in this and other chapters.

The foundation stuff

The questions that measure your basic knowledge of networking form 16 percent of the total test, the largest single group of questions on the exam. These questions measure the following:

- ✔ **Your understanding of basic network structure:** star, bus, mesh, and ring topologies, their characteristics, advantages, and disadvantages, and the characteristics of network segments and backbones.

- ✔ **Your ability to identify major network operating systems (NOS):** Microsoft Windows NT, Novell NetWare, and UNIX, their clients, and NOS directory services.

- ✔ **Your ability to associate network protocols with their functions:** IPX, IP, and NetBEUI.

- ✔ **Your ability to define fault tolerance and high availability concepts and terminology:** mirroring, duplexing, stripping (with and without parity), volumes, and tape backup.

- ✔ **Your ability to define the OSI Model's layers:** identifying the protocols, services, and functions that operate at each layer.

- ✔ **Your ability to recognize and describe the characteristics of networking media and connectors.**

Peeling away the OSI layers

Questions relating to the OSI Model comprise twenty percent of the test, a significant portion of the test. The questions on the layers of the OSI measure the following:

- ✔ **Physical layer**
  - Your ability to identify the differences and usage of Physical layer network components, including hubs, MAUs, switching hubs, repeaters, and transceivers
  - Your ability to apply and explain your knowledge in selecting an appropriate course of action when a network interface card fails on installation or replacement

- ✔ **Data Link layer**
  - Your knowledge of bridges, what they are, and how and why they are used
  - Your knowledge and understanding of the IEEE Project 802 specifications

- • Your knowledge of the function and characteristics of MAC addresses

✔ **Network layer**

- • Your ability to explain routing and network layer concepts

✔ **Transport layer**

- • Your knowlege of the distinction between connectionless and connection-oriented transports

- • Your understanding of the reason for and activity of name resolution

Understanding TCP/IP fundamentals

This is the key emphasis area on the test, which is why it provides 28 percent of the questions. The questions from this area expect you to demonstrate your knowledge of the following:

✔ TCP/IP operations

✔ TCP/IP addressing

✔ TCP/IP configuration

✔ TCP/IP utilities

Remotely connecting to a network

This area of the exam accounts for only five percent of the test and deals with the concepts, protocols, advantages and disadvantages, and configuration of remote connectivity tools. Be prepared to show that you can connect using the following:

✔ Point-to-point protocols and carrier types

✔ Dial-up networking

Keeping it secure

Don't be fooled by the fact that only six percent of the test is dedicated to security issues — the subject of network security pops up in several other areas of the test. The questions in the security-specific exam area require you to identify the good practices that ensure network security, including the following:

✔ Security models (user level and share level)

✔ Standard password practices and procedures

✔ Data encryption

✔ Firewalls

Implementing and installing the network

This is the first of the three areas that measure your knowledge of networking administration and management practices. The questions in these areas are based on scenarios and situations, and require you to apply your understanding of the procedures, processes, practices, and tools commonly used by network administrators. This area, with its double-action name, represents six percent of the test and asks you to demonstrate your knowledge of these points:

✔ Administrative actions prior to network implementation

✔ The impact of environmental factors on computer networks

✔ The identity of common peripheral ports and common network components from illustrations or descriptions

✔ Compatibility and cabling issues

Keeping the network running

This area of emphasis, which accounts for six percent of the exam questions, focuses on the actions used by a network administrator to keep network software and hardware versions current and to ensure the integrity of the system and its resources. The questions from this area measure your knowledge of these two support and maintenance activities:

✔ Test documentation available to support vendor patches, fixes, upgrades, and so on.

✔ Standard operational and administrative practices.

Looking for trouble

This is the last emphasis area of the exam, but hardly the least. In fact, it is a close third, with 11 percent of the test, to just two larger areas (basic knowledge and TCP/IP fundamentals) on the exam. You need to know the following to do well in this area:

✔ The steps that make up a systematic approach to identifying network problems and the choice of the best next action step.

- The use of physical and logical error and trouble indicators

- Common network troubleshooting resources

- The symptoms and causes of common problems

- The tools commonly used to isolate and resolve network equipment problems

✔ The appropriate tools used to resolve network problems.

I love It When You Talk Network!

Here are some network terms, and their definitions, that you really should know before starting your preparation for the Network+ exam. These terms and their meanings help you build the basic foundation of knowledge you need before tackling more specific networking concepts and practices. Each of the concepts, terms, processes, procedures, and actions that I introduce in this chapter shows up again in other chapters of the book, and that's where I provide a full explanation for your study pleasure.

After you study the material in each section, use the bulleted lists and tables for a quick hop, skip, and jump through each topic area. If you find an item that you're not completely comfortable with, concentrate your review on that section.

Servers, workstations, nodes, and cables

The three most basic elements of any network are servers, workstations and other network nodes, and cabling used to connect them all together. Here's what each piece of the puzzle adds up to:

✔ **Cable:** The physical medium over which information is transmitted between nodes in a network. The five main types of cable used in networking are coaxial, shielded twisted pair (also referred to as just twisted pair), unshielded twisted pair, IBM, and fiber optic.

✔ **Server:** A network computer from which workstations (clients) access and share files, printing, communications, and other services. Servers can be dedicated to a single service, such as file servers, print servers, application servers, Web servers, and so on.

- ✔ **Node:** Any addressable network points, including workstations, peripherals, or other network devices. Commonly used interchangeably with the noun *workstation*.

- ✔ **Workstation:** A personal computer, connected to a network by a cable, that runs application or utility software and uses data stored locally or provided by a network server. Also known as a client.

Server

A *server* is a specially designated computer in a network, one chosen to perform a special task to service the resource needs of the workstation (client) computers on the network. A server can perform a variety of functions on behalf of a network. A server can be a printer server, a file server, an application server, a fax server, a World Wide Web server, and so on. Servers are looked into a little deeper later in this chapter in "Hello, I'll be your server."

Workstations and nodes

As defined earlier, a workstation is a computer attached to the network and a node is an addressable workstation, peripheral, or other device attached to the network. In general usage, node commonly refers to a workstation. On the Network+ exam, a mention of node is cause for you to consider all things that may relate to a network node.

Network classifications, types, and domains

I cover this topic in much more detail in Chapter 3, but here are some additional names used with workstations and servers on networks. You can expect to see these terms on the exam.

Host

A *host* is a server to which workstations are attached. A host server is usually a computer configured as a central controller to the rest of the network. The term host typically is applied to the computer that controls or coordinates resource access and usage by the network workstations.

Domain controller

In the context of a Windows NT network, a *domain* is a collection of hardware and software resources and the user accounts that have access to the resources. The resources may include multiple servers, printers, CD-ROM drives, RAID, and other devices.

In this arrangement, one server is designated as the primary domain controller (PDC) and manages the user logons and permissions for the domain resources. One or more of the other servers are designated as backup domain controllers (BDCs), which obviously serve as backup to the PDC, but also maintain the user account database. Like the first runner-up in a beauty pageant, a BDC can be promoted to PDC if the PDC is for some reason unable to fulfill its official duties.

Resources are made available to the domain through share names, which are assigned to the resource by the network administrator. To access any resource on a domain, a user needs two things: the appropriate access permissions and the share name of the device.

Peer

Any workstation in a peer-to-peer network is a *peer*. Workstations are peers because they are equal. Gee, I can't come up with a way to make this stuff tough. Peers are peers because they operate at the same level. True democracy at work, nobody's the lord and nobody is the peasant. They are all lords or peasants, depending on your viewpoint and cynicism.

Client

Workstations that make requests on the server for a function the server provides upon request are *clients* of that server. Clients, when they are strictly clients, do not share their own resources with the network. What I mean by "when they are strictly clients" is that in some network situations, a computer can be a client in some instances and become a server in others.

I'm sure that in some ways you can liken this relationship to professionals, such as doctors and lawyers, and their clients. However, perhaps a more accurate example is when I take my shirt and the button that fell off to a seamstress for her specialized button-replacement services. Like a server on a network handling specialized requests from its clients, the seamstress provides just the service I need. Anything smaller than inserting a half-height hard disk in a full-height drive bay is just about beyond my hand-eye coordination anymore.

If many servers are on a network, they conceivably may be clients to one another. Peer-to-peer workstations can be clients or servers, or both, depending on whether they are asking for or providing resources to the other peer workstations on the network.

Workstation II

Workstations and clients are synonymous. These terms are commonly used interchangeably and the Network+ exam treats them likewise. Just remember that workstations and clients are the same and do not share their resources to the network.

Hello, I'll be your server

Several different types of servers can exist on a network, each one performing a different sort of task for the network and its workstations. Servers are usually thought of as the hardware that houses it, but the server is actually the software that performs, controls, or coordinates a service or resource. So, one computer (server) actually can be considered as many different (software) servers to network clients. Table 2-3 lists the most common types of servers implemented on a network.

Table 2-3	Server Types
Function	*Description*
File server	A centralized computer that stores network users' data files
Print server	A centralized computer that manages the printers connected to the network and the printing of user documents on the network printers
Communications server	A centralized computer that handles many common communications functions for the network, such as e-mail, fax, or Internet services
Application server	A centralized computer that shares network-enabled versions of common application software eliminating the need for the software to be installed on each workstation
Database server	A centralized computer that manages a common database for the network, handling all data storage, database management, and requests for data

Broadband versus baseband

I need to interrupt your studies for a brief definition of broadband and baseband signaling. *Baseband networks* use only one channel to support digital transmissions. This type of network signaling uses twisted-pair cabling. Most LANs are baseband networks.

Broadband networks use analog signaling over a wide range of frequencies. This type of network is unusual, but many cable companies now offer high-speed Internet network access over broadband systems. You may resume your studies now.

A Bit about Binary Numbers

The binary number system is the foundation upon which all logic and data processing in computers and networks is built. For no other reason than that, you should know something about it. I'll assume you know that the *binary number system* consists of only two digital values (0 and 1) and that the computer can store only one binary value in each bit (binary digit).

All addresses, including network addresses, are stored as binary values in computers, with each bit occasionally taking on special meanings. Chapter 13 goes into these special meanings in detail, but in general, the bits can be used to represent the network identity (also called the NETID) and host identity (the HOSTID) of a network address.

Putting every bit in its place

Binary values are created by raising the number 2 to various powers. Actually, this is true for all number systems. For example, the decimal number system is based on values of the decimal number 10 raised to increasing powers: The decimal number 101 represents (reading right to left), 1 times 10^0 (1) plus 0 times 10^1 (0) plus 1 times 10^2 (100), which equals one hundred and one in decimal numbers.

```
Decimal 101 = 1 X 10² + 0 X 10¹ + 1 X 10⁰ = 101
```

The same digits 101 in binary form represent (again reading right to left) 1 times 2^0 (1) plus 0 times 2^1 (0) plus 1 times 2^2 (4), which results in the equivalent of the decimal value 5.

```
Binary 101 = 1 X 2² + 0 X 2¹ + 1 X 2⁰ = 5
```

The powers of two set the value of each digit in the binary number, starting with 2 to the 0 power on the right-most (or least significan) digit, and increasing to the left-most (or most significant) digit, as shown in Table 2-4.

Table 2-4	Powers of Two
2^n	*Decimal Value*
2^0	1
2^1	2
2^2	4
2^3	8

(continued)

Table 2-4 *(continued)*	
2^n	**Decimal Value**
2^4	16
2^5	32
2^6	64
2^7	128

A one in any position of a binary number indicates that the value of that position is "turned on" and should be added into the total of the entire binary value. Using the information in Table 2-4, the binary number 11011011 represents the decimal value 219, and the binary number 11111100 equates to the decimal value 252.

Braving Boolean algebra 101

Not to worry, I'm not making you do algebra, at least not the kind you remember from high school. *Boolean algebra* applies binary logic to yield binary results. Working with subnet masks, you only need four basic principles of Boolean algebra:

- 1 and 1 = 1
- 1 and 0 = 0
- 0 and 1 = 0
- 0 and 0 = 0

What I mean by "1 and 1" is that when two numbers have ones in the same position, in Boolean algebra, they combine to produce a one in the same position of the result.

Think of the ones as representing true and the zeros representing false. In Boolean algebra, true and true makes true, true and false is false, and of course false and false is definitely false. Got it? The only way to end up with a 1 is to combine two 1s. Everything else results in a 0.

So why am I telling you this? Good question. Later in the book, in Chapter 13 to be exact, I attempt to explain subnet masking and how it is applied to identify network and host identities. One of the procresses used to do this is Boolean algebra.

Keeping things at parity

While I'm on the subject of bits, this would be a good place to discuss the concept of parity. *Parity* is a methodology used to help ensure that the data stored or transferred was actually the data written or sent. Parity uses an additional bit for every 8 bits of data. There are two parity protocols in use — odd parity and even parity. Parity checking works like this:

✔ For every eight bits of data, there is an additional bit used to set the parity.

✔ If the system is using even parity, the extra bit is set on to create an even number of positive (ones) bits.

✔ In odd parity, the extra bit is set on to create an odd number of one bits.

The limitation with parity methods is that while they can detect an error, parity processes can't do anything about the error. The method doesn't identify which of the bits are wrong and which are correct. It only knows that the number of one bits is wrong.

Defining a Network Operating System

The Network+ test doesn't require that you be an expert on either of the popular network operating systems (NOS) — Microsoft Windows NT Server and Novell NetWare. However, you do need a good basic knowledge and understanding of the administrative functions performed in any NOS. The three chapters in Part VI provide the information you need for the test.

The *network operating system* (NOS) is a core element of any network. It is the software that manages, permits, and facilitates the sharing of resources on the network by the network users.

Some desktop clients, such as Windows 9*x* (short for Windows 95 and 98) and Windows 3.*x*, also provide peer-to-peer network support through their file and print sharing services, but I wouldn't go so far as to call them network operating systems. Chapter 5 covers network operating systems in more detail.

Part II
The Basics of Networking Technology

The 5th Wave — By Rich Tennant

EXPERIMENTING WITH THE WIRELESS LASER BEAM NETWORK

"Okay—did you get that?"

In this part . . .

Like most technology, networking has its own language, and your ability to speak and understand this language is an essential part of the Network+ certification. I won't go so far as to say that networking should be your first language, with English a distant second, but I will say that without an extensive networking vocabulary, you may struggle on the Network+ exam. This part of the book should be a first stop in your exam preparation.

Chapter 3

The Essentials of Networking

Exam Objectives

▶ Describing common network classifications

▶ Listing common network cable types

▶ Detailing common network connectivity devices

▶ Explaining fault-tolerance approaches

*T*he Network+ exam, not surprisingly, packs in all shapes and sizes of common networking, communications, and fault-tolerance terminology and concepts. After all, that's the stuff the test covers. So, plan to focus the first part of your preparations for this test on developing a good understanding of networks, cabling, connectivity devices, and fault-tolerance terminology, concepts, and usage.

Although you may not see questions that require you to identify, describe, or define the devices, terms, concepts, and technologies included in this chapter, you can count on finding these terms included in scenarios, multiple-choice answers, or in any other way that those pesky test-weavers may dream up. My personal estimate is that the Network+ exam is about one-third memorization (lists, layers, properties, and so on), one-third terminology and concepts ("what is . . ." and "which of the following is — or is not," and so on), with the remaining one-third application and administration situation-based questions ("given . . . , what do you recommend . . .?"). Allocating your preparation time accordingly is a wise move.

Providing you with a solid foundation of basic definitions, concepts, and terminology is the purpose of this chapter. I can't promise to make you an expert in any of the topics included, but I certainly can get you ready for the test, and isn't that why you're here?

Quick Assessment

Describing
common
network
classifica-
tions

1 The two most common classifications of networks are _____ and _____.

2 A _____ is a network in which computer workstations are directly connected to each other to share resources.

3 Server-based networks are also called _____.

Listing
common
network
cable types

4 A _____ cable forms the main trunk of a network to which workstations and peripherals are directly attached.

5 Category _____ cable is UTP cable that supports transmission speeds up to 100 Mbps.

Detailing
common
network
connectivity
devices

6 A(n) _____ hub amplifies the signal it passes on to its ports.

7 The network connectivity device used to connect two different LANs is a _____.

Explaining
fault-
tolerance
approaches

8 RAID is the acronym for _____.

9 RAID 5 is also called _____.

10 Using multiple disk controllers in a disk mirroring application is called disk _____.

Answers

1 *local area networks (LANs), wide area networks (WANs).* See "Classifying a Network."

2 *Peer-to-peer.* Review "Network types."

3 *Client/server.* Check out "Network types."

4 *Backbone.* Take a look at "Stringing It All Together."

5 *5.* Check out "Stringing It All Together."

6 *Active.* See "Hubs."

7 *Bridge.* See "Bridges."

8 *Redundant Array of Independent Disks.* Look up "Redundant Array of Independent Disks (RAID)."

9 *Disk Striping with Parity.* Review "Redundant Array of Independent Disks (RAID)."

10 *Duplexing.* Check out "Disk duplexing."

Classifying a Network

The term network has many meanings and usages. Even on the Network+ test, the word *network* is used to mean different things in different scenarios and contexts. Be sure you have a good understanding of each of the following different classifications and types of networks.

The following two classifications of networks are likely candidates for the test:

- **Local area network (LAN):** A LAN is made up of two or more nodes situated in a relatively small area and connected for the purpose of data- and resource-sharing.
- **Wide area network (WAN):** A WAN interconnects LANs and nodes that are located over a large area using dedicated long-distance and usually high-speed lines.

Network types

The following are the two basic types of networks:

- **Peer-to-peer (peer-based) networks:** Two or more computers connected with cabling for the purpose of directly sharing data and hardware resources. In this arrangement, each computer can be either a client (when requesting resources) or a server (when providing resources).
- **Server-based (client/server) networks:** A network of connected computers and peripherals with a centralized server that facilitates the sharing of network data, software, and hardware resources.

Domains

Another server-related term you can expect to see is *domain*. It is used a couple of different ways on the Network+ exam. Although three different common usages of this term exist within networking, you need to worry about only two: the Windows NT domain and the Internet domain. The third usage does not appear on the test.

- **Windows NT domain:** A group of network servers and devices that appear to end-users as a single network.
- **Internet domain:** An element of the Domain Name Server (DNS) naming hierarchy. I cover Internet domains in more detail in Chapter 11.
- **NetWare domain:** The memory segment within NetWare used to separate NetWare Loadable Modules (NLMs) from the operating system.

Internet domains

The highest level of domains defined by the DNS is standardized to group domain names by the type of organization or geographical location. The top-level Internet domains are

- ✔ **.com** — for companies intending to make a profit (such as `idgbooks.com`)
- ✔ **.edu** — for schools, colleges, and universities (such as `uwashington.edu`)
- ✔ **.gov** — for the not-secret government agencies (such as `whitehouse.gov`)
- ✔ **.int** — for international organizations outside of the U.S. (such as `europa.eu.int`)
- ✔ **.mil** — for the U.S. Armed Forces (such as `pentagon.mil`)
- ✔ **.net** — for networking services providers (such as `innw.net`)
- ✔ **.org** — for charitable and other nonprofit organizations (such as `redcross.org`)

International domain country codes you don't need to know for the exam

International domains are identified by a two-letter country identifier, which is designated in ISO 3166, an international standard you also don't need to care about. Here are some of the more common ones:

- ✔ **.au** — Australia
- ✔ **.br** — Brazil
- ✔ **.cn** — China
- ✔ **.fr** — France
- ✔ **.de** — Germany
- ✔ **.hk** — Hong Kong

- ✔ **.no** — Norway
- ✔ **.ru** — Russian Federation
- ✔ **.ch** — Switzerland
- ✔ **.uk** — United Kingdom
- ✔ **.zw** — Zimbabwe

Stringing It All Together

A veritable smorgasbord of more than 30 different applications of cable exists for use in all forms of networking. The Network+ exam has some specific questions on cabling and cable types, and Chapter 5 details what you need to know. However, cable types and the terms that relate to them are used throughout the test. Here are some of the cable types and terms you encounter on the Network+ test:

- **Adapter cable:** Connects a token ring network interface card (NIC) to a token ring hub or Multistation Access Unit (MAU).

- **Backbone cable (most commonly called "the backbone"):** Forms the main trunk of a network to which individual workstations and peripherals can be directly attached.

- **Category *n* cable (where *n* represents a category number):** Defined in a set of cabling standards developed by the Electronics Industry Association (EIA) and the Telecommunications Industry Association (TIA). The categories you need to know are

  - **Category 3:** Unshielded twisted-pair (UTP) cable used for speeds up to 10 million bits per second (Mbps). 10BaseT networks require at least Category 3 cable.

  - **Category 4:** The lowest grade of UTP cabling acceptable for 16 Mbps token ring networks.

  - **Category 5:** UTP cable used for network speeds up to 100 Mbps.

- **Coaxial cable:** Has a central solid wire surrounded by insulation. A braided-wire conductor sheath surrounds the insulation, which is then covered with a plastic jacket. Supports high bandwidth with little interference.

- **Drop cable:** A four-pair Attachment Unit Interface (AUI) cable that connects an NIC to an Ethernet network backbone using a clamping connector.

- **Fiber-optic cable:** Made of glass- or plastic-fiber strands, surrounded by a protecting jacket that facilitates high-bandwidth transmission by modulating a focused light source. Commonly used to connect Fiber Distributed Data Interface (FDDI) networks and local area network (LAN) backbones.

- **IBM cable:** A cable standard developed by IBM that defines cables as Type 1 through Type 9, also designated as I-1 through I-9. IBM cabling is used for token ring and general-purpose wiring. The types you need to know about are

  - **IBM Type 3 cable:** UTP with two, three, or four pairs of solid wire.

- **IBM Type 5 cable:** Fiber-optic cable.
- **IBM Type 9 cable:** STP with two pairs of solid or stranded wire that is covered with a plenum (see below) jacket.

✓ **Patch cable:** Common to token ring networks, where it is used to connect two MAUs to each other; also used to connect Ethernet hubs together.

✓ **Plenum cable:** Used for connections through conduits because its fireproof plastic jacket doesn't give off toxic fumes at high temperatures.

✓ **Ribbon cable:** Connects internal disk and tape drives. It is constructed with wires placed side-by-side in an insulating material. One edge of the cable is usually colored red or blue to mark wire number one.

✓ **Riser cable:** The most common fiber-optic cabling, riser cable is used to run a connection vertically, such as between floors of a building.

✓ **Thick coaxial cable:** A coaxial cable with a diameter of one centimeter (a little less than one-half inch) that is used with Ethernet networks. Also called thickwire, thicknet, and yellow wire.

✓ **Thin coaxial cable:** A coaxial cable with a diameter of five millimeters (about one-fifth of an inch) that's used with Ethernet and ARCNet networks. Also called thinwire and thinnet.

✓ **Twisted-pair (TP) cable:** A cable with two or more pairs of insulated wires twisted together at a rate of six twists per inch. In each pair of wires, one wire carries the signal and the other is grounded. The two common types of TP cable are shielded twisted-pair and unshielded twisted-pair cable.

- **Shielded twisted-pair cable:** A TP cable constructed with a foil shield and copper braid around the pairs of twisted copper wires to protect against electromagnetic interference (EMI) and radiofrequency interference (RFI). This type of cable is commonly used with token ring networks.

- **Unshielded twisted-pair cable:** A cable with no outer foil shield to protect against EMI or RFI. A cable with a high number of twists has lower crosstalk (interference picked up from another wire).

A Primer on Connectivity Devices

Concentrate on the network interface card (NIC), the functions and usage of repeaters, hubs, routers, bridges, and brouters, and the layer of the OSI Reference Model (see Chapter 7) on which they operate. These devices are discussed in detail in Chapters 8, 9, 10, and 11. Here is a list of these devices and their OSI Model layers:

- ✔ **Repeaters** — Physical layer
- ✔ **Bridges** — Data Link layer
- ✔ **Switches** — Data Link layer
- ✔ **Routers** — Network layer
- ✔ **Gateway** — Application layer

Networks are interconnected by cabling and networking connectivity devices that are added to improve network performance or to extend it beyond media or hardware limitations. In the following sections, I define many of the most commonly used connectivity devices. You can find detailed descriptions of each device in Chapters 8 through 11 that cover the Physical, Data Link, Network, and Transport layers of the OSI Model respectively.

Repeaters

A repeater, a Physical layer device, is by far the simplest of the network connectivity devices. In effect, a repeater is merely an electronic echo machine without any other intelligence. It simply retransmits whatever it hears, literally in one ear and out the other.

The primary reason that you use a repeater in a network is to extend the maximum distance of the transmission medium and protect against attenuation. *Attenuation* is the natural tendency for a signal to weaken as it travels over a cable. The longer the cable, the weaker the signal becomes. By regenerating the signal every so often, the rejuvenated signal is able to reach its destination.

Each type of cable has a different maximum distance limit, which is caused by signal attenuation (see Chapter 6). Table 3-1 lists the distance limits of the more common cable media in an Ethernet network. Plan to know these maximum cable lengths for the Network+ exam, especially UTP.

Table 3-1	Maximum Cable Distance for Ethernet Networks
Cable Media	*Maximum Segment Distance*
Thin coax	185 meters (a little over 600 feet)
Thick coax	500 meters (about 1650 feet)
UTP	100 meters (a little over a football field)
Fiber-optic	2,000 meters (pretty far — about a mile and a quarter)

All segments of cable between the server (or repeater, or active hub, and so on) and a workstation contribute to the maximum distance of the particular cable type. Suppose that a workstation on an Ethernet UTP network has 85 meters of cable from the server to a patch panel, then a 5-meter cable to a passive hub, and a 15-meter cable to its NIC. Total cable length is 105 meters, which exceeds the 100-meter maximum distance for UTP and is reason enough for this workstation to fail or perform poorly.

Patch panels

The most common configuration for cabling between the workstations of a network segment and the hub is to use a patch panel as the front-end for the cables that go to the workstations. A patch panel is a clustering device onto which network cable wires are individually "punched down" on one side of a connector and a cable plug. For example, an RJ-45 may be placed on the other side of the connector. Patch panels allow a great deal of flexibility in configuring and troubleshooting cable runs.

Short cables, called patch cables, are then used to connect the patch panel ports to a corresponding hub port. The benefit of this arrangement is that you can easily move the workstation to another port or, perhaps, to another hub simply by moving the patch cable.

You don't need to know patch panels or patch cables in any particular detail, but you can count on the configuration that I describe in the preceding paragraphs to show up in a question or two.

Token ring media filters

A media filter is used on token ring networks to convert from Type 1 (shielded twisted-pair) cable to Type 3 (unshielded twisted-pair) cable or the reverse.

Hubs

As illustrated in Figure 3-1, a *hub* is a network device used to connect workstations and peripheral devices to the network. Each workstation or device is plugged into one of the hub's ports. A hub receives a signal from one port and passes it on to all of its other ports and to whatever is attached to the port. For example, if an eight-port hub receives a signal on port 4, it immediately passes the signal to ports 1, 2, 3, 5, 6, 7, and 8.

Hubs, which are common to Ethernet twisted-pair networks, especially 10BaseT and 100BaseT configurations, are commonly configured with 8, 16, or 24 ports. There are four types of hubs.

✔ **Active hub:** This type of hub acts like a repeater to amplify the signal being passed on as well as serving in a traffic cop role to avoid signal collisions. An active hub is a powered device with a power cord.

✔ **Passive hub:** This type of hub does not amplify transmission signals, it merely passes them along. A passive hub does not need power and therefore does not have a power cord.

✔ **Hybrid hub:** This is a hub that can mix media types (thinwire, thickwire, and UTP) and serve as an interconnect for other hubs.

✔ **Smart (intelligent) hub:** This is an active hub with a bigger brain. Smart hubs include some administrative interface, often including SNMP (Simple Network Management Protocol) support or the ability to segment the ports into different logical networks.

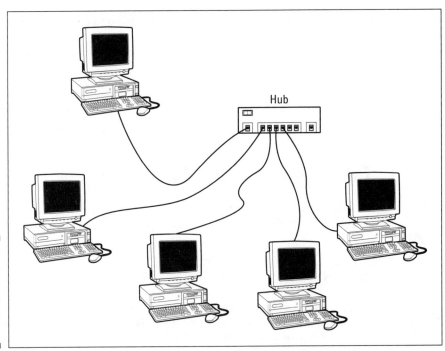

Figure 3-1:
A hub
connecting
computers
to a
network.

Bridges

You use a *bridge* to connect two different LANs or two similar network segments and make them appear to be one network. The bridge builds a routing table (also called a bridging table) of physical device addresses that is used to determine the correct network destination for a message. Because a bridge sends messages only to the part of the network on which the destination node exists, the overall affect of a bridge on a network is reduced network traffic and a reduction of message bottlenecks.

Routers

You say potato, I say potawto . . . Depending on where you're from, you also may pronounce the word *router* a bit differently from your fellow Earth occupants. If you're from England, you're likely to say "rooter," but we Yankees pronounce the word "rowter," which rhymes with pouter.

No matter how you express it, a *router* directs, or routes, packets across networks. A router works with the logical or network address of a message to determine the path that a message should take to arrive at its destination. I cover the process in more detail in Chapter 10.

You use routers to control broadcast storms on a network. When too many workstations broadcast too many messages to the whole network rather than to a single workstation, the result is a broadcast storm. By routing messages only to certain segments of the network, a router helps prevent broadcast storms.

Not all network protocols are routable. You need to know which are which for the Network+ exam. Table 3-2 shows which protocols are and which aren't routable.

Table 3-2	Routable and Nonroutable Protocols
Protocols	*Routable?*
AppleTalk	Yes
IP	Yes
IPX	Yes
NetBEUI	No

NetBEUI is not routable! Remember this, know this, and don't forget this!

Brouters

A *brouter* is a hybrid device that combines the functions of a bridge and a router. It operates on two layers of the OSI model: the Data Link layer (as a bridge) and the Network layer (as a router). A brouter is just what it sounds like: a cross between a bridge and a router. It can act like a router for routable protocols and like a bridge for nonroutable protocols.

I mention this device for two reasons: to remind you that it exists and that you can expect to see a question about it on the test. You may find brouter included in the list of multiple-choice answers on a couple of questions as well.

Gateways

A gateway, which is usually a combination of hardware and software, enables two networks with different protocols to communicate with one another. Gateways are used in a number of situations involving the conversion of the characteristics on one environment to another, including architecture, protocols, and language. Three different types of gateways exist.

- ✔ **Address gateway:** Connects networks with different directory structures and file management techniques.

- ✔ **Protocol gateway:** Connects networks that use different protocols; the most common gateway.

- ✔ **Format gateway:** Connects networks using different data format schemes, for example, one using the American Standard Code for Information Interchange (ASCII) and another using Extended Binary-Coded Decimal Interchange Code (EBCDIC).

A gateway is usually a dedicated server on a network because it typically requires large amounts of system resources.

Network interface cards (NICs)

The most basic of network connectivity devices are *network interface cards* (NICs), also called *network adapters*. A NIC is the piece of hardware installed in every computer, and other devices, that both attaches the node to the network cabling and connects it to the network system. The primary purpose of the NIC is to transmit and receive data to and from other NICs.

Here's a handful of characteristics of NICs that you need to know for the Network+ exam.

- ✔ **MAC (Media Access Control) address:** Each NIC is physically encoded with a unique identifying address that is used to locate it on the network.

- ✔ **System resources:** A NIC is configured to the computer with an IRQ, an I/O address, and a DMA channel. A NIC commonly uses IRQ3, IRQ5, or IRQ10, and an I/O address of 300h.

- ✔ **Transceiver type:** Some NICs are capable of attaching to more than one media type, such as UTP and coaxial.

- ✔ **Data bus compatibility:** NICs are designed with compatibility to a particular data bus architecture.

Transceiver types

Some NICs have their transceivers (the device that transmits and receives data from the network) on-board the adapter card itself. Others, especially those supporting thick coaxial media, attach to an external transceiver. The NIC uses an AUI (adapter unit interface), also called DIX (Digital-Intel-Xerox), connector on a transceiver cable linked to a tapping (or vampire) connector that pierces the network cable. Figure 3-2 illustrates this arrangement.

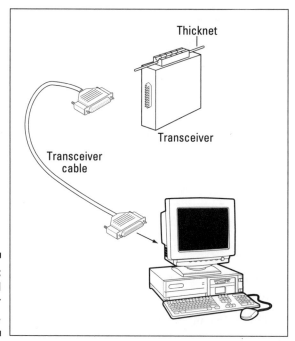

Thicknet

Transceiver

Transceiver cable

Figure 3-2:
An external transceiver connection.

NIC connectors

Often the media type in use on the network can control other hardware decisions — for example, not only the type of NIC, but also the type and style of connectors linking it to the network media. Table 3-3 shows the connectors appropriate for each type of media.

Table 3-3	NIC/Media Connector Types
Media	*Connectors Used*
Thinnet	BNC T connectors (see Figure 3-3)
Thicknet	AUI connectors (take a look at Figure 3-2)
UTP	RJ-45
Fiber-optic	ST connectors

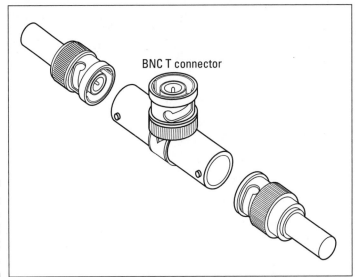

BNC T connector

Figure 3-3:
BNC T con-
nector used
on thinnet
cable.

Be sure you know all of these Ethernet media aliases:

✓ Thinnet is also called thin coaxial, thinwire, and 10Base2.

✓ Thicknet is also called thick coaxial, thickwire, and 10Base5.

✓ Twisted-pair (TP) can mean STP or UTP or 10BaseT or 100BaseT.

✓ Fiber-optic is also 10BaseF.

It's Not My Fault

In the world of networking, the term fault tolerance means that a computer, whether workstation or server, is resilient to failure and hardware or environmental failures. The focus of fault tolerance on the Network+ exam is primarily in two areas: hard disk fault tolerance and power fault tolerance.

Hard disk fault tolerance consists of a number of disk management strategies that protect against the loss of data in the event of a disk drive failure in varying levels of security. RAID (Redundant Array of Independent Disks) technology and disk duplexing are used as fault-tolerance strategies.

A *disk volume* is a logical grouping under a single drive letter of hard disk partitions or areas of freespace located across different physical disk drives.

Redundant Array of Independent Disks (RAID)

Memorize the name associated with each RAID level (for example, RAID 0 is disk striping, RAID 1 is disk mirroring, and so on) and the minimum number of disk drives each strategy requires. Table 3-4 summarizes the characteristics of the three RAID strategies that you need to remember.

Table 3-4	RAID Characteristics	
Level	*Common Name*	*Minimum Number of Disk Drives*
RAID 0	Disk striping	1
RAID 1	Disk mirroring	2
RAID 5	Disk striping with parity	3

The implementation of RAID technology minimizes the potential for data loss in the event of disk drive problems or failure. Standard RAID strategies are categorized as RAID 0 through RAID 5, plus RAID 10, but for the Network+ test, concentrate only on the following three.

 ✔ **RAID 0 (disk striping):** Data is written in stripes across multiple volumes. The good news is that disk striping is relatively inexpensive and provides fast reads and writes. The bad news is that if you loose one of the physical drives, you loose all the data in the stripe set, which is all the stripes in the array. In other words, no fault tolerance, which is pretty bad for a fault-tolerance strategy.

- ✔ **RAID 1 (disk mirroring):** Duplicates (mirrors) a disk partition from one physical drive to another drive. When one partition changes, the mirror automatically updates. The good news is that you maintain a redundant, exact copy of the data, and you get high speed reads and writes. The bad news is that you need at least two disks, and only one is available for use, which makes the cost of both a bit steep.

- ✔ **RAID 5 (disk striping with parity):** The most popular RAID strategy for fault tolerance. RAID 5 extends RAID 4 to store parity information (see Chapter 2) across the array disks. The good news is that if you lose a disk drive, you're not likely to lose any data (although system performance will suffer as the data is reconstructed in memory). The bad news is that you need at least three disks.

Disk duplexing

Disk mirroring can involve duplication of data on disk drives sharing the same disk controller card. Disk duplexing, which is also considered to be RAID 1, goes one step further and separates the two disk drives to their own disk controllers. If the common disk controller fails in a mirroring strategy, the data from both drives is unavailable. Duplexing provides better fault tolerance because in the event of hard disk or disk controller failure, the data stored on the other disk is still available.

Data backups

Creating a backup of the data on a disk is another form of disk fault tolerance. Instead of spreading the data around on the disk drives, the data is captured on media that can be stored physically separate from the system. Magnetic tape is the most common media used for data backups.

You will need to know the various types of backups, when they should be used, and where the backup media should be stored. Chapter 20 covers tape backups in more detail.

Power fault tolerance

You can use a variety of products to help protect a system from data loss due to power fluctuations or failures. These products run the gamut from small and inexpensive (and usually ineffective) to large, bulky, expensive, and protective. Most networks use tools located somewhere between these two extremes. Common power fault-tolerance hardware includes the following types of equipment.

✔ **Surge suppressor:** Essentially a plug strip that also provides protection from voltage spikes and overvoltage surges from the primary power supply.

✔ **Power (line) conditioner:** A device that keeps the power within a range of acceptable voltages, suppressing spikes and filling in low voltage (brownout) conditions.

✔ **Uninterruptable Power Supply (UPS):** Designed to provide an emergency power source in case the power fails completely. Many UPS units also combine the features of surge suppressors and line conditioners. There are three types of UPS devices.

- **Standby UPS:** Uses a small amount of the AC supply to maintain a battery backup, but otherwise performs surge suppression on a passed-through power line.

- **Inline UPS:** Passes power through and out of a battery backup unit with the advantage of being instantaneously available in the event of a power failure.

- **Interactive (intelligent) UPS:** Connects to a computer through a serial port that is used to signal a loss of power, a weak UPS battery, or other conditions to UPS utility software running on the computer.

Prep Test

1 Which of these unshielded twisted-pair cabling can you use for 10BaseT networks with transmission speeds of up to 10 Mbps?

A ○ Category 3 cable

B ○ Category 4 cable

C ○ Category 5 cable

D ○ IBM type 5 cable

2 A network that interconnects multiple local area networks using long-distance connectivity and high-speed lines is a

A ○ Campus area network.

B ○ Global network.

C ○ Wide area network.

D ○ Peer-to-peer network.

3 A network of ten or fewer workstations connected by cable for the direct sharing file and hardware resources is which type of network?

A ○ Server-based

B ○ Peer-based

C ○ Peer-to-server

D ○ Server-to-peer

4 A network bridge operates at which layer of the OSI Model?

A ○ Physical layer

B ○ Data Link layer

C ○ Network layer

D ○ Transport layer

5 The connectivity device that is used to provide flexibility in cable management and troubleshooting is the

A ○ Hub.

B ○ Repeater.

C ○ Patch panel.

D ○ Transceiver.

6 The connectivity device that passes an amplified signal to each of its ports is a

A ○ Passive hub

B ○ Repeater

C ○ Active hub

D ○ UPS

7 Which of the following network protocols is not routable? (Choose all that apply.)

A ❑ AppleTalk

B ❑ IP

C ❑ IPX

D ❑ NetBEUI

8 Each network interface card is uniquely identified by its

A ○ Transceiver type

B ○ MAC address

C ○ IP address

D ○ WINS address

9 Which disk organization strategy do RAID 1 and RAID 5 share?

A ○ Disk mirroring

B ○ Disk duplexing

C ○ Disk striping

D ○ Disk striping with parity

10 What piece of equipment provides an emergency power supply as well as over-voltage protection to a computer?

A ○ Surge suppressor

B ○ Line conditioner

C ○ Uninterruptable power supply

D ○ Battery backup

Answers

1 *A.* Category 4 and IBM Type 3 cable are primarily used for token ring networks. Category 5 cable supports speeds up to 100 Mbps. *See "Stringing It All Together."*

2 *C.* A wide area network (WAN) uses a variety of means to interconnect local area networks. A WAN usually involves some form of long-distance connection but does not require high-speed lines, though most use them. *Look over "Classifying a Network."*

3 *B.* A peer-to-peer or peer-based network has a practical limit of ten computers that are connected by cabling for sharing files and hardware. *Check out "Network types."*

4 *B.* Memorize the types of connectivity equipment, protocols, and software that operate at each layer of the OSI Model. Bridges and switches operate at the Data Link layer. *Review "A Primer on Connectivity Devices."*

5 *C.* The patch panel is used primarily to organize cabling as well as to provide ease of cable management and troubleshooting. *Take a look at "Patch panels."*

6 *C.* Passive hubs only pass through whatever signal comes in — no regeneration involved. An active hub regenerates the signal before passing it along to its ports. *See "Hubs."*

7 *D.* Count on seeing this question (or one very much like it) on the test. In fact, that NetBEUI is nonroutable may even surface in a situational question as well. *Look over "Routers."*

8 *B.* The device driver for a network interface card works at a sublayer of the Data Link layer called the Media Access Control (MAC) sublayer, which is why the physical address of a NIC is called its MAC address. *Review "Network interface cards (NICs)."*

9 *C.* RAID 1 implements disk striping and RAID 5 implements disk striping with parity. However, the two fault-tolerance strategies have little more than disk striping in common. *Check out "Redundant Array of Independent Disks (RAID)."*

10 *C.* An uninterruptable power supply (UPS) usually performs surge suppression and some line conditioning, in addition to providing an emergency power source. *Take a look at "Power fault tolerance."*

Chapter 4

Networking Basics

• •

Exam Objectives

▶ Understanding basic network structures

▶ Differentiating common network topologies

▶ Defining network backbones and segments

• •

*B*efore you dive into the really technical and complicated networking stuff, consider taking a refreshing dip with some fundamental networking concepts. If you don't know the basics, trying to understand, and especially remember, the more advanced network concepts and technologies may dampen your spirits a tad — or even put you in over your head. The basics include the general network topologies and common network structures and their concepts and terminology. By building on a foundation of networking basics, you can engineer a deep and demonstrable knowledge and understanding of networking technology and practices. Wow! Talk about deep!

Don't get me wrong, the information in this chapter is on the test! It's just that this kind of stuff may appear as background data to a scenario-based question, or it may show up as a "____ is a _____ that _____ and ____" type of thing. To put it more plainly, know your basics for the Network+ exam!

The Network+ test assumes a fair share of fundamental knowledge when it poses questions on troubleshooting, fixing, installing, designing, and upgrading networks. You may have trouble, for example, providing a brilliantly deduced answer to a question about the best approach to improving performance on an Ethernet network if you're not keen on Ethernet standards, media, and so on.

For no other reason other than being sure your understanding and definitions match those used on the exam, you really should begin your preparations for the Network+ exam by reviewing the fundamental concepts and terminology included in this chapter and in Chapter 3. Heck, it can't hurt, it can only help, and, you just never know, you could learn something!

Quick Assessment

Understan-
ding basic
network
structures

1 A _____ is two or more computers connected by a transmission media for the purpose of sharing resources.

2 The two basic types of networks are _____ and _____.

3 A _____ network works best with a maximum of ten workstations.

4 Granting access to files and hardware on an individual workstation is _____ security.

5 A server that shares network-enabled versions of common application software is a _____ server.

6 The two most common network classifications are _____ and _____.

Differentia-
ting common
network
topologies

7 The three most common network topologies are _____, _____, and _____.

8 A topology in which the nodes regenerate the signal when sending it on is a(n) _____ topology.

Defining
network
backbones
and
segments

9 Two computers attached to the same terminated network cable are located on the same network _____.

10 In a bus structure, the cable that runs the length of the network is its _____.

Answers

1   *Network.* Start with "Starting at the Beginning."

2   *Peer-to-peer (or peer-based) and server-based (or client/server).* Peer at "Peer-based and server-based networks."

3   *Peer-to-peer network.* Check out "How many workstations can it have?"

4   *Share-level.* Review "Who controls security?"

5   *Applications.* Take a look at "Hello, I'll be your server."

6   *Local area network (or LAN) and wide area network (or WAN).* See "Network Classifications."

7   *Bus, ring, and star.* Look over "Network Topologies."

8   *Active.* Check out "Won't you wear my ring around your net?"

9   *Segment.* Review "Cable termination."

10   *Backbone.* See "Cable termination."

Covering Networking Basics

Even if you knew the Father of Ethernet personally and truly understand the basic concepts of networking, the common network topologies, and their usage, you should still review this chapter. Sometimes the way that I understand something works for general purposes, but my knowledge may not be insightful enough to answer some of the questions on a test. I recommend that you review the networking fundamentals in this chapter as a part of your test preparation. You should also give this info a quick review before you take the test, just in case.

I start you off with the most basic of network basics: *A network is two or more computers connected by a transmission media for the purpose of sharing resources.* This is on the test!

You absolutely must understand the concept of this definition. One computer cannot be a network. A network is two or more computers connected by some form of communications media so that they can share data, software, or hardware resources. Think about it. What better reason to connect up two computers than to enable one to access something the other one has?

Figure 4-1 illustrates this concept: Adam's computer is connected to Eve's computer so that Adam can use Eve's new killer laser printer. In this configuration, Adam and Eve can also share data on each other's hard disk. May look frighteningly simple, but the two computers in Figure 4-1 form a network!

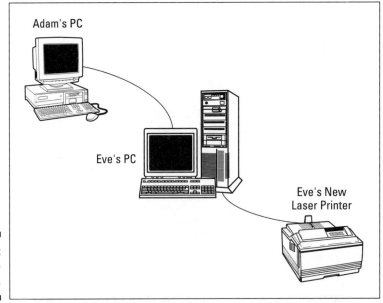

Figure 4-1:
A simple network.

Adam's PC

Eve's PC

Eve's New
Laser Printer

Sharing resources (yes, data is a resource) is what networks are all about. Users want access to the resources that they need to carry out tasks on their computers. Because networks are now so advanced, most users tend to take the network — and resource accessibility — for granted. Whether the required resource is software, data, or access to a particular piece of hardware, such as Eve's printer, the user wants the network to put everything within fingertip reach, as if the resource were directly connected to the user's own personal computer.

Peer-Based and Server-Based Networks

Without looking at the heading, what are the two types of networks? Your reward for not peeking is the following easy-to-understand description of each:

- ✔ **Peer-to-peer** — a.k.a. peer-based networks. In my "in the beginning" example, Adam and Eve created a peer-to-peer network where neither is the master nor the slave. Peer-to-peer networks are a voluntary, you-trust-me-and-I'll-trust-you affair.

- ✔ **Server-based** — a.k.a. client/server. A server-based network has a centralized server or host computer that tends to the resource needs of the workstations attached to the network, its clients. Figure 4-2 illustrates a simple server-based network. These networks can be complicated and enigmatic beasts that take on a personality of their own. They are also the subject of nearly all the questions on the Network+ exam.

Table 4-1 lists a few of the factors that differentiate peer-based and server-based networks.

Table 4-1	Peer-to-Peer versus Client/Server Networks	
Factor	*Peer-to-Peer*	*Server-Based*
Number of workstations	2–10	Limited only by the network hardware and software in use
Relative cost	Inexpensive	Can be very expensive, depending on network size
Security	User-managed	Centrally administered
Administration	User-managed	Centrally administered
Data backups	Each user responsible for backing up his or her own data	Backups centrally created

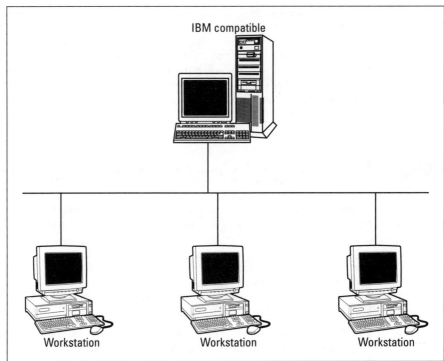

IBM compatible

Figure 4-2:
A simple
server-
based
network.

Workstation   Workstation   Workstation

How many workstations can the network have?

A peer-to-peer network is usually effective only with a maximum of ten work-stations. With more workstations, the management tasks involved in enabling each user to share resources with all the other users and to maintain the security for access to their computers become so much of a headache that everyone mutinies and appoints a central administrator to fuss with it all.

The number of workstations supported by server-based networks varies, but for the sake of comparison, consider the amount virtually unlimited. Many factors can each impose a limit on the number of workstations on a network. These factors, all of which I cover later in this book (in Chapters 6 and 8), include the type of cable used, the network operating system, and how much money you're willing to spend on connectivity devices.

How much does it cost?

Gilster's Law of Network Cost Estimation is: You never can tell, and it all depends. The cost of a network totally depends on the types of cabling, equipment, and software that you use to build the network.

A peer-to-peer network is a relatively low-cost affair. At minimum, all that you need is a standard parallel or serial cable and Windows to set up a file- and print-sharing peer-based network between two computers. If you decide to *daisy-chain* (connect several computers to one another) three or more computers, network interface cards and more cable add to the cost, but that's all there is. You really can't get much fancier than that.

On the other hand, the cost of a server-based network really invokes Gilster's Law. The cost can range from nearly the same cost as a peer-to-peer network to thousands — even millions — of dollars, depending on the size, scope, and class of network involved.

Who controls security?

Aha! Now you're treading on where the difference truly lies — security. In a peer-based network, security – that is, the who and when of permissible access to a computer and use of its resources – is controlled by the owner/operator of each workstation. Security is granted to individual users on the peer network one at a time and one folder at a time. Permission to share a folder is granted by the owner to each user in the Network Neighborhood. In Windows 9*x,* this permission is given using the Shared Files Properties function shown in Figure 4-3, which you access from the Windows Explorer by right-clicking on the folder to be shared and choosing Sharing.

Access granted by the owner (user) of a workstation to the files and hardware resources on a particular workstation is a called *share-level security.* I discuss security levels in more detail in Chapter 16.

The full responsibility for security (no small job, I might add), falls directly on the network administrator. This poor soul, I mean, this highly trained and skilled professional is responsible for assigning and managing the permissions and rights of network users and groups of users so that they have access to network resources, such as software, data, and hardware. Something akin to herding cats.

The access granted by the network administrator to network resources — such as data, software, or hardware — using the rights of individual users or groups is called *user-level security.* In other words, permission to access a resource is granted directly to an individual user (or group of users). Chapter 16 provides more information on both user-level and share-level security.

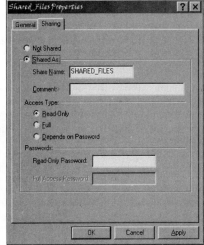

Figure 4-3:
The Shared
Files
Properties
dialog box is
used to
share a file.

Who's in charge here?

In a peer-to-peer network, each peer (which is to say, each user) is in charge of his or her own workstation, playing gatekeeper to the other users on the network.

Server-based networks have a central administrator, which depending on the size of the network, may actually be a group of administrators. Nevertheless, the central administrator is responsible for the function, security, and integrity of the entire network, including the workstations.

Networks Near and Far

You only need to worry about two network classifications for the Network+ exam: local area networks (LANs) and wide area networks (WANs). You may see other classifications of networks mentioned here and there on the test (usually as wrong answers), but focus on the differences between just these two:

✓ **Local area network (LAN):** A LAN connects workstations (also called nodes) in a relatively small geographical area — usually a single office, department, or building for the purpose of data and resource sharing.

✓ **Wide area network (WAN):** A WAN connects nodes and interconnects LANs located over geographically large areas, such as states, countries, and even globally, using dedicated long-distance, high-speed lines. The Internet is *the* WAN.

Network classifications you don't need to know

You may stumble across a mention of these three network classifications on the exam, but no need to sweat the details. These classifications specifically define types of local area and wide area networks, and their scope is evident in their names.

✔ **Campus area network (CAN):** This type of network connects network nodes located in different physical locations of a geographically small area without using remote communications connectivity. A CAN takes its name from its use to interconnect buildings on a corporate or collegiate campus into a network.

✔ **Global area network (GAN):** This type of network connects network nodes located in multiple countries or on multiple continents. Obviously, this requires remote communications connectivity.

✔ **Metropolitan area network (MAN):** This class of network connects network nodes that are located within the same metropolitan area (defined as being a 50- to 75-mile-wide area). May or may not require remote communications connectivity, but likely does.

Please Accept My Topologies

Imagine an aerial view of a network. Picture the network's general shape. The pattern of connections that tie the workstations to the network is its *topology*. Here are the most common network topologies:

✔ **Bus:** Nodes are connected to a central cable, called a *backbone,* that runs the length of the network.

✔ **Ring:** The primary network cable is installed as a loop, or *ring,* and the workstations are attached to the primary cable at points on the ring.

✔ **Star:** Each workstation is connected directly to the central server with its own cable, creating a starburst-like pattern.

✔ **Mesh:** Each workstation is directly connected to the server and all other workstations, creating a mess, I mean, mesh of network connections. This topology is not very common, but you may find it mentioned on the test.

Exam-wise, here's what you need to remember about topologies in general.

✔ The bus topology is commonly used for Ethernet networks. Figure 4-4 illustrates a bus topology.

✔ The ring topology is the basis for the token ring network structure. Figure 4-5 illustrates a ring topology. This one was on the test I took.

✔ The star topology, common to ARCNet networks, is today used with both Ethernet and token ring networks to cluster workstations with hubs or MAUs, which are then attached to the primary network cable. Figure 4-6 shows this arrangement.

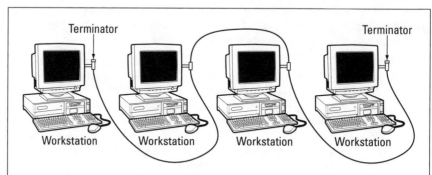

Figure 4-4:
The bus topology.

Riding the bus

In a network using the bus topology, all of the nodes are connected to a backbone, the primary network cable, that runs the length of the network. In its simplest form, the backbone cable runs from one computer to the next. It runs from the first computer in the network to the last computer in the network (refer to Figure 4-4). Bus topologies have three primary characteristics: signal transmission, cable termination, and continuity.

Signal transmission

To avoid problems, only one computer at a time can transmit a signal on a bus network backbone (check out Chapter 9). Politely, when one node is "talking," the other nodes are "listening." As the signal travels down the cable, each node examines the signal to see if it was sent to them. If not, the signal passes on down the cable uninterrupted.

Because bus network nodes only listen for messages sent to them and do not actually pass signals along by regenerating the signal, the bus topology is considered to be a *passive* network structure. Also remember that the bus topology is commonly known as Ethernet, and therefore, Ethernet networks are passive networks.

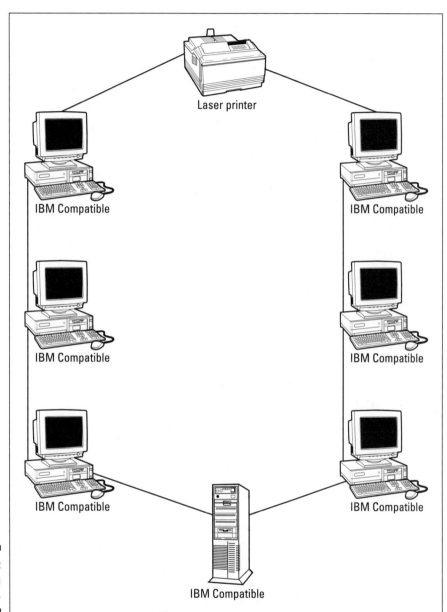

Figure 4-5:
The ring
topology.

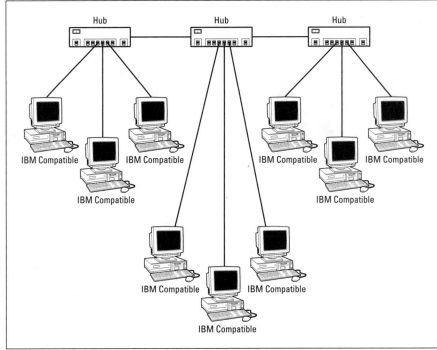

Figure 4-6:
The star
topology
used with
the bus
topology
(also called
a star-bus
topology).

Cable termination

Without something to stop it from bouncing back and forth on the network backbone, a signal would ricochet indefinitely, preventing any other signals from being sent. By definition, only one signal should be on the backbone at a time. Terminating the cable at each end helps prevent a message from riding the bus indefinitely. The terminator is a resistor that is placed on each end of the backbone cable to absorb errant signals and clear the cable.

If the backbone cable breaks or has an open end (an open connection, for example), the network is sure to malfunction because signals are too busy bouncing about to reach the terminators.

The cable that runs the length of a network is its *backbone*. Workstations and other networked devices can attach directly to the backbone or be connected through hubs and other clustering devices.

If the network is connected to another network through a bridge, router, or other connectivity device, the terminated cable is also known as a *segment*. Two computers on the same wire are on the same segment. Two computers on two different wires may be on the same network, but are on separate segments of the network.

Continuity check

As long as a bus network's cable has no open ends and is properly terminated, the network continues to function. However, if one of the nodes on the
network fails, as long as its cable connections are intact, the network cable is
operable. This doesn't mean that any problems the failed node is causing
magically disappear, it only means the network cable is still okay.

Won't you wear my ring around your net?

As depicted in Figure 4-5, the ring topology looks like a, well, it looks like a
ring. What can you say? The primary network cable forms a loop that, in
effect, has no beginning or end, which eliminates any termination problems
on the network. A signal placed on the network cable travels around the ring
from node to node until it reaches its destination. In reality, a ring structure
rarely is installed in a perfectly round shape, but you already guessed that
amazing truth, right?

In contrast to the bus topology, the ring topology is an *active* topology. Each
node on the ring network receives the signal, examines it, and then regenerates it onto the network. Because of this, if a computer on the network fails
and is unable to regenerate the signal, the entire network is affected and continuity is lost.

Passing the token

You may have had the pleasure of attending one of those meetings where
some object is used to control who can talk. I went to one once where a small
pine tree branch was passed around a circle. The person holding the pine
branch was supposed to share his thoughts on a particular subject. Well, as
lame as this sounds, it works very nicely for the ring topology, except that
the object passed around is called a *token*. Strangely enough, this process is
called *token passing*.

Like the bus network, only one ring network node can send data at a time.
Only the node holding the token can transmit to the network. The node
proves it has the token by embedding it in the message it sends. Kind of like a
hall pass, in a way. None of the other nodes can send messages to the network because they cannot access the token. The destination node of the
message includes the token in its response to the sender. The sending node
releases the token when its message session is completed.

I want to see stars!

Once upon a time, terminals were directly connected to mainframes by individual pieces of wire that resulted in a configuration of wires emanating from

the central unit — and there you have the look of a starburst. Ah, the good old days! This same configuration is the basis for the star topology in which network nodes are directly connected to the central server.

The star topology can be used as the structure for an entire network, but this setup is rare these days. ARCNet networks (a legacy networking type) apply the star topology. However, the primary reason ARCNet is not very popular these days is because of the way it uses the star topology: Each workstation has a direct wire (called a home-run) to the server; when the server is gone, so are the workstation's network services.

It is far more common for the star topology to be used in conjunction with another topology. You can use the star topology to improve the configuration and performance of the bus and ring topologies by creating clusters of workstations that attach to the bus or ring backbones. The result: hybrid or mixed topologies, such as the star-bus and the star-ring (also called the ringed-star).

- ✔ **Star-bus:** Used with bus (Ethernet) networks. A hub is used as the central or clustering device, which is then attached to the network backbone (see Figure 4-7). This is the most common topology of Ethernet networks.

- ✔ **Star-ring:** Used with ring (token ring) networks. A multistation access unit (MAU) is used to cluster workstations and to connect with the next MAU to complete the ring. Used instead of a pure ring structure, the star-ring is the most common form of ring networks.

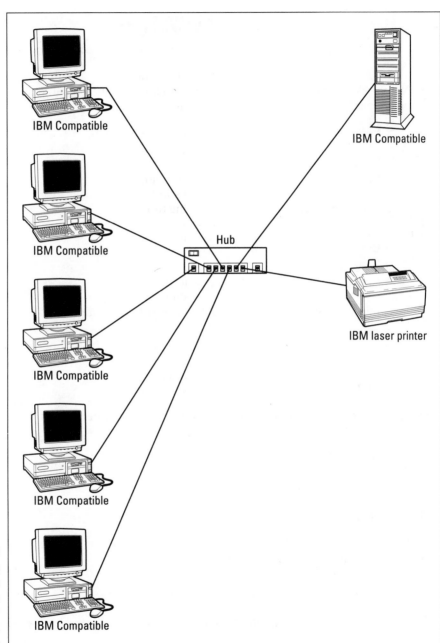

Figure 4-7:
A hub is
used to
cluster
devices.

Prep Test

1 Networks on which of the following topologies fail when a cable breaks? (Choose two answers.)

A ❏ Star

B ❏ Bus

C ❏ Ring

D ❏ Star-bus

2 Which of the following topologies must be terminated?

A ○ Star

B ○ Bus

C ○ Ring

D ○ Star-bus

3 An Ethernet network most commonly uses which topology?

A ○ Star

B ○ Bus

C ○ Ring

D ○ Star-bus

4 The topology most commonly used with a token ring network is the

A ○ Star

B ○ Star-bus

C ○ Ring

D ○ Star-ring

5 The primary purpose of a network is to

A ○ Interconnect computers for ease of administration

B ○ Provide central access to workstation hard disks

C ○ Share resources

D ○ Provide increased security for all workstations

6 Which of the following enables users to access files and to share a printer on a peer-based network?

A ○ Share-level security

B ○ User-level security

C ○ User permissions

D ○ User account policies

7 The recommended upper limit for the number of workstations that can be included in a peer-to-peer network is

A ○ 5
B ○ 10
C ○ 12
D ○ Unlimited

8 Which of the following are common types of network servers? (Choose five answers.)

A ❑ File server
B ❑ Application server
C ❑ Local server
D ❑ Communications server
E ❑ Print server
F ❑ Database server
G ❑ All of the above

9 An Ethernet network is a(n) _____ network.

A ○ Active
B ○ Passive
C ○ Active-passive
D ○ Passive-aggressive

10 The method used to control the transmission of signals to a ring network is

A ○ Backbone termination
B ○ Segment termination
C ○ Token passing
D ○ Token termination

Answers

1 *B and C.* Bus backbone cables continue to operate even if a node fails, but are not available if the cable is broken between the termination points. A ring cable cannot operate if the cable or a node fails. *See "Please Accept My Topologies."*

2 *B.* Bus cables must be terminated to eliminate signal bounce. *Review "Cable termination."*

3 *D.* The bus topology is the basic topology used in nearly all Ethernet networks, but the star-bus hybrid is the specific topology used in most implementations. *Review "Mixed topologies."*

4 *D.* The pure ring topology is rarely implemented. Instead, the star-ring is used. *See "Mixed topologies."*

5 *C.* Although answers A, B, and D are seemingly valid reasons to create a network, the primary objective of a network is to share data, software, and hardware resources. *Look over "Covering Networking Basics."*

6 *A.* Users can designate folders and devices as shared devices on their workstations and make them available to network users. *Review "Who controls security?"*

7 *B.* Beyond ten workstations, the administration tasks become too much for most users. *See "How many workstations can it have?"*

8 *A, B, D, E and F.* These servers provide dedicated services to share and manage specific functions and resources on the network. *Review "Hello, I'll be your server."*

9 *B.* Because its workstations only "hear" messages and do not regenerate them, bus topology networks (such as an Ethernet network) are considered passive networks. *Look over "Signal transmission."*

10 *C.* The node in possession of the token is the only one that can send a message. The other workstations must wait until the token is available. *See "Passing the token."*

Chapter 5

Network Operating Systems

●●●

▶ Differentiating the major network operating systems (NOSs)

▶ Identifying popular client operating systems

▶ Describing NOS directory services

▶ Associating IPX, IP, and NetBEUI with their functions

●●●

A test developed to measure knowledge and understanding of networking technology undoubtedly drills you on the inner workings of all the major network operating systems, right? Not so. The Network+ exam deals with network operating systems in a rather strange way. Apparently, Network+ concedes testing of specific Windows NT and Novell NetWare operations to the MCP/MCSE and CNA/CNE tests, preferring to target itself to generic functions and administrative tasks common to all NOS. You need to know something about each major NOS. You don't need to prepare yourself at the level of the MCSE NT Server 4.0 or the Novell CNA exams to be ready for the Network+ test. In the area of network operating systems, Network+ is more like the MCP/MCSE Networking Essentials.

In this chapter, I detail what you have to know about the major NOS, which includes Novell NetWare, Windows NT Server, and the UNIX operating system and their directory services, clients, and protocols. Even if you consider yourself proficient in any or all of these systems, I recommend that you review the entire chapter. For the sake of space (each of these systems is a book in itself!), I weave the generic among the NOS particulars.

Quick Assessment

Differentiating the major network operating systems (NOS)

1 A(n) _____ is a specialized piece of system software that runs on a network server.

2 Under NetWare, the physical disk is divided into logical groupings called _____.

3 The two file systems supported by Windows NT are _____ and _____.

4 _____ is the UNIX protocol used to send datagrams over a serial connection.

Identifying popular client operating systems

5 The most popular client operating systems are _____.

6 _____ is another name for protocol clients.

Describing NOS directory services

7 Directory services in Novell NetWare are provided by _____.

8 Windows NT directory services are provided by the _____.

Associating IPX, IP, and NetBEUI with their functions

9 IPX refers to _____ and IP refers to _____.

10 The basic protocols of Windows NT are _____ and _____.

Answers

1 *Network operating system (NOS).* Review "What You Need to Know about NOSs."

2 *Volumes.* See "NetWare file systems."

3 *FAT, NTFS.* Check out "Windows NT file systems."

4 *UDP.* Take a look at "UDP and ICMP, and we all get along."

5 *Windows operating systems.* Look over "Workstation operating systems and clients."

6 *Redirector.* See "Smoke, mirrors, and redirection."

7 *NDS (NetWare Directory Services).* Check out "NetWare Directory Services (NDS)."

8 *Windows NT Explorer.* Review "Exploring Windows NT directory services."

9 *Internet Packet Exchange, Internet Protocol.* Take a look at "The IPX/SPX protocols."

10 *NetBIOS, NetBEUI.* Look over "Windows NT network messaging."

What You Need to Know about NOSs

Call me cut-to-the-chase Gilster: Here are the key points to remember about network operating systems:

- ✔ Novell NetWare, Windows NT Server, and UNIX are the three most popular NOSs.

- ✔ Windows (all the various flavors) and MS-DOS are the clients most commonly used to connect each NOS to a Windows-based workstation.

- ✔ NetWare uses NDS (NetWare Directory Services) and Windows NT uses the Explorer and NTFS (and other file systems) for directory and file services.

I don't dig deep into protocols or network operations in this chapter, leaving that coverage to later chapters dealing with cable (Chapter 6) and network models and architectures (Parts III and IV).

A network operating system (NOS) is a specialized piece of system software that runs on a network server to provide the following services:

- ✔ Connects computers and peripheral devices into a local area network (LAN) and services their requests for resources

- ✔ Manages who can access data and shared network resources (such as printers, CD-ROM, disk drives, software, and so on)

- ✔ Monitors the performance and activities of the network

You need to know three NOS systems for the Network+ test: Novell NetWare, Microsoft Windows NT Server 4.0, and UNIX (or its little brother, Linux). You may also see the Mac/OS included in a list or a situation, but the Network+ test won't ask any questions about its NOS functions.

Based on the definition of a network operating system that I include earlier in this section, Novell NetWare is the only one of the bunch that is truly and solely an NOS. The others (Windows NT, Mac/OS, and UNIX/Linux) are actually multipurpose operating systems. As you prepare for the Network+ exam, concentrate only on their network operating system functions.

Enlisting in the NOS Services Core

Network operating systems generally provide a whole host of core services, and although you don't need to know the list inside and out, you can use the following bulleted items to organize your overall knowledge of an NOS — the big picture, as they say.

✔ **File services** provide shared access to directories and files and fault-tolerance services on network storage devices.

✔ **Print services** provide a common utility for local and remote printing on shared network printers and manage print queues, devices, forms, and user access.

✔ **Directory services** provide users with transparent access to network resources and services, which means that users do not need to know where data or resources are physically located. Directory services create the illusion that all resources are local. Novell NetWare includes NetWare Directory Services (NDS), and Windows NT uses its Explorer.

✔ **Security services** provide network security and data protection for local and remote access, including user-level (password-based), share-level (permissions-based), and data encryption services.

✔ **Messaging services** provide message (e-mail) store and forward services and support for mail-enabled applications. This service, along with security services, is fast becoming a primary NOS service as internetwork computing continues to evolve.

✔ **Routing services** provide multiprotocol routing services, including options for common LAN protocols (IP, IPX, and AppleTalk).

✔ **Network administration services** provide SNMP (Simple Network Management Protocol) and resource and directory structure management tools.

Scoping Out Novell NetWare

On the Network+ exam, IntraNetWare, the newest incarnation of Novell NetWare, is still referred to by its older, more established, and commonly used name — Novell NetWare.

A popular local-area network (LAN) operating system developed by Novell Corporation, NetWare supports a variety of different types of LANs, including Ethernet, and token ring networks. Like most operating system software, Novell has gone through some changes, enhancements, and fixes in its history. In fact, Novell has a variety of versions, including Novell ZenWorks, NetWare 3.*x,* NetWare 4.*x,* NetWare IntraNetWare, and recently NetWare 5. Any NetWare questions on the Network+ test are not version specific. You'll be well prepared for this part of the test if you have a good general understanding of NetWare's functions and services.

Don't read this and keep studying

I don't deliver lengthy histories of NetWare, Windows NT, and UNIX because frankly, you don't need all that stuff for the test, and I wouldn't dream of distracting you from your studies. If you're anything like me, you probably subconsciously seek out all the interesting trivial details of subjects as a diversion to actually hitting the books.

You can find loads of background material on the World Wide Web. I recommend that you visit the following sites if you crave historical background on these products:

NetWare — `www.netware.novell.com/discover`

Windows NT—`www.microsoft.com/ntserver`

UNIX — `www.yahoo.com/computers/operating_systems/unix/`

Remember that the Network+ test is not the CNE exam. You don't need to know NOS versions or match them to their functions for the test. In fact, you don't need to know much beyond these facts:

- ✔ The IPX protocol, also known as the IPX/SPX protocol, is the primary protocol of NetWare (see "NetWare messaging services," later in this chapter).

- ✔ NetWare arranges files and dates in both physical and logical file systems (see "NetWare file systems," later in this chapter).

- ✔ NetWare uses the NetWare Directory Services (NDS) to manage resources on the network (see "NetWare Directory Services (NDS)," later in this chapter).

NetWare file systems

A *file system* is the way an NOS handles and stores files or, in this case, how NetWare stores and handles files on the network. NetWare divides the physical disk media into logical groupings called volumes. A *volume,* which represents a fixed-size amount of hard disk space, is the highest level in the NetWare file system. A volume may be created on any hard disk that has a NetWare partition, and a NetWare server can support up to 64 volumes on a network.

Two kinds of volumes exist in the NetWare file system: physical and logical. A *physical volume* is made up of up to 32 volume segments that can be stored across one or more hard disks. To further complicate this, a disk drive can hold up to 8 volume segments from one or more physical volumes. A *logical volume* is divided into directories and is used to locate files. The NetWare installation creates the first volume, which is named SYS.

A colon follows the volume name in directory paths; for example, the path to the PUBLIC directory on the SYS volume is SYS:PUBLIC. This format is much like the DOS device designator (such as A:).

NetWare file and directory attributes

You can protect data on two levels: what can be done to files and directories (the subject of this section) and who has access to them (I cover this hot topic in the upcoming "Keeping out the nasties with NetWare security" section).

You should be familiar with the file attributes included in Table 5-1, which compares a few of the file attributes used in NetWare and Windows NT. As shown in the table, minor differences exist between NetWare rights and Windows NT file permissions. For the Network+ exam, you don't need to know any file attributes beyond what is included in Table 5-1.

Table 5-1	File Properties Used in NetWare and Windows NT		
NetWare Attribute	**Windows NT Permission**	**Meaning**	**Purpose**
A	A	Archive	Directory or file is new or has been changed and needs to be backed up.
H	H	Hidden	A file that cannot be viewed with directory list commands.
RO	R	Read-only	Restricts access to read-only and prevents changes to the file.
RW	-	Read-write	Directory or file can be viewed, changed, or deleted. No direct Windows NT equivalent (absence of read-only attribute enables same action).

(continued)

Table 5-1 *(continued)*

NetWare Attribute	Windows NT Permission	Meaning	Purpose
SH	-	Shareable	More than one user can access the file at a time; handled in Windows NT by creating a network share.
SY	S	System	Operating system files.

The entries marked with a dash indicate NetWare rights that are not supported or are implemented differently in Windows NT.

NetWare print services

Network print services are a part of the transparent world created for network users. Figure 5-1 is a simplistic illustration of the difference between what the user believes and network reality.

NetWare controls printing through a mechanism called a printer queue. The queue accepts and holds requests for print services until the printer in question becomes available. One or more print servers on the network hang on to incoming print jobs until the printer is free to receive the order.

Figure 5-1: The user's view of printing versus the network reality.

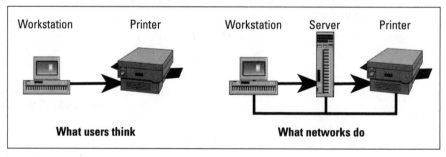

Workstation   Printer   Workstation   Server   Printer

What users think   **What networks do**

The PCONSOLE utility manages NetWare printer queues. PCONSOLE is a command-line utility that allows you to monitor and administer the network printer queues.

NetWare Directory Services (NDS)

In general, an NOS directory service is used to identify the resources on a network, such as e-mail addresses, computers, and printers, and make them accessible to users and server- and client-based applications. Ideally, the directory service shields the user from the network's physical topology and protocols, creating a transparent working environment. The Windows 95/98 Explorer is an example of a simple directory service.

Network directory services generally fall under the ITU (International Telecommunications Union) X.500 standard. However, because this standard is so large and complex, virtually none of the network directory services in use comply totally.

NetWare Directory Services (NDS) delivers most NetWare core services. NDS serves as an agent for the user in requesting and accessing network resources. When the user logs on, NDS captures information about the user to facilitate any requests the user makes — then or later — for system resources. Users can go blissfully about the business of what they want to do rather than concern themselves with how their wishes are carried out.

From a network administrator's point of view, NDS helps manage users, applications, and the network resources that users can access. Through NDS, the administrator creates and controls a database of users and resources, including resources in remote locations. Although NDS is an integrated part of a NetWare installation, it can be installed on a Windows NT network and on several flavors of UNIX as well.

Keeping out the nasties with NetWare security

Any NOS worthy of that designation must provide some means for keeping out the mean-and-nasties while enabling the good-and-deserving to access the resources they require. NetWare is no different: It uses a two-level model of SUPERVISOR and non-SUPERVISOR (a.k.a. users, peons, pests, nags, and so on) accounts.

The all-knowing, all-powerful SUPERVISOR

Supervisor-level accounts (SUPERVISOR and ADMIN) are the omnipotent, anointed rulers of the NetWare network. Supervisor accounts have the power to add and remove users from the network and to set which network resources each user can and cannot access.

Supervisor accounts also have the ability to run administrative software utilities for a wide range of security, fault-tolerance, and user management functions.

Groups and users

On a NetWare system, a login account represents each user, and every account can have its own set of resource access rights. You turn to group accounts to collectively administer users who rely on the same software and access the same directories and files. On all NetWare systems, all users automatically belong to the PUBLIC group. However, to restrict access to accounting files, a group named BEANCNTR may be created and include only the accounting office users. All file rights and permissions assigned to BEANCNTR are then automatically extended to the users in this group.

You can protect data not only by assigning file attributes (see "NetWare file and directory attributes," earlier in this chapter), but also by giving specific groups or individual users access to certain volumes, directories, and files. Assigning rights to group or user accounts is the mechanism by which you can keep all other users out of the accounting files, except those in the BEANCNTR group.

User security rights work with file attributes to determine who has access to a file and what they can do with it. Table 5-2 provides a list of the NetWare user security rights that you can assign to NetWare files and directories.

Review Table 5-2 for background information only. What you need to know about user rights is that much of data resource security is set through assignment of user rights, also known as *user-level security*.

Table 5-2	NetWare Security Rights
Name	*Description*
ACCESS CONTROL	This is like granting supervisor-level rights to a user for a particular directory or file.
CREATE	This enables a user to make subdirectories and create files.
ERASE	This enables a user to delete a file or directory, provided the file is not read-only.
FILE SCAN	The user can use the DIR command to view the contents of a directory.
MODIFY	The user can change files, including renaming them, and change their attributes.
READ	The user can open or execute files.
SUPERVISOR	The user has all other rights.
WRITE	The user can write to files that do not have read-only attributes set.

User account restrictions

Using NWADMIN, NWADMN32, NETADMIN, or SYSCON, depending on the NetWare version, you can set a variety of other access and login limits on a user account. These restrictions include the number of active login accounts a user can open, a designated workstation for a user, and the time of the day or the days of the week an account is valid. You can also set password characteristics, an account expiration date, or a limit on disk space used.

No, not that kind of messaging services

Although most people think of e-mail when they hear the term *messaging,* the word actually refers to the technology employed by the network to move service requests and data around the network. As far as e-mail goes, NetWare supports the protocols that enable e-mail clients and mail-enabled applications, but its primary messaging functions are carried out through the IPX protocol.

The IPX/SPX protocols

The Internetwork Packet Exchange (IPX) and its companion protocol Sequenced Packet Exchange (SPX), commonly referenced as IPX/SPX, provide a combined function that ensures that a network message — a packet — gets to its intended address. IPX routes packets across the network to their destinations and directs replies and returning data to their appropriate locations; SPX verifies arrival of routed material. The IPX protocol works well with many different network topologies, which is one reason why Microsoft created its own version of IPX for Windows NT (see "IPX and TCP/IP," later in the chapter).

IPX is a best-effort protocol, which means that it does not include a message acknowledgement system to guarantee delivery of a message. This is where SPX comes in. SPX enhances IPX by supplying acknowledgement services. SPX requests verification (in the form of a checksum or calculated control sum) from the destination location and then compares that value with the sum that it calculated before sending the message. If the two match, the packet reached its destination intact. If the two sums do not match, SPX has IPX resend the packet. SPX also manages larger messages that must be broken into smaller packets, verifying their sequencing as well.

One of IPX's stronger features is its ability to use different frame types. This feature can be a problem if two NetWare servers try to communicate using different frame types. Unless two NetWare networks or servers use the same frame types, they cannot communicate. For the test, you don't necessarily need to know the different packet formats supported by NetWare, but do remember that in order to communicate, two NetWare systems must use the same packet type.

Don't confuse IPX with IP (Internet Protocol). IP is the TCP/IP protocol that provides the mechanism for transferring data across an internetwork, and IPX is the native transport protocol of NetWare.

IPX burst mode

Trying to use IPX to send messages over a wide area network can inspire frustration. Because IPX requires each packet to be acknowledged before it sends the next packet, routing messages over slower transmission links, such as telephone lines, can be extremely slow. The remedy for this snail's pace is the use of packet burst mode, which requires an acknowledgement only after a burst (bundle) of packets are received correctly at their destination.

Getting around with routing services

NetWare provides support for multiprotocol routing services through a suite of software tools called the IntraNetWare bundle. The elements included with the IntraNetWare suite are

- **NetWare MultiProtocol Router with WAN Extensions** provides concurrent routing support for IPX, TCP/IP, and AppleTalk, NetBIOS, and SNA/LLC2 (Systems Network Architecture/Logical-Link Control Type 2) protocols and applications. The WAN extensions package provides NetWare with the ability to connect over ISDN (Integrated Systems Digital Network), frame relay, or ATM (Asynchronous Transfer Mode) without an external router.

- **NetWare IPX/IP Gateway** enables network clients to connect to the Internet to access resources without running a TCP/IP client. The gateway translates between NetWare's native IPX protocol (used to communicate on the local network) and the IP protocol (used to communicate with remote network hosts).

- **RIP (IPX)** is NetWare's version of the standard Routing-Information Protocol (RIP) used to determine the best path for a message to follow to its destination.

- **NetWare Web Server** enables the NetWare server to act as a World Wide Web server, including browser-level access to NDS.

- **FTP Services for NetWare** enables the NetWare server to provide file transfer protocol support to local and remote users.

Not much happening here

A NetWare network, like any other network, requires performance of a considerable number of administrative tasks and responsibilities, that are the same regardless of which network operating system is in use. The Network+

exam focuses on certain generic administrative functions, such as user administration, security policies, password control, resource management, and data integrity. Chapters 19 and 20 discuss the administrative duties that you should be familiar with for the Network+ exam.

Checking Out Windows NT Server

Like NetWare, Windows NT has several versions still in use around the networking world. The most popular current version is Windows NT Server 4.0. Although not mentioned by name on the test, 4.0 is the version covered by the exam. Later versions, Windows NT 5.0 or the ever-imminent Windows 2000, and some of the newer Windows NT features, such as Active Directory, are not covered on the test.

So, focus your studies on Windows NT Server 4.0, especially user accounts and group management (spend some time in Chapter 20).

Windows NT looks very much like the Windows graphical user interface (GUI) found on nearly all desktop computers these days. However, beyond its pretty face, the similarities begin to fade. Make no mistake about it, Windows NT Server was designed to compete with Novell NetWare as a network operating system and provides each of the NOS core services (listed earlier in this chapter in "Enlisting the NOS Services Core").

Whereas NetWare has NDS to provide the lion's share of its core services, Windows NT relies on a family of specialized services to provide its core functions. Table 5-3 lists the Windows NT service that provides each of the NOS core services.

Don't memorize this table. I include this information as background material and as a tool to compare the Windows NT architecture to Novell.

Table 5-3	Windows NT Core Services
Core Service Area	*Windows NT Service*
File services	NTFS (New Technology File System)
Print services	Windows NT File and Print Services
Directory services	The Windows NT Explorer and the User Manager for Domains
Security services	The Security Access Manager and the Remote Access Services

(continued)

Table 5-3 (continued)

Core Service Area	Windows NT Service
Messaging services	Microsoft Exchange, Outlook, Mail, and other add-on products
Routing services	Routing Information Protocol (RIP)
Administration services	User Manager for Domains and Windows NT Control Panel

Getting the FAT out of the Windows NT file system

Windows NT gives you a choice of two file systems: FAT (file allocation table) or NTFS (New Technology File System). FAT is the easier and less expensive way to go, in terms of hardware and labor. The FAT file system enables users to store and read files on server disk drives, but little data protection exists beyond basic user-level security. Because of this limitation, NTFS is the file system of choice for Windows NT Server servers.

NTFS is a driver that loads at the I/O layer of Windows NT to process input/output requests for its files, directories, and volumes and provides file- and directory-level security.

FAT also provides share-level security identical to that offered by Windows 9x. Network shares located on an NTFS drive provide additional share-level security features to the network administrator (see "Share and share alike," later in this section).

The disk bone is connected to the partition bone . . .

Windows NT supports a fairly simple hierarchical organization of hard disk drives. At the top of the storage tree is the physical storage media itself. Using FDISK.EXE (yes, the old DOS FDISK), the hard disk is divided into one or more partitions. No matter how many disks are installed on a computer, at least one primary partition (usually designated drive C) must serve as the boot partition for the system. Any other partitions created on the disks are extended partitions.

Okay, here is the wrinkle in this otherwise simple hierarchy: Each extended partition can also be subdivided into as many as 23 logical partitions, each of which can be assigned a drive letter. One or more partitions form a volume, which is assigned to a file system, such as NTFS or FAT. And that brings you back full circle.

Share and share alike

Network shares enable users to access data and resources on the network. Although they are part of the file system, network shares create a new level of security called *share-level security.* Users can access data on the network only after assignment of the appropriate user-level security and creation of a network share for the directory or file the user wants to access. The definition of share-level security for Windows NT may be slightly different than that given earlier for a peer-to-peer network (see Chapter 4), but the difference is subtle. In the peer-based network, the workstation owner allowed the shares. On a Windows NT network, both the network administrator *and* the workstation or resource owner may grant share-level access.

The share name for a file or directory is usually the same as its file system name, but different names can be assigned. For example, if you're so inclined, you can assign the directory BEANCOUNTER the share name ACCTONLY. Users can then use the shorter name to access the shared resource using the following syntax:

```
\\SERVER_NAME\SHARE_NAME or \\THUNDER_BIT\ACCTONLY
```

The general syntax used for share names is the Universal Naming Convention (UNC), which consists of two backward slashes followed by the server name followed by a backward slash followed by the share name, as shown in the first example. The second sample shows the share for the ACCTONLY share (folder) on the THUNDER_BIT server.

It's a hard (copy) world

Windows NT Server print services involves four components: print servers, print queues, print jobs, and oddly enough, printers. Actually, two types of printers exist: physical printers and logical printers. To confuse things further, you have three types of physical printers: server-attached, network-attached, and workstation-attached. These three configurations are also known as server printer, network printer, and remote printer, respectively. The good news is that beyond the naming quagmire, Windows NT printing works very well. It's just a matter of organization.

Print servers are either computers dedicated to that task or a network workstation that takes on an additional duty. Print queues form the line of print jobs (stuff to be printed) submitted by the user, with each job awaiting its turn on the printer. When the user sends something to the printer (refer to Figure 5-1), the print server stores it in the queue for the destination printer until the printer is available.

For the exam, know the following three printer configurations for printers on a Windows NT Server network:

- ✔ **Server-attached (server printer):** This is just what it sounds like, a printer attached directly to the server computer.

- ✔ **Network-attached (network printer):** You can attach several printers directly to the network as an addressable node on the network. These printers use special network adapters, such as the HP JetDirect card, to connect to the network.

- ✔ **Workstation-attached (remote printer):** This is a printer cabled directly to a network workstation. In order for other network users to access the printer, the workstation user (owner) must make the printer available via share-level permissions (see "Securing the NT world" later in this chapter).

Windows NT workstations do not need a driver installed locally for a network- or server-attached printer. Windows NT print services uses a server-based printer driver to prepare the print job for the printer, making sure that the printer receives instructions and formatting that the printer understands in its own language.

Exploring Windows NT directory services

Veteran Windows users, those folks who have experience with a Windows version that includes a number 9 in it, are likely to be familiar with the Windows NT Explorer. At first glance, NT Explorer looks exactly like the Explorer found in Windows 95 and 98. Beneath its facade, though, Windows NT Explorer clearly separates itself from the Explorer pack.

The Windows NT Explorer is the file and directory management tool for Windows NT Server. Using a special set of tools and utilities found only on the Windows NT version, you can add or delete directories (called folders) and network shares or alter the structure of the network. With NT Explorer, you can also manage file permissions, auditing, and ownership properties.

File permissions (refer to Table 5-1) control the actions that a user can perform on a file or directory. Auditing sets up a tracking procedure that logs access and other activity on a share, file, or directory. Only the owner of a network resource can change its properties. On occasion, the administrator must take ownership of a resource to solve a problem.

Securing the NT world

Security on Windows NT Server and Novell NetWare operates in much the same way, with three levels: user-level, share-level, and resource permissions. Users and groups are assigned rights to access shared network resources. Permissions govern the type of actions permitted on a resource. User rights are reestablished with each logon.

Share-level security

You can create network shares for a directory, file, printer, CD-ROM drive, and so on to enable users to access that network resource. A network share can be restricted to certain groups or accounts or left open to all network users. Network share-level security can be set only for network resources. Local resources, those attached or inside a local workstation, can be shared in the same manner by the workstation user (owner).

Table 5-4 lists the share permissions that the Windows NT administrator has at his or her disposal.

Table 5-4	Share Permissions
Permission	*Description*
No Access	This is a kind of backhanded permission. With this permission "granted," a user or group cannot see or access the shared resource.
Read	Read-only access is granted. No changes can be saved to the shared file.
Change	This share permission enables users to make changes to a shared file or directory.
Full Control	Whoa, there! You have just assigned full access and control to a share (including the ability to remove it).

Mother, may I?

File and directory permissions are a part of share-level security on a network. They control what can — and cannot — be done on a file or directory. Just because users have access to files doesn't mean that they can have their way with them. You may want to limit some users to read-only permission to a file, and you may actually trust some others. The file permissions shown earlier in Table 5-1 provide you with sufficient background information for the Network+ exam because file rights and permissions are not tested directly.

Clinging to the NetBEUI

At its most basic levels, Windows NT uses two protocols, NetBIOS (Network Basic Input/Output System) and NetBEUI (NetBIOS Extended User Interface), that have a singular purpose: to carry network messages around the network. However, NetBEUI is somewhat limited if you want the network to grow or connect to the outside world through, for example, the Internet.

NetBEUI is a nonroutable, connection-oriented protocol that works well on small networks. *Nonroutable* means that the protocol cannot be used to connect with another physical network without the nonroutable protocol first passing through a bridge. *Connection-oriented* means that the protocol operates with a form of point-to-point connection much like the connection used to dial up another computer over a modem. One benefit of a connection-oriented protocol is that the sender receives confirmation when a packet arrives at its destination.

IPX and TCP/IP

Windows NT Server also supports virtually every one of the popular networking protocols in use, including IPX, TCP/IP, and AppleTalk. This support is provided through three protocol bundles: NWLink (NetWare Link), Microsoft Services for Macintosh, and Microsoft TCP/IP.

NWLink is the Microsoft version of the NetWare IPX. Often called Microsoft IPX, NWLink is fully compatible with IPX.

Microsoft TCP/IP (Transmission Control Protocol/Internet Protocol) implements the hugely popular open protocol suite used primarily for the Internet, and TCP/IP is gaining some favor as a LAN protocol as well. I devote much of this book (especially Part IV) to coverage of TCP/IP, so I spare you the details here.

For the Network+ test, you need to know that Windows NT Server supports and implements TCP/IP protocols and IP address resolution as its default protocol.

Other Windows NT protocols

Windows NT also supports DLC and AppleTalk, which is not a fact that's likely to be a focal point on the Network+ test, but you do need a casual familiarity with the names and purposes of these protocols. They show up in situations and multiple-choice answer lists.

DLC (Data Link Control) is a protocol used to connect networks and workstations to mainframe computers or to network-attached printers.

AppleTalk is the Apple Macintosh networking protocol. This protocol is implemented on a Windows NT Server network as Services for Macintosh. Another Apple Macintosh network protocol you may see on the test is TokenTalk, the token ring equivalent of the Ethernet AppleTalk.

Getting around with Windows NT routing services

Routers are either dynamic or static. Dynamic routers, such as a TCP/IP or IPX router, are protocol dependent (see Chapter 10 for information on routers). Windows NT implements dynamic routers for both IPX (RIP IPX) and TCP/IP (RIP) using a choice of frame (packet) standards: IEEE 802.2, IEEE 802.3, or auto-detect. IEEE 802.2 and 802.3 are standards for Logical Link Control formats and bus networks, respectively. The auto-detect method looks at the packet and determines which format it uses.

Managing users and not much else

The User Manager for Domains utility is the Windows NT tool used to manage group and user accounts, rights, and permissions on a Windows NT Server network with multiple domains. Beyond this, Windows NT administrative services are not specifically covered on the Network+ exam. Instead, the Network+ exam covers network administration activities in a general way without specifically mentioning particular network operating systems.

Giving UNIX the Once-over

For the Network+ test, you don't need to know a whole lot about the UNIX operating system itself (or its work-alike — Linux). What you do have to keep in mind is the way this operating system supports networking, especially internetworking.

UDP and ICMP, and we all get along

TCP/IP on UNIX is no different than TCP/IP on any other operating system or NOS. However, in UNIX networking services, you have some alternatives, the most common of which are the User Datagram Protocol (UDP) and the Internet Control Message Protocol (ICMP). The UNIX world calls data packets *datagrams*.

UDP is a connectionless protocol designed for applications that don't need messages divided into multiple datagrams or that don't care about the sequence in which messages are received. UDP, which works with IP, is a direct replacement for TCP. However, UDP doesn't track what has been sent so that messages can be resent if necessary.

ICMP serves to transmit error messages and messages intended for TCP/IP itself. For example, if you attempt to connect to an Internet host server, you may receive an ICMP message that states, "Host unreachable."

Sharing files over the Network File System (NFS)

The Network File System (NFS) provides network services using a mechanism called *remote procedure call* (RPC). NFS enables users to access files on remote hosts in the same way they access files on their local systems. The remote file access is completely transparent to the user and is compatible with a variety of server and remote host architectures. The true benefit of NFS is that centrally stored files can be mounted, or linked, to the local workstation when it is logged on. To the user, the file is just as close at hand as any local file. Using NFS to access files is very effective for sharing large or commonly accessed files, which can be installed in a single location and then shared throughout the network.

Creating one from many with the Network Information System (NIS)

The Network Information System (NIS) is a UNIX service that distributes information, such as that contained in the user accounts and groups files, to all servers on a network. NIS makes the network appear to be a single system, with the same accounts supported on all servers. Using NIS to organize a network eliminates the need for the user to know, or find out, just where on the network resources are located. Resources all appear to be present on what seems to be a single network.

Workstation Welfare: For the Good of the Client

No matter which network operating system is running on the network servers, each workstation requires its own operating system, preferably one that is compatible with the NOS and its protocols. In some situations, the NOS has to adjust to the OS running on its clients.

As a group, the Microsoft Windows operating systems are the most popular client operating systems. Windows systems (Windows 3.*x*, Windows 9*x*, and Windows NT Workstation) include client software to enable the workstation to communicate with a network running the IPX, TCP/IP, or NetBEUI protocol. Later releases of Windows also include clients and services providing cross-platform support for file, directory, and print services for NetWare and Macintosh AppleTalk networks.

The Linux operating system is growing more popular as a workstation (and network) operating system. Part of the reason for its popularity is the fact that it too includes clients for TCP/IP, IPX, and NetBEUI networks.

Network-specific client-based protocols are also called *redirectors,* which basically describes what they do. Messages sent to the network are redirected (properly formatted and structured specifically for a certain protocol) to the protocol that the redirector is associated with. A workstation may run multiple clients, depending on the number and type of servers it has access to and the NOS and protocols running on the servers.

Cross-Platform Connectivity

Windows NT Server and NetWare servers on the same network, you say? Surely not. Actually, the scenario is not unusual, especially if the network is being migrated to one or the other. Both of these NOSs include utilities and services packages to provide for cross-platform connectivity on the network.

Microsoft Windows NT Server includes a variety of cross-platform connectivity services to enable all Windows NT clients to access a NetWare server. These services are:

- ✔ **Gateway Service for NetWare (GSNW)** enables a Windows NT server to act as a gateway for Windows clients to access resources on a NetWare server.

- ✔ **Client Service for NetWare CSNW**, which is included in Windows NT Workstation, enables a client to access and use file and print services from a NetWare server.

- ✔ **File and Print Services for NetWare (FPNW)** enables a Windows NT server to be seen as a Novell NetWare 3.*x*-compatible server by NetWare clients for file and print services.

- ✔ **Directory Service Manager for NetWare (DSMN)** enables user and group accounts to be managed on both the Windows NT and NetWare servers, with the changes of one updated automatically to the other.

Prep Test

1 Which of the following are among the more popular network operating systems? (Choose three.)

A ❏ UNIX/Linux

B ❏ MS-DOS

C ❏ Windows NT Server

D ❏ Windows 98

E ❏ NetWare

2 Which of the following is a valid NetWare path to the public directory on the SYS volume?

A ○ \\SYS\PUBLIC

B ○ \PUBLIC\SYS

C ○ SYS\\PUBLIC

D ○ SYS:PUBLIC

3 NetWare printer queues are managed by which utility?

A ○ PRINTERS

B ○ PCONSOLE

C ○ PDIRECTOR

D ○ QUEUEMGR

4 The driver that loads at the I/O layer of Windows NT to process input/output requests for its files, directories, and volumes and to provide file- and directory-level security is

A ○ NDS

B ○ NFS

C ○ GSNW

D ○ NTFS

5 A valid example of a Windows NT share name is

A ○ \\SERVER\SHARE_NAME

B ○ \SHARE_NAME\\SERVER

C ○ /SERVER/SHARE_NAME

D ○ /SHARE_NAME//SERVER

6 Which of the following is NOT a type of Windows NT printer configuration?

A ○ Server printer
B ○ Network printer
C ○ Domain printer
D ○ Remote printer

7 Microsoft's version of NetWare's IPX protocol is called

A ○ Client Services for NetWare
B ○ Gateway Services for NetWare
C ○ NWLink
D ○ TCP/IP

8 Which of the following describe the UDP protocol? (Choose two.)

A ❑ Connectionless
B ❑ Guaranteed delivery
C ❑ Datagram packets
D ❑ Open format packets

9 What mechanism is used by NFS to provide network file services?

A ○ PRC
B ○ NDS
C ○ U812
D ○ RPC

10 The UNIX protocol used for messages that are not divided over several datagrams is

A ○ ICMP
B ○ UDP
C ○ RPC
D ○ TCP

Answers

1 *A, C, and E.* Although other operating systems and network operating systems are in use, these three are definitely the most popular on the Network+ exam. *See "What You Need to Know about NOS."*

2 *D.* The volume name is used in directory path names. Following the MS-DOS device pattern, a colon follows the volume name. *Check out "NetWare file systems."*

3 *B.* Take a look at *"NetWare Print Services."*

4 *D.* Another choice for the file system in Windows NT is FAT (file allocation table). *Review "Windows NT file systems."*

5 *A.* Network shares enable users to access data and shared devices on the network. *Look over "Share and share alike."*

6 *C.* Printers can be attached to the server, directly to the network, or to a workstation (remote printer). *See "Printers."*

7 *C.* Microsoft reverse engineered IPX/SPX to create its own version of this popular network protocol. *Check out "IPX and TCP/IP."*

8 *A and C.* The UDP protocol is used in situations where a message does not need more than one packet and delivery does not need to be guaranteed. *Take a look at "UDP and ICMP, and we all get along."*

9 *D.* RPC (remote procedure call) enables users to access remote system files and resources. *Review "Sharing files over the Network File System (NFS)."*

10 *B.* The User Datagram Protocol (UDP) directly replaces TCP and works with IP to send and receive Internet packets. *Look at "UDP and ICMP, and we all get along."*

Chapter 6

Network Media Primer

▶ Identifying common network media and connectors

▶ Listing the characteristics of common network media

▶ Describing the media and function of a network backbone

▶ Defining a network segment

Many so-called experts suggest that all networks are bound for wireless-ness someday. The possibility surely exists, especially when converting to wireless media costs about the same as dealing with wired cable — the reliability results are equal. But until that time, you can expect networks to exist on a cable-based infrastructure and the Network+ exam to ground its questions accordingly.

Nearly as important as the network operating system or the topology chosen for the network, the cable media sets the data transmission speed, the network's overall distance, the number and type of connectivity devices required, and the number of devices the network can support. For this reason, CompTIA has decided, and rightly so, that any network technician worth his or her weight in RJ-45 connectors has to show familiarity with network media.

You don't need to be an expert or anything. However, you do need to know the construction of the most commonly used media and be able to identify each cable from an illustration. No sweat, you say! Wait, there's more—you also need to know the characteristics, limitations, advantages and disadvantages, and the conditions under which each type of cable is an appropriate choice for a network. That's all!

This chapter focuses on helping you fine-tune your vast knowledge of cabling, cable types, and connectors and all of the technical stuff about each kind. And forget about that wireless stuff, I was only kidding! I don't want to give you bad dreams.

Quick Assessment

Identifying common network media

1 The three most popular general types of cable media used in networks are _____, _____, and _____.

2 The amount of data a cable can carry in a certain amount of time is its _____.

3 _____ is the most common specific type of cable used in networks.

Listing the characteristics of common network media

4 Some cable types are highly susceptible to electromagnetic and radio frequency _____.

5 The maximum segment length of 10BaseT cable is _____.

6 Category 3 and Category 5 cable are both a type of _____ cable.

7 The core of a(n) _____ cable contains strands of glass or plastic.

8 100BaseTX indicates a data speed of _____ Mbps.

Defining a network segment

9 A(n) _____ is a group of workstations, servers, or devices that have been isolated by a bridge or router.

Describing the media and function of a network backbone

10 The _____ serves as the trunk line for an entire network.

Answers

1 *Coaxial, twisted-pair, and fiber-optic.* Review "The big three of cabling."

2 *Bandwidth or data transmission speed.* Check out "Technical cable stuff."

3 *Unshielded twisted pair (UTP).* See "Unshielded is not unheralded."

4 *Interference.* Take a look at "Technical cable stuff."

5 *100 meters.* Review "The Ethernet Cable Standards."

6 *UTP.* See "Unshielded is not unheralded."

7 *Fiber-optic.* Look over "You Need Your Fiber."

8 *100.* Speed over to "Living in the Fast Ethernet lane."

9 *Network segment.* Check out "Networks in pieces all around."

10 *Backbone.* Review "Backbones and Segments."

The Fascinating World of Cables

Networks use cables made of two materials: copper and glass. Yes, the same stuff you find in pennies and windows. Both substances are relatively inexpensive and abundant, but more importantly they are excellent conductors. Copper is a great conductor of electricity and glass is a super conduit for light, which brings me to the reason for cable media in the first place.

In order for one computer to carry on a conversation with another computer, both computers must be able to transmit and receive electrical impulses representing commands or data. In a networked environment, whether peer-based or server-based, the computers and peripherals of the network are interconnected with a transmission medium to enable data exchange and resource sharing. Cable media has laid the foundation on which networks grew — literally.

The big three of cabling

Perhaps the best news I have for you in this entire book, beyond the fact that you don't have to memorize the name of every NOS that ever existed, is that you need to know only three cable types:

- **Coaxial (coax) cable:** This type of cable is a little like the cable used to connect your television set to the cable outlet. Actually, networks use two types of coax cable: thick coaxial cable and thin coaxial cable. I explain each type in the upcoming section, "Coaxial Cables through Thick and Thin."

- **Twisted pair (no, not the upstairs neighbors):** Twisted pair cable is available in two types: unshielded twisted pair (UTP) and shielded twisted pair (STP). UTP is similar to the wiring used to connect your telephone. I explain each of these cable types in the "Twisted Pair" section later in the chapter.

- **Fiber-optic:** Glass fibers carry modulated pulses of light to represent digital data signals. Although a few different types of fiber-optic cables exist, you care about only one specific kind, and it's generally referred to as fiber-optic.

So okay, my three types of cable turned into five with the variations within coaxial cable and twisted pair. Unfortunately, these variations do not have the same characteristics and performance — I cover those details in later sections of this chapter.

Technical cable stuff

All network cabling has a set of general characteristics that guide you in picking the most appropriate cable for a given situation. Here are definitions for the ones you may find on the Network+ exam:

- **Bandwidth (speed):** This is the amount of data a cable can carry in a certain period of time. Bandwidth is often expressed as the number of bits (either kilobits or megabits) that can be transmitted in a second. For example, UTP cable is nominally rated at 10 Mbps, or ten million bits per second.

- **Cost:** This is always a major consideration when choosing a cable type. The Network+ exam deals with this characteristic on a comparative basis. The relative cost comparisons for the major cable media are:

  - Twisted-pair cable is the least expensive, but has limitations that require other hardware to be installed.

  - Coaxial cable is a little more expensive than TP, but it doesn't require additional equipment, and it is inexpensive to maintain.

  - Fiber-optic cabling is the most expensive, requires skilled installation labor, and is expensive to install and maintain.

- **Maximum segment length:** Every cable is subject to a condition called *attenuation*, which means that the signal weakens and can no longer be recognized. Attenuation occurs at a distance specific to every type of cable. This distance (measured in meters) is the maximum segment length for a cable medium, or the distance at which signals on the cable must be regenerated.

- **Maximum number of nodes per segments:** Each time a device is added to a network, the effect is like another hole being put in the cable. Like leaks from pinholes in a balloon, having too many devices attached to a network cable reduces the distance at which attenuation begins. Therefore, each type of cable must limit the number of nodes that can be attached to a cable segment.

- **Resistance to interference**: The different cable media have varying vulnerability to electromagnetic interference (EMI) or radio frequency interference (RFI) caused by electric motors, fluorescent light fixtures, your magnet collection, the radio station on the next floor of your home or office, and so on. As the construction of the cable and its cladding (coverings) varies, so does its resistance to EMI and RFI signals.

Just for clarification, a network segment is created each time you add a network device that regenerates or redirects the message signals being transmitted over the network. An example of such a device is a router, switch, or bridge. I discuss the types of devices used to create a network in Chapters 8, 9, and 10.

About the only way that I know to remember the information in Table 6-1 is to memorize it. You can count on seeing a variety of questions that use this information in one way or another.

Memorize the characteristics of thin and thick coaxial cable, unshielded twisted pair cable, and fiber-optic cable, especially as they are used in an Ethernet network as defined in IEEE 802.3. Be sure you know all of the other names coax cable goes by. Table 6-1 should help you with this.

Table 6-1	Cable Types and Their Characteristics			
Cable Type	*Bandwidth*	*Max. Segment Length*	*Max. Nodes/ Segments*	*Nodes' Resistance to Interference*
Thin coaxial	10 Mbps	185 meters	30	Good
Thick coaxial	10 Mbps	500 meters	100	Better
UTP	10–100 Mbps	100 meters	1,024	Poor
STP	16–1,000 Mbps	100 meters	1,024	Fair to Good
Fiber-optic	100–10,000 Mbps	2,000 meters	No limit	Best

Coaxial Cables through Thick and Thin

Although recently deposed as the ruling network cable type, coaxial cable is still a popular choice for networks. Coaxial is inexpensive, easy to work with, reliable, and moderately resistant to interference, which makes it a good choice in many situations.

Coaxial cable is constructed with a single solid copper wire core, which is surrounded by an insulator made of plastic or Teflon material. A braided metal shielding layer (and in some cables, another metal foil layer) covers the insulator, and a plastic sheath wrapper covers the cable. The metal shielding layers act to increase the cable's resistance to EMI and RFI signals. Figure 6-1 illustrates the construction of a coaxial cable.

Study Figure 6-1 carefully. The test may require that you identify coaxial cable from a drawing.

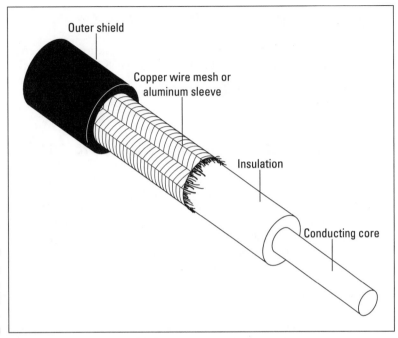

Outer shield

Copper wire mesh or
aluminum sleeve

Insulation

Conducting core

Figure 6-1:
The layers
of a coaxial
cable.

The Institute of Electrical and Electronics Engineers (IEEE) 802 project
defines coaxial cable as either thick or thin. Coaxial cable is used primarily in
Ethernet networking environments (see Chapter 4), where folks refer to the
cable as either thicknet or thinnet. Other names coaxial cable goes by are the
generic coax and 10Base5, thickwire, and yellow wire (all nicknames for thick
coaxial cable), and 10Base2, thinwire, and cheapnet (aliases for thin coaxial
cable).

What's this 10Base stuff?

In the Ethernet world, the designation of cable is also descriptive of its characteristics. Thick coax cable is designated as 10Base5, thin coaxial cable is
10Base2, and UTP is generally 10BaseT. The 10Base part indicates that these
cables carry 10 Mbps bandwidths and that they carry baseband (digital) signals. For coax cable, the 5 and 2 mean 500 meters and 200 meters, the
approximate maximum segment length of the cable. Actually, the maximum
segment length of thin coax is 185 meters, but 200 works better in this case,
and besides, it's easier to remember. The T in 10BaseT refers to twisted pair
cable. See "The Ethernet Cable Standards," later in this chapter, for more
information.

Now back to thicker subjects

The coaxial couple carries one additional designation: Thick coax is also designated as RG-11 or RG-8, and thin coax as RG-58 (the coax used for television service is RG-59, by the way). The RG stands for Radio/Government and is the rating of the cable based upon the type and thickness of its core wire.

Does this cable make me look fat?

Thick coax is the more rigid of the coaxial twins (fraternal, no doubt). It is about 1 centimeter (about four-tenths of an inch) in diameter and is commonly covered in a bright yellow covering, the origin of its "yellow wire" nickname. The thicker hide makes the cable more resistant to interference and attenuation, resulting in a longer segment length and the ability to support a greater number of nodes on a segment compared to its thinner sibling. That's it, I'm not fat, I'm just thick.

Connecting thick coaxial cable to workstations is a fairly complicated simple process. What I mean is that the whole business really is simple, but darned complicated to explain. An external transceiver attached to a piercing connector (appropriately called a "vampire" tap) is clamped on the thick wire, making a connection directly to the central core wire. Then a transceiver cable (also called a drop cable) is used to connect to a computer's network adapter card with an AUI (Attachment Unit Interface) connector. Figure 6-2 illustrates how simple this really is, despite my convoluted description.

Table 6-2 details the characteristics of thick coaxial cable.

Table 6-2	Thick Coaxial Cable Characteristics
Characteristic	*Value*
Max. Segment Length	500 meters (about 1,640 feet)
Bandwidth (Speed)	10 Mbps
Number of Nodes per Segment	100
Connector Type	AUI (Attachment Unit Interface)
Interference	Good

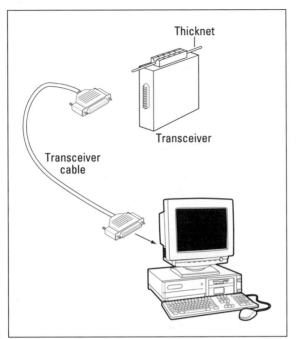

Thicknet

Transceiver

Transceiver
cable

Figure 6-2:
A thick coax
connection.

You can never be too thin

In contrast to its thicker relative, thin coaxial cable — commonly called thinnet cable — is lightweight and flexible. This thin friend is about two-tenths of an inch in diameter and is easily installed. Second only to UTP in popularity among cabling used for networks, thinnet is the right candidate for daisy-chaining computers together using a British Naval Connector "T" connector (BNC -T), shown in Figure 6-3. Daisy-chaining refers to connecting computers in a series by running the thinnet cable from one computer to the next.

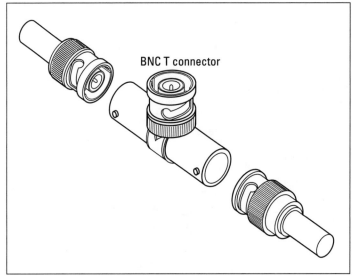

BNC T connector

Figure 6-3:
A BNC -T
connector.

Table 6-3 summarizes the characteristics of thin coaxial cable.

Table 6-3	Thin Coaxial Cable Characteristics
Characteristic	*Value*
Max. Segment Length	185 meters (a little over 600 feet)
Bandwidth (Speed)	10 Mbps
Number of Nodes per Segment	30
Connector Type	BNC (British Naval Connector)
Resistance to Interference	Good

The Twisted Pair

Although its title sounds like the bad name of an even worse movie, this section covers the most popular cabling in use for networks — twisted pair copper wire. This wire possesses all the attributes of a truly popular cable: It is the lightest, most flexible, least expensive, and easiest to install of any of the popular network media. The bad news is that is quite vulnerable to interference and has attenuation problems as well. But, given the right network design and implementation, these problems can be overcome.

As I mention in "Technical cable stuff" earlier in this chapter, you can use two types of twisted pair wire in networks: unshielded (UTP) and shielded (STP), both shown in Figure 6-4. Of the two, the more common choice is unshielded, which is particularly popular in Ethernet (bus) networks. Unshielded twisted pair wire is just about what its name implies, two unshielded wires twisted together.

Unshielded is not unheralded

For use in networks, unshielded twisted pair (UTP) is clearly the most common pick among cabling types. For all the reasons presented in the introductory paragraph of this section, unshielded provides the most installation flexibility and ease of maintenance of the big three cabling media. You may hear UTP referred to as 10BaseT Ethernet cable, which loosely translated means "The moon is made of green iMacs." However, for the Network+ exam, you should remember the more literal meaning, which is 10 megabits using baseband transmission over twisted pair copper lines.

Figure 6-4:
A two-wire unshielded twisted pair cable and a four-wire shielded twisted-pair cable.

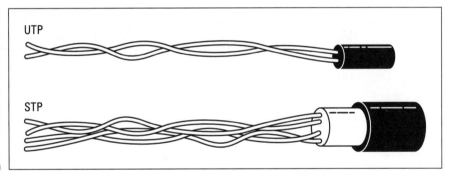

The Electronics Industries Association and the Telecommunications Industries Association (EIA/TIA) define UTP cable according to five categories, or "cats" as the real techies call them (as in Cat 3 or Cat 5):

 ✔ **Category 1 and 2:** Not used in networking, this isn't here and you didn't see it, so just walk away slowly, and you won't get hurt on the test.

 ✔ **Category 3:** A 4-pair cable supporting bandwidth up to 10 Mbps — the minimum standard for 10BaseT networks.

 ✔ **Category 4:** A 4-wire cable commonly used in 16 Mbps token ring networks.

 ✔ **Category 5:** A 4-wire cable with bandwidth up to 100 Mbps, used for 100BaseTX and ATM (asynchronous transfer mode) networking.

Isn't that a phone plug?

UTP uses an RJ-45 connector, as shown in Figure 6-5, which looks much like the little clip connector on your telephone, only a bit bigger.

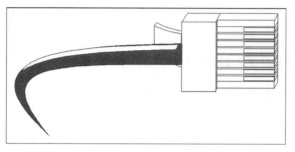

Figure 6-5:
UTP cable
requires
an RJ-45
connector.

The complete UTP

Table 6-4 summarizes the characteristics of UTP cable:

Table 6-4	Unshielded Twisted Pair Cable Characteristics
Characteristic	*Value*
Max. Segment Length	100 meters (not much over 320 feet)
Bandwidth (Speed)	10–100 Mbps
Number of Nodes per Segment	1,024
Connector Type	RJ (registered jack)-45
Resistance to Interference	Poor

Shielding the network from the shocking truth

The other half of the twisted pair is shielded twisted pair cable (STP). The magical way you can tell shielded apart from its sister cable: STP is the one with each of its wire pairs swaddled in a grounded copper or foil wrapper that helps shield them from interference. This wrapping of interference protection makes STP more expensive than UTP, but it does support higher transmission speeds and carry signals over longer distances.

STP is most commonly used in token ring networks. In fact, IBM has its own standards for twisted pair cable for ring networks. The IBM cable standard includes nine categories that range from a two-pair shielded cable (Type 1) to a UTP cable (Type 3), a fiber-optic cable (Type 5), and a fire-safe cable (Type 9). See Chapter 3 for a closer connection to cables.

Don't confuse UTP Category 3 or 5 (Cat 3 and Cat 5) with IBM Type 3 or Type 5 cabling. Cat N cables are used in Ethernet networks, and IBM Type N cables are used in token ring networks. To help you remember the differences between these two cable standards, I came up with IBM — IBM's Basic Media — and CAT (N) — "Creates a Twisted (Network)." Perhaps, you think the difference between these two acronyms isn't all that tough to remember in the first place. Well, I tried!

You Need Your Fiber

A fiber-optic cable carries data in the form of modulated pulses of light. Imagine turning a flashlight on and off a couple of million times a second: That strobe effect demonstrates how data travels through this kind of cable. The core of fiber-optic cable consists of two extremely thin strands of glass. Glass cladding covers each strand, helping to keep in the strand of light moving through the strand. The two strands transmit signals with each strand carrying light either up or down the cable run. A plastic outer jacket covers the cable, giving it a home to call its own. Figure 6-6 shows the makeup of a fiber-optic cable.

Figure 6-6:
Fiber-optic cable —
inside
and out.

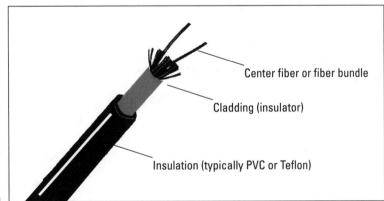

Center fiber or fiber bundle

Cladding (insulator)

Insulation (typically PVC or Teflon)

Because it uses light and not electrical signals, fiber-optic cable is not susceptible to electromagnetic or radio frequency interference, which gives it
incredibly long attenuation and maximum segment lengths. Network backbones commonly use fiber-optic cable. Table 6-5 summarizes the
characteristics of fiber-optic cable.

Table 6-5	Fiber-Optic Cable Characteristics
Characteristic	*Value*
Max. Segment Length	2 kilometers (a little over a mile)
Bandwidth (Speed)	100 Mbps to 2 Gbps
Resistance to Interference	Excellent

Don't fret over the fact that Table 6-5 doesn't have all of the same entries
included in those for UTP and coaxial cables. These are the characteristics
that you need for the test.

The Ethernet Cable Standards

So, what's in a name, you ask? If you're talking Ethernet cable, the name tells it
all: bandwidth/speed, transmission mode, and segment length (coaxial cable)
or cable type (TP or fiber-optic). Table 6-6 breaks down the meaning of each
of the Ethernet cable designations that you're likely to see on the Network+
exam. The "10Base" part of each standard indicates that it supports a 10 Mbps
transmission speed and uses a baseband (digital) transmission mode.

Table 6-6	Basic Ethernet Cable Standards	
Cable	*Maximum Distance*	*Cable Material*
10Base2	185 meters (the 2 is for approximately 200)	Thinnet coaxial
10Base5	500 meters	Thicknet coaxial
10BaseF	2,000 meters	Fiber-optic
10BaseT	100 meters	UTP

Where does the name *Ethernet* come from?

You really don't need to know this info, so if you're cramming for the exam, quit reading and get back to work. However, if you're leisurely reading through this part of the book, here's a bit of trivia you can use to amaze your friends and coworkers.

Like quite a bit of today's computer technology, the groundwork for Ethernet was developed by Xerox research. Originally a design for a wireless network (Get it? Ether, air?), the name *Ethernet* was a registered trademark of Xerox

Corporation. A more refined and developed version of Ethernet (Ethernet II) was widely used in early networking. Another name used for Ethernet during this time was DIX, which represented its earliest adopters and sponsors: Digital, Intel, and Xerox.

You may hear another story attributing the development to work that was performed by the University of Hawaii as well. In any case, the name Ethernet is now just a name without any specific meaning.

To complicate life further, variations of 10BaseF and 10BaseT standards are likely to show up on the exam. Here are the ones you may encounter on test day:

- ✔ **100BaseT:** Along with 100BaseX, the generic terms for *Fast Ethernet.*
- ✔ **100BaseTX:** A two-pair wire version of 100BaseT.
- ✔ **100BaseT4:** A four-pair wire version of Fast Ethernet.
- ✔ **100BaseFX:** Fast Ethernet using two-strand fiber-optic cable.
- ✔ **100BaseVG:** A new 100 Mbps standard over Category 3 cable.
- ✔ **100BaseVG-AnyLAN:** Hewlett Packard's proprietary version of 100BaseVG.

Backbones and Segments

Affectionately called the *backbone,* the cable that runs the entire length of a network interconnects all the computers, printers, servers, and other devices of the network. Visualize the skeleton of a fish: All the little-catch-in-your-throat bones attach to one big ol' backbone. A network backbone serves the same purpose, without the smell, connecting and interconnecting all of a network's resources. The backbone serves as the trunk line for the entire network.

Cables commonly used for backbones are 10Base5, 10BaseF, 10BaseT, 100BaseFX, and 100BaseTX.

FDDI ditty dee

Network backbones commonly use Fiber Distributed Data Interface (FDDI) technology. FDDI is pronounced "F – D – D – I," but some folks insist on making the letters into the word "fiddy." Is nothing sacred? FDDI is a 100 Mbps fiber-optic network access method that is excellent for moving traffic around the trunk of a network.

FDDI implements networks as two rings. You can attach workstations to one or both rings of the backbone. The two rings serve as redundant network trunks — if one ring breaks or fails, the other takes over, routing around the trouble spot. If both rings break, the remaining pieces bond together to form a new ring. Although the regrowth potential sounds like something akin to lizard tails or space aliens, FDDI's ability to regenerate the network backbone is what makes it so popular.

Networks in pieces all around

Throughout the Network+ exam, the term *segment* pops up as a reference to discrete portions of a network, usually represented by a single run of cable, a group of workstations, or even a local area network in a WAN. The most common reason for creating a network segment is to improve network performance or security by installing bridges or routers in strategic locations around the network, which I discuss in Chapters 9 and 10 respectively.

A cable segment is a single run of cable with terminators at each end. A network segment is a group of workstations, servers, or devices that are isolated on the other side of a bridge or router to improve the overall network's performance or security.

Prep Test

1 Which of the following are characteristics of 10Base2 cable?

A ○ 10 Mbps bandwidth

B ○ 500 meters maximum segment length

C ○ 1,024 maximum nodes per segment

D ○ Poor interference resistance

E ○ None of the above

2 The Base portion of the designation 10BaseT refers to

A ○ Broadbaseband

B ○ Baseband

C ○ Broadband

D ○ It is a basic cable type.

3 Thin coaxial cable commonly uses which type of connector?

A ○ AUI

B ○ BNC

C ○ Ferrule

D ○ RJ-11

4 STP cable is most commonly found in which type of network?

A ○ Ethernet

B ○ FDDI

C ○ Star

D ○ Token ring

5 A Fast Ethernet standard that uses four-wire UTP cable is

A ○ 10BaseT

B ○ 100BaseTX

C ○ 100BaseFL

D ○ 100BaseT4

6 Which of the following are 100 Mbps Ethernet standards that use Category 3 cabling? (Choose two.)

A ❑ 100BaseT

B ❑ 100BaseVG

C ❑ 100BaseVG-AnyLAN

D ❑ 100BaseFX

7 Which of the following are cable standards commonly used as a network back-bone? (Choose four.)

A ❏ 10Base5

B ❏ 10Base2

C ❏ 10BaseF

D ❏ 100BaseFX

E ❏ 10BaseT

F ❏ 100BaseT4

8 Which of the following characteristics apply to FDDI? (Choose one.)

A ○ 100 Mbps

B ○ Fiber-optic backbone technology

C ○ Implements only one ring similar to token ring

D ○ Implements two network rings

9 UTP cable uses which type of connector?

A ○ RJ-11

B ○ AUI

C ○ RJ-45

D ○ RG-58

10 Which cable media uses modulated pulses of light to transmit data?

A ○ Thinnet

B ○ Thickwire

C ○ 10BaseT

D ○ Fiber-optic

Answers

1 *A.* Thick coax has a 500-meter maximum segment length, and UTP supports 1,024 nodes per segment and has poor resistance to interference. *See "Technical cable stuff."*

2 *B.* Baseband transmission is a digital signal; broadband is an analog signal. *Check out "What's this 10Base stuff?"*

3 *B.* Thin coax uses BNC T connectors. *Connect up with "You can never be too thin."*

4 *D.* Shielded twisted-pair cable is commonly used in token ring networks. *Review "Shielded twisted pair."*

5 *D.* Fast Ethernet is any of the 100BaseX standards. 100BaseT4 uses four-wire cable to implement Fast Ethernet. *Speed over to "The Ethernet Cable Standards."*

6 *B and C.* Essentially, these two standards are the same. 100BaseVG-AnyLAN is Hewlett Packard's proprietary standard for Fast Ethernet using Category 3 cabling. *Check out "The Ethernet Cable Standards."*

7 *A, C, D, and F.* You can use 10Base2 and 10BaseT as backbones, but they suffer from fairly short attenuation spans. *Look over "Backbones and Segments."*

8 *A, B, and D.* FDDI implements two counter-rotating rings. *Take a look at "FDDI ditty dee."*

9 *C.* RJ-11 connectors are used on telephone (two-pair) cable, AUI connectors are used with coaxial cable, and RG-58 is the standard for thinnet cable. *See "The complete UTP."*

10 *D.* Light — optic, get the connection? Expect this question on the test. It is one of the few giveaways the test has to offer. *Review "You Need Your Fiber."*

Part III
The Layers of the OSI Model

The 5th Wave — By Rich Tennant

"We take network security very seriously here."

In this part . . .

*I*n general, a network technician works in only four of the seven layers of the OSI Reference Model: the Physical, Data Link, Network, and Transport layers. Don't misunderstand, you do need to know about all seven layers, but the exam focuses primarily on just these four layers. The other three layers (Session, Presentation, and Application) are dealt with as one big layer called *the upper layers.*

Remember that the OSI model is not a thing but more of a how or why. In each of the four "lower" layers, you need to know what the layer defines and which of the real-world elements, such as protocols and networking devices, operate on that layer. This part gives you all the answers.

Chapter 7

The OSI Model

Exam Objectives

▶ Defining the layers of the OSI model

▶ Identifying the protocols, services, and hardware of each layer

*I*n 1984, the International Standards Organization (ISO) spruced up its specifications for connecting network devices and released the Open System Interconnection Reference Model, which goes by the nickname of Open System Interconnect, or OSI model. The ISO OSI (nice and easy to remember, huh?) model is the internationally accepted standard for networking. It provides the networking world with a common and standard blueprint for designing, implementing, and operating networking hardware and software. The model also provides the basic operating and interconnection rules for all network operating systems, network messaging, and communications connectivity devices.

So, the rationale behind the OSI model's starring role on the Network+ test is pretty simple and straightforward. To omit OSI from the test would be akin to talking Internet without mentioning TCP/IP. One is essential to the other.

Questions relating directly to the OSI model and its layers make up at least 20 percent of the Network+ test. That exam emphasis is your first clue to the importance of knowing the OSI model, its layers, what each does, and with what it does it. This chapter gives you an overview of the OSI model, its makeup, and the four layers featured prominently on the test.

Quick Assessment

Defining the layers of the OSI model

1 The seven layers of the OSI model are (bottom to top): _____, _____, _____, _____, _____, _____, and _____.

2 The OSI layer that deals with matching data packets to media capabilities is the _____ layer.

3 A _____ is a unit of data packaged for movement from one OSI layer to another.

4 The _____ layer addresses data for delivery and converts network addresses into physical addresses.

5 A _____ is added to the outbound packet at each layer and removed by each layer on the receiving end.

6 A repeater is an example of a(n) _____ layer device.

Identifying the protocols, services, and hardware of each layer

7 A common Data Link layer device is a _____.

8 A router operates at the _____ layer.

9 Of the three main types of protocols, TCP is a _____ protocol.

10 The primary protocol on the Network layer in the TCP/IP suite is _____.

Answers

1 _Physical, Data Link, Network, Transport, Session, Presentation,_ and _Application._ Review "Betting on the OSI's lucky 7."

2 _Transport._ Check out the "Betting on the OSI's lucky 7."

3 _PDU (or protocol data unit)._ See "PDUs, packets, frames, and datagrams."

4 _Network._ Take a look at "Betting on the OSI's lucky 7."

5 _Header._ Look over "Up one side and down the other."

6 _Physical._ Review "Gettin' physical."

7 _Bridge._ See "A bridge over troubled layers."

8 _Network._ Take a look at "Internetworking devices."

9 _Transport._ Look over "Transport protocols."

10 _IP (Internet Protocol)._ Check out "How TCP/IP stacks up."

OSI: The Networking Supermodel

The OSI model is not a standard in the sense that it can be implemented directly like an Ethernet or token ring. The model is more of a blueprint or framework for the ways in which networking devices, protocols, and services ought to interact with one another.

Just like my favorite dessert, the OSI model consists of seven layers. However, much to my sweet tooth's dismay, it is more like an onion than a cake, with each layer encompassing and hiding the preceding layer. Figure 7-1 illustrates the seven layers of the OSI model.

7. Application layer
6. Presentation layer
5. Session layer
4. Transport layer
3. Network layer
2. Data Link layer
1. Physical layer

Figure 7-1:
The Network+ exam focuses on the seven layers of the OSI model.

Betting on the OSI's lucky 7

At this point, you probably have the urge to play 777 on the lottery. But before you lay down big bucks on a sure bet, understand that it's only coincidence that the seven layers of the OSI model show up in Chapter 7. Here is a brief overview of each OSI layer:

- ✔ **Physical layer:** This is the bottom layer for the OSI model, and, as its name suggests, this layer is concerned with the physical nature of a network, which includes cabling, connectors, network interface cards, and the processes that convert bits into signals for sending and signals to bits when receiving. Chapter 8 covers the particulars of this layer.

- ✔ **Data Link layer:** This layer is concerned with providing context to the Physical layer's bits by formatting them into packets, providing for error checking and correction, and avoiding transmission conflicts on the network. Chapter 9 goes into agonizing detail on this layer.

✔ **Network layer:** This layer handles addressing of data for delivery and converting network addresses into physical addresses. Routing of messages on the network and internetwork also occurs at this layer. Chapter 10 gives you all you need on this layer.

✔ **Transport layer:** This layer of the OSI model deals with network computers communicating with each other and matching the message to the capabilities and restrictions of the network medium. At this layer, network messages are chopped into smaller pieces for transmission and reassembled at their destination, hopefully in the correct order. The Transport layer supports the delivery of messages as well as error detection and recovery. Chapter 11 packs the power to carry you away to OSI ecstasy.

✔ **Session layer:** The Session layer manages communication "sessions," including *handshaking* (which connection-oriented devices use to establish a session), security, and the mechanics of an ongoing connection.

✔ **Presentation layer:** This layer, the sixth of the OSI model, is where raw data messages are packaged in generic form so they can withstand the rigors of being transmitted over a network. Incoming messages are broken down and formatted appropriately for the receiving application.

✔ **Application layer:** This is the seventh and top layer of the OSI model. As its name suggests, this layer interfaces with applications that want to gain network access. Do not confuse the Application layer with Microsoft Office, WordPerfect, Corel Draw, or end-user application software. Applications like Windows NT Server or NetWare and certain network services, such as FTP, HTTP, TELNET, and SMTP function at this layer.

Primarily, applications use the top three layers of the OSI model (Session, Presentation, and Application). The bottom four layers (Physical, Data Link, Network, and Transport) are used for moving data from one network device to another. The Network+ test focuses on the bottom four layers.

How to remember the OSI layers and bring the pizza

You need to know the seven layers in sequence, either top to bottom or bottom to top. Remembering the layers of the OSI model is as easy as memorizing a clever little saying. Here are a few possibilities:

✔ **"Please Do Not Throw Salami (or Sausage if you prefer) Pizza Away."** This works for bottom to top. My personal favorite: the saying and the pizza.

✔ **"APpS Transport Network Data Physically."** APS refers to Application, Presentation, and Session. This one spells out the layers that the Network+ test emphasizes.

✔ **"All People Seem To Need Data Processing."** Another top-to-bottom reminder.

✔ **"Please Do Not Tell Secret Passwords Anytime."** I know, the mnemonic magic is waning!

PDUs, packets, frames, and datagrams

The official OSI name for the packets of data passed around on networks is PDU. You can take your pick from several versions of what PDU means, including the original "protocol data unit," the easily remembered "packet data unit," and the heavyweight "payload data unit." A PDU is a unit of data that is packaged for movement from one OSI layer to another as it winds its way from its source to its destination. In certain instances, PDUs can be tagged with very specific terminology, such as data frames, or frames for short, when the Data Link layer passes them to the Physical layer. You may also hear PDUs referred to as packets, frames, or datagrams — the names are interchangeable in common usage.

Up one side and down the other

Bear in mind that the OSI model itself is never directly implemented. However, its protocols define how data packets are transferred between the hardware and software of a network and on to other networks. As depicted in Figure 7-2, when a packet is sent over the network, it travels down through the OSI layers of the originating network from the Application layer to the Physical layer. At the Physical layer, the packet is physically transmitted to the Physical layer of the receiving network. At the receiving end, the packet passes back up through the layers from the Physical layer to the Application layer.

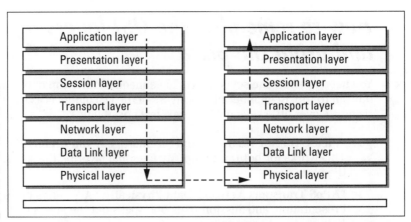

Figure 7-2:
The route a packet takes through the OSI model layers.

As the packet passes down through the sending side layers, each layer performs its own brand of magic on the packet, formatting it, adding a CRC (Cyclic Redundancy Check) or another error-checking mechanism, breaking it into smaller pieces, and more. Each layer also adds its own header to the message. When transmitted by the Physical layer, the original message, if it is still in one piece, has six headers attached to it — souvenirs of its travels. In case you're wondering why a packet gathers only six headers instead of seven, it's because the Application layer is too lazy to add one before sending the packet to the Presentation layer.

The header from each layer is intended to provide instructions to the counterpart layers at the other end. For example, the Transport layer of the sending side provides a header with instructions on sequence and reassembly for the receiving side Transport layer. As the packet passes up through the receiving side layers, the packets are stripped away until the original message is delivered to the destination application.

Layers of Hardware

Each of the devices that make up networks beyond your desktop computer all operate on one or more layers of the OSI model. I can't say it enough: The OSI model is a framework or blueprint for the way things ought to work. Some hardware strictly conforms, and other hardware follows the guidelines a bit more loosely. *Some* conformity is required, however, if interoperability (the ability to communicate smoothly) with other networks is expected. The OSI model provides, just have to say it again, the ever-important framework for connecting devices on a network.

Gettin' physical

The Physical layer is concerned with moving bits on the physical media. Therefore, it deals only with the hardware affecting the physical movement of data from point A to point B. The networking devices that operate at the Physical layer are

- **Network interface cards (NIC):** The NIC by itself — that is, the hardware device without its software drivers — operates at the Physical layer.

- **Network media (cabling):** The medium used to transport the message bits on the network is also a Physical layer element. This is true with all media — copper wire, glass fiber, or wireless signals.

- **Repeaters:** This device, much like my Aunt Sally, repeats everything it hears, energizing the message with new life in the process. Repeaters are used to solve attenuation problems in cables.

> ✔ **Hubs:** Hubs come in two flavors: passive and active. A *passive hub* receives data on one of its ports and passes the data along to its other ports without regenerating the signal. An *active hub* combines the actions of the passive hub with a repeater to regenerate the signal passed along.

Chapter 8 provides a deeper look into these devices.

A bridge over troubled layers

Since the Data Link layer deals with addressing packets on the local physical network, the devices that operate on this layer are focused on this task. The primary Data Link layer device is a bridge.

A *bridge* is used to connect two or more network segments — often dissimilar ones — together to form a larger individual network. Another way to look at this definition is that a bridge is used to segregate a part of a network into a segment. In general, a bridge uses a routing table to determine on which part of a network a destination address is located. Bridges operate by using the Media Access Control (MAC) physical address of NICs and other network devices to determine if a packet is eligible to cross the bridge to the other side.

Another device that operates at the Data Link layer is a switch. A *switch,* also called a multiport bridge, is a smart bridge. It uses MAC addresses to determine the port a message should be sent on and sends it only to that port. See Chapter 9 for more information on bridges and switches.

Internetworking devices

Networking devices that operate at the Network layer of the OSI model are concerned with network addressing on large networks that are physically made up of many separate networks. Network layer devices use addressing information to effectively join networks into a large internetwork.

The primary device that operates at this layer is a *router,* which is more intelligent than a bridge and uses its smarts to calculate an efficient route for a network packet. Another Network layer device is a *brouter,* which is a hybrid of a bridge and a router. I examine routers and brouters more closely in Chapter 10.

Transport me to the gateway

There are no bad gateways, only misunderstood gateways. A gateway can be hardware or software or both, but its main purpose is to join two dissimilar systems that have similar functions but cannot otherwise communicate. For example, a PC workstation and a mainframe. Although a gateway operates at the transport layer, it can also operate at any of the top four layers of the OSI model.

Table 7-1 summarizes the OSI model layers and the hardware that operates at each layer.

Table 7-1	The Hardware at Each OSI Model Layer
OSI Layer	*Device(s)*
Physical	NIC, cable and transmission media, repeater, and hub
Data Link	Bridge and switch
Network	Router, brouter
Transport	Gateway
Upper Layers	Gateway

Ain't It Suite?

In general, networking protocols follow the OSI model and its layers. Network servers have suites of protocols that perform the actions and activities of each layer as a packet passes down or up the OSI model. One more time with feeling: A protocol defines the rules that control how two computers, networking devices, or programs transfer data between them.

Protocol suites have a different protocol for each layer of the OSI model. Of the three types of protocols — application protocols, transport protocols, and network protocols — you need to know the transport and network protocols and the layers on which they operate for the exam. Figure 7-3 illustrates the general relationship of the three protocol types to the OSI model's layers.

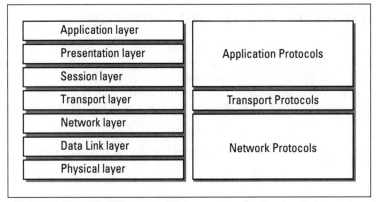

Figure 7-3:
The three
main types
of protocols
match up to
the OSI
model
layers.

Network protocols

These protocols provide for packet addressing and routing information, error-checking and correction, and they enforce the rules for communicating within a specific network environment. Network protocols provide *link services* to other protocols operating at other layers. The following are common network protocols that you can't possibly escape — in everyday practice or on the exam:

- ✔ **IP (Internet Protocol):** You know, the IP of the famous TCP/IP duo. IP provides addressing and routing information and is a Network layer protocol.

- ✔ **NWLink (NetWare Link) and IPX (Internetwork Package Exchange):** The Novell NetWare protocol and Microsoft IPX clone for packet routing and forwarding.

- ✔ **NetBEUI (NetBIOS Extended User Interface):** Provides transport services for NetBIOS.

- ✔ **DLC (Data Link Control):** Used for network-connected mainframes and Hewlett Packard printers.

Transport protocols

Transport protocols actually do a lot more than their name implies. They not only provide reliable end-to-end transport and delivery of data packets, but also perform error detection in the delivery system. Common transport protocols are

- ✔ **TCP (Transmission Control Protocol):** TCP is commonly misnamed the Transport Control Protocol, which is understandable. It is the TCP/IP protocol responsible for guaranteeing the transport and delivery of packets across networks. TCP is a universal protocol that runs on virtually any system, which is one of its major strengths.

- ✔ **SPX (Sequenced Packet Exchange) and NWLink:** In the Novell IPX/SPX protocol suite, SPX is the TCP, and IPX the IP. Like TCP, SPX is used to guarantee data delivery. NWLink is Microsoft's version of the IPX/SPX protocol for Windows NT Server systems.

- ✔ **NetBIOS/NetBEUI (Network Basic Input/Output System)/(NetBIOS Extended User Interface):** NetBIOS manages communications between computers, and NetBEUI provides the data transport services. NetBIOS and NetBEUI are Microsoft protocols used on Windows networks.

Application protocols

These protocols provide application-to-application services at the upper layers of the OSI model. Some common application protocols are

- ✔ **SMTP (Simple Mail Transport Protocol):** This member of the TCP/IP gang is responsible for transferring electronic mail.

- ✔ **FTP (File Transport Protocol):** Another one wearing the TCP/IP colors. FTP is used to transport files from one computer to another.

- ✔ **SNMP (Simple Network Management Protocol):** YATP (yet another TCP/IP protocol) that is used to monitor network devices.

How TCP/IP stacks up

The most commonly used protocol suite is TCP/IP, also known as the Internet Protocol, not to be confused with IP, the Internet Protocol. Huh? That's why it is still commonly called TCP/IP. Although TCP/IP has been around about ten years longer than the OSI model, it matches up very nicely with the layers of the OSI model. Funny how that works out, huh?

Table 7-2 contains a layer-by-layer breakdown of the TCP/IP suite.

Table 7-2	TCP/IP and the OSI Model
OSI Model Layer	*TCP/IP Protocol(s)*
Physical layer	Physical hardware device connectivity
Data Link layer	NIC driver and ODI/ NDIS
Network layer	IP, ICMP, ARP, OSPF, and RIP
Transport layer	TCP, DNS, and UDP
Upper layers	Telnet, FTP, and SMTP

The TCP/IP suite protocols included in Table 7-2 are

- **ODI/NDIS (Open Data-Link Interface/Network Driver-Interface Specification):** A Data Link layer interface that enables NIC drivers to connect to dissimilar networks and have them appear as one. ODI is the Novell protocol, and NDIS is the Microsoft protocol for NIC interconnection.

- **IP (Internet Protocol):** A Network layer protocol that provides source and destination addressing and routing.

- **ICMP (Internet Control Message Protocol):** A Network layer protocol that carries control messages, such as error or confirmation messages.

- **ARP (Address Resolution Protocol):** A Network layer protocol that converts IP addresses to MAC physical addresses.

- **OSPF (Open Shortest Path First):** Used by TCP/IP routers to determine the best path through a network.

- **RIP (Routing Information Protocol):** Helps TCP/IP routers to use the most efficient routes to nodes on the network.

- **TCP (Transmission Control Protocol):** The primary TCP/IP transport protocol that accepts messages from the upper OSI layers and provides reliable delivery to its TCP peer on a remote network.

- **DNS (Domain Naming System):** A Transport layer Internet name-to-address resolution service that allows users to use human-friendly names.

- **UDP (User Datagram Protocol):** Another Transport layer that can be used in place of TCP to transport simple single-packet messages.

Treat this bulleted list two ways: one, as part of your study materials right before the test to refresh your knowledge of TCP/IP suite protocols; and two, as a guide to what I cover in more appropriate detail in later chapters.

Prep Test

1 Applications use which of the following layers of the OSI model? (Choose three.)

A ❑ Network layer

B ❑ Application layer

C ❑ Transport layer

D ❑ Session layer

E ❑ Presentation layer

F ❑ Physical layer

2 The OSI model layer that formats data packets and provides for error checking and correction is the

A ○ Network layer

B ○ Data Link layer

C ○ Transport layer

D ○ Session layer

3 Which of the following mnemonic sayings represents the OSI model's layers from bottom to top?

A ○ Please Don't Toss Out Salami Pizza Anytime.

B ○ All People Seem To Need Data Processing.

C ○ Please Do Not Throw Salami Pizza Away.

D ○ Sleepy, Grumpy, Sneezy, Doc, Bashful, Rudolph, and John-Boy.

E ○ None of these sayings represents the OSI model layers.

4 As a PDU is passed from layer to layer, what is added or removed from the packet by each succeeding layer?

A ○ Header

B ○ Trailer

C ○ Error-checking bits

D ○ Protocol ID bits

5 Which of the following are Physical layer elements? (Choose all that apply.)

A ❑ Network interface card

B ❑ Unshielded twisted pair cable

C ❑ Hub

D ❑ Bridge

6 The device used to join two dissimilar network segments is a

A ○ Router

B ○ Switch

C ○ Bridge

D ○ Hub

7 Which of the following are considered to be Transport protocols? (Choose all that apply.)

A ❑ SMTP

B ❑ TCP

C ❑ FTP

D ❑ IPX

E ❑ NetBEUI

8 The protocol that enables network interface card drivers to connect to dissimilar networks and have them appear as one is

A ○ OSPF

B ○ RIP

C ○ NDIS

D ○ ICMP

9 TCP/IP is an acronym for

A ○ Transmission Control Protocol/Internet Protocol

B ○ Transport Control Protocol/Internetworking Protocol

C ○ Transport Control Protocol/Internet Protocol

D ○ Transmission Control Protocol/Internetworking Protocol

10 The Network layer device that determines and sends packets over the most efficient route available is a

A ○ Bridge

B ○ Switch

C ○ Active hub

D ○ Router

Answers

1 *B, D, and E.* The upper layers of the OSI model are grouped together as the application-oriented layers. *See "Betting on the OSI's lucky 7."*

2 *B.* The Data Link layer prepares network packets for their trip across the data links of networks. *Review "Betting on the OSI's lucky 7."*

3 *C.* By all means, find a saying that is easy to remember. If you're just smart enough to remember the layers of the OSI model, keep in mind that you need to know the layers in sequence — top to bottom or bottom to top. I never can remember those dwarfs. *Look over "How to remember the OSI layers and bring the pizza."*

4 *A.* Each layer adds its layer to the outbound PDU to provide instructions to its counterpart layer on the receiving end, which strips the header away. *Check out "Up one side and down the other."*

5 *A, B, and C.* A bridge is a Data Link layer device. *Take a look at "Gettin' physical."*

6 *C.* A bridge joins two dissimilar network segments that perform similar functions but cannot otherwise communicate into a single network. *See "A bridge over troubled layers."*

7 *B and E.* This is not a trick question: NetBEUI includes NetBIOS and is used to mean both. Another common Transport layer protocol is SPX. *Review "Transport protocols."*

8 *C.* Microsoft's NDIS along with Novell's ODI, like OSI, are a specification for network interface card drivers that enable them to work in multiple platform and protocol environments. *Look over "How TCP/IP stacks up."*

9 *A.* The deck is stacked against you: TCP is a Transport layer protocol used to transport PDUs across networks. Nevertheless, the official name is Transmission Control Protocol — you just have to remember it. *Take a look at "Transport protocols."*

10 *D.* Plain as the nose on your face: Routers route packets over networks on the Network layer. *See "Internetworking devices."*

Chapter 8

The Physical Layer

● ●

Exam Objectives

▶ Installing and configuring a network interface card (NIC)

▶ Connecting network media to an NIC

▶ Identifying Physical layer devices

▶ Using Physical layer devices appropriately

● ●

*T*he name of the Physical layer just about sums it up. This layer contains the physical devices and transmission media that physically carry the electronic signal (or light) that makes up the data being sent from one computer to another. This includes the wireless physical media, although wireless is not a big deal on the Network+ exam.

The Network+ exam expects that you know how to install an NIC into a computer, configure it using the appropriate hardware or software methods, and assign to it the right system resources. You also need to be able to connect the physical cable media to the NIC and then test the NIC and the connection. Because the Network+ test is meant to attest to a technician's field-readiness, "virtual" proof of performance seems like a reasonable expectation.

A network begins to *be* only after somebody buys a network card, sticks it into his or her computer, and then attaches a cable to the NIC. And, wonder of wonders, the network isn't born into reality until another person does the same thing on the same cable. Until the physical parts of the network are in place, no network exists.

The jungle drums, the fires used for smoke signals, and the telegrapher's key — all prime candidates for the OSI models of their times, had such framework existed in those days. All the modern ways you can communicate and share data are wonderful and almost magic, but in every case (at least for now) they all require that physical equipment, computer hardware, cable, and what-have-you to function — not so different from the good old days.

In this chapter, I give you an overview of the network components that operate at the OSI model's Physical layer. You can't possibly imagine the amount of restraint required to spare you the pain of reading the clever phrase "let's get physical" over and over and over . . .

Quick Assessment

1 Two hardware methods used to configure a NIC are _____ and _____.

2 Most _____ network adapters are plug-and-play.

3 An IRQ setting commonly available for use by the NIC is _____.

4 _____ or _____ are shared memory areas commonly assigned to NICs.

5 The _____ connector is used with 10BaseT cabling.

6 10Base2 cabling uses the _____ connector.

7 A _____ is used to regenerate a signal before its attenuation point.

8 The maximum segment distance for 10BaseT cabling is _____ meters.

9 A(n) _____ hub passes along all inbound signals to its other ports without regenerating the signal.

10 The hub is connected to the patch panel by _____ cables.

Answers

1   *Jumpers and DIP switches.* See "Configuring an NIC."

2   *PCI.* Check out "Plug-and-play and software configuration."

3   *IRQ5 or IRQ10.* Review "Interrupt requests."

4   *C800h, D800h.* Take a look at "Shared memory address."

5   *RJ-45.* Look over "Cables and Connectors."

6   *BNC T-connectors.* Check over "Cables and Connectors."

7   *Repeater.* Review "Can you repeat that?"

8   *100.* See "Can you repeat that?"

9   *Passive.* Look at "Active or passive."

10 *Patch.* Check out "Connecting Up the Physical Layer."

The Network Interface Card (NIC)

Until you breathe NIC life into a network, nothing happens. This section takes you through the general steps that you can use to select the proper NIC, install it in your system, configure it, and install its device driver. Just in case you have been living in a cave in the Borneo jungle and haven't heard the term before, a network interface card (NIC), also called a network adapter, connects a computer to a network. It is an expansion card that you insert into an available expansion slot in the computer and attach the network cabling to. Insert an NIC, plug in the network cable, and you're on your way to being networked.

Getting an NIC without getting nicked

Options abound when you set out to secure the NIC you need, want, and deserve. This list of considerations can help deliver you in the right direction (and help you maneuver through the test):

- **Expansion bus adapter:** Although you're kind of partial to that nifty USB (Universal Serial Bus) connector, the NIC must fit into an available bus expansion slot on your computer's motherboard and only comes in a few matching formats, as shown in Figures 8-1 through 8-5, which illustrate the more common types of NIC adapter card formats.

- **Compatibility:** Beyond merely plugging into an open expansion slot, the NIC needs to be compatible with your motherboard's data bus. 32-bit cards don't work to their utmost efficiency on an 8- or 16-bit system.

- **Plug-and-play:** If your system supports plug-and-play (PnP) devices, by all means, get a PnP NIC (what a catchy ring, don't you agree?).

- **Connectors:** If you haven't decided on your cable type, you probably haven't figured out your topology or network protocols, both of which are priorities. After you decide all that topology/protocol stuff, you can look for an appropriate NIC to connect to the cable media. If you are still just a little undecided between coaxial and unshielded twisted pair (UTP), you may want to pay the extra cost and get an NIC that can connect to both.

- **Interoperable:** Just like you are somewhat assured of not being electrocuted by an electrical product with a UL label, you can be confident that an NIC with a NE2000 compatibility is bound to work with about any network.

- **Conformity:** At the risk of breaking your rebel spirit, I suggest that you make all the NICs in a network the same. Such consistency is not required — and may even be arguable — but uniformity does tend to level the troubleshooting playing field.

Don't waste your time memorizing every performance and configuration fact about each type of network interface card (network adapters). What you need to know are the general characteristics that I discuss in this section.

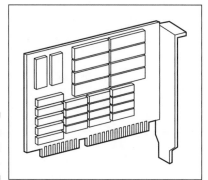

Figure 8-1:
ISA network
adapter.

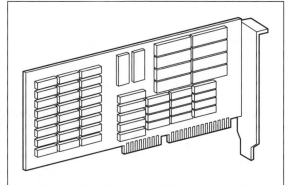

Figure 8-2:
EISA
network
adapter.

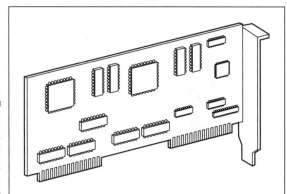

Figure 8-3:
VESA
(VL-Bus)
network
adapter.

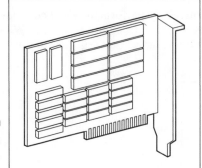

Figure 8-4:
PCI adapter.

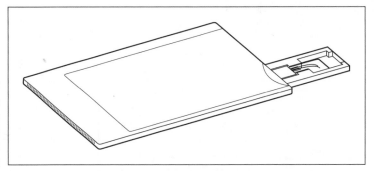

Figure 8-5:
PCMCIA
(PC-Card)
adapter.

Here are some guidelines for figuring out the expansion slots available on a computer:

- ✔ A 386 or older computer more than likely has an ISA slot. If the computer has seen life as a server in the past, it may have an EISA slot.
- ✔ A 486 computer should have both VESA (VL-Bus) and ISA slots.
- ✔ An IBM PS/2 computer definitely has MicroChannel Architecture (MCA) slots.
- ✔ A Pentium computer has both ISA and PCI slots.

Configuring an NIC

For the exam, knowing how to configure an NIC is more important than having all the details about what to use, assuming you know why you're doing what you're doing in the first place. You configure each specific NIC differently to fit its computer host and the network to which it is to be connected. Some are plug-and-play, some are hardware-configured, some are software-configured, and others combine two or more of the above.

Jumping to configurations

You configure some NICs by changing the position of a jumper. A *jumper* is a small block that is placed on little posts to turn on a certain value or indicator. Figure 8-6 shows a three-pin jumper with a block covering two pins. You can usually find the positions and corresponding values for the blocks and pins in the NIC documentation or on the manufacturer's Web site.

The manufacturer's Web site is a good location for configuration, troubleshooting, and upgrade information for both hardware and software components. This fact may show up in a question on the test.

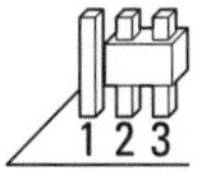

Figure 8-6:
A jumper is used to set NIC settings.

1–2–3–dip, 1–2–3–switch

Another device used to configure an NIC using hardware settings is a DIP (dual-inline packaging) switch. As illustrated in Figure 8-7, the toggle switches on a DIP switch can be used to set one or more setting values for the NIC.

Can NIC come to plug-and-play?

Most PCI network cards are plug-and-play, and coincidentally, so are most Windows NT and 95/98 workstations and servers. If your computer has an available PCI slot to use, that's the way to go.

Not all newer network adapters are plug-and-play, although the majority are. Even many plug-and-play NICs are not PnP-compatible on a Windows NT system. Those that aren't compatible usually have configuration software with them to detect the available resources and configure the adapter accordingly. However, even some plug-and-play and software-configured adapters need adjustments after you install them.

Assigning system resources

An NIC is no different than other input/output devices when it comes to configuring for interaction and communication with the motherboard systems and the CPU. This configuration, whether by hardware, software, or through plug-and-play, assigns the NIC four important system resources: an interrupt request, a base input/output port address, a direct memory channel, and a shared memory area.

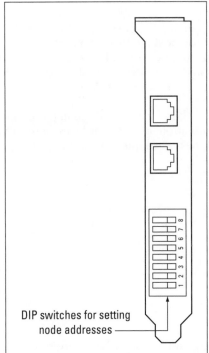

Figure 8-7:
A DIP
switch is
used to set
NIC
settings.

DIP switches for setting
node addresses

Interrupt requests (IRQ)

Network interface cards request services from the system via an interrupt request line. Table 8-1 lists the common IRQ assignments for most computers. Notice that although no IRQ is specifically assigned to the NIC, some (IRQs 5, 10, 11, and 15) are available for use. Remember, sharing IRQs between devices is usually a bad thing. A plug-and-play NIC that is installed in a Windows 9*x* workstation is automatically assigned system resources, including an IRQ. Even though this is the technician's dream, it can turn into a nightmare. You probably should review PnP IRQ assignments for potential conflicts.

Table 8-1	Common IRQ Assignments
IRQ	*Common Use*
0	System timer
1	Keyboard
2	Video adapter
3	COM2 or COM4
4	COM1 or COM3

IRQ	Common Use
5	Available (Sound card, if present)
6	Floppy disk controller
7	LPT1
8	Real-time clock
9	Cascaded to IRQ2
10	Available (primary SCSI controller, if present)
11	Available (secondary SCSI controller, if present)
12	Bus mouse
13	Math coprocessor
14	Primary hard disk controller
15	Available (secondary hard disk controller, if present)

Be familiar with the IRQ settings and know that IRQ 5, 10, 11, and 15 are eligible for NIC use.

Base input/output (I/O) ports

The scenario's simple: The IRQ grabs the attention of the CPU, which enables the movement of data via the I/O (Input/Output) port. Like the IRQ, the I/O port requires unique assignment. Some common base I/O port addresses are listed in Table 8-2. The *h* in the port address means only that it is a hexadecimal address.

Table 8-2	Common I/O Port Assignments
Port Address (Hexadecimal)	**Common Use**
200h	Game port
230h	Bus mouse
270h	LPT3
280h	Network interface card
2B0h	LPT1
2F8h	COM2
300h	Network interface card

(continued)

Table 8-2 *(continued)*	
Port Address (Hexadecimal)	*Common Use*
310h	Network interface card
370h	LPT2
3F8h	COM1

You don't need to memorize the information in Table 8-2, but do remember the addresses that are open for NIC use.

Direct memory access (DMA)

A DMA resource assignment enables a device to write to primary memory without working through the CPU, which can really speed up the process. If a device can write its data directly to RAM, without the need to wait on the CPU to transfer the data, the CPU is able to do other more CPU-intensive things, such as execute instructions. The result is a more efficient use of computer resources.

Shared memory address

The shared memory address identifies a small area in memory that the system can use as a buffer to store data until the NIC is ready for it. This address is usually set to either C800h or D800h and does not require configuration. Usually, the internal system of a computer runs just a little faster than the network to which the NIC is transferring the data. I think of the NIC as the coal-shoveler on an old-time train. The shared memory address area is the storage area that holds the data for the NIC, who is shoveling as fast as it can.

Driving the NIC home

After you install and configure the NIC — and confirm that the host system isn't in the mood to reject the card — you need to install a device driver. Most NICs come with their own device drivers, and some operating systems even have generic versions for you to use. The most important consideration is making sure that the device driver is compatible with the ODI/NDIS (Open Data-Link Interface/Network Device Interface Specification) standards (see Chapter 7 for more information on OSI/NDIS).

NDIS is a Microsoft standard that has both a 16-bit and a 32-bit version. ODI, also available in 16-bit and 32-bit flavors, is the Novell driver standard. These standards enable the NIC to be bound to as many protocols as necessary inside the system.

Cables and Their Connectors

Chapter 6 covers cables and their connectors thoroughly, but I summarize the cable types and their connectors here so that you have all the Physical layer information at your disposal for last-minute studying. Table 8-3 lists the common network media types along with their connectors.

Table 8-3	Network Media and Their Connectors
Cable Type	_Connector(s) Used_
10Base2 (thinnet)	BNC (British Naval Connector) T-connectors
10Base5 (thicknet)	AUI (attached unit interface) and BNC N-connectors
10BaseF (fiber-optic)	FC, D4, or media interface connector (MIC)
10BaseT (twisted-pair)	RJ-45

NIC connections

In general, network interface cards have only one connection, but you can find some that have two (or more) connections. Those adapters with two or more different connectors allow the card to connect to different media types but only one type at a time. This allows you some flexibility for connecting a computer into a network that has more than one media type installed.

The terminators

Ethernet networks (see Chapter 9) must be terminated with a terminating plug. The terminating plug absorbs signals, preventing them from bouncing back onto the network and increasing the chances for data collisions. Terminators are used on Ethernet networks that use coaxial cable media (see Chapter 6 for more information on coaxial cable media).

Connectivity Devices

At the heart of the Physical layer is a variety of network connectivity devices that provide for network construction and flexibility. These devices are repeaters and hubs.

Can you repeat that?

You use repeaters to overcome the effects of attenuation on coaxial and twisted pair cable. A repeater's role is simple: It repeats. Whatever it hears from one side it repeats to the other side, reenergizing the signal in the process. A repeater becomes necessary when a workstation or network segment must be located more than the media's maximum segment distance from the last workstation or segment. Table 8-4 lists the maximum distance for Ethernet cabling. As you can see, 10BaseT is a likely candidate for a repeater.

Table 8-4	Ethernet Media Maximum Distances
Media	*Maximum Distance*
10Base2	185 meters
10Base5	500 meters
10BaseF	2,000 meters
10BaseT	100 meters

Have you hubbed your network today?

A hub sets up a star-wired arrangement for workstations and devices and provides a multiport connection to the network. Figure 8-8 illustrates how computers can connect to a network through a hub. You also can use a hub to connect workstations into a peer-to-peer network.

Hubs are known to live their lives as either passive hubs or active hubs. A passive hub merely passes along to all of its other ports whatever it hears on any one of its ports (remind you of any relatives you know and love?). For example, on a four-port passive hub, whatever signal comes in on port 2 is sent, without being energized, to ports 1, 3, and 4.

An active hub works like a multiport repeater (as it's sometimes called). Like a passive hub, it passes along what it hears, but with the added bonus of reenergizing the signal (now, that describes my family!).

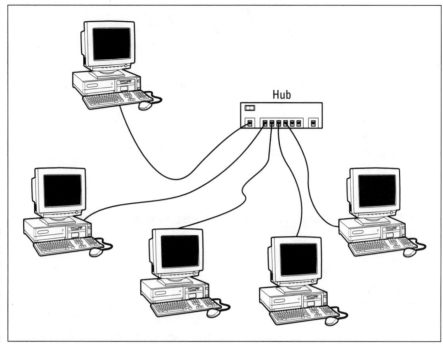

Figure 8-8:
A hub
connecting
computers
to a
network.

Hub

The Physical Layer Connection

Most networks use 10BaseT (unshielded twisted pair cable), with the cabling
connected into a patch panel, which is then connected to a hub or switch using
a patch cable. This arrangement provides flexibility and supports ease of troubleshooting and repair for the network. Here's how the whole enchilada works:

- ✔ Workstations are connected into RJ-45 wall jacks using short 10BaseT
  cables called patch or drop cables.

- ✔ The wall jacks are connected by 10BaseT cable to a punch-down block
  located in the same room as the hubs.

- ✔ The punch-down blocks (located on the back of the patch panel) are
  directly connected to corresponding RJ-45 ports on the face of the patch
  panel.

- ✔ Another short patch cable, also called a patch cord, is used to connect
  the RJ-45 port on the patch panel to the hub.

To determine whether your cabling approach fits within the cabling type's
maximum cable segment length, you add up all the cable segments involved
in getting the signal from the server to the workstation. Inserting a repeater
or active hub resets the cable length beginning point. The exam presents
cable distances in meters.

Prep Test

1 Which of the following expansion adapters are used for network interface cards? (Choose four.)

A ❑ EISA

B ❑ AGP

C ❑ VESA

D ❑ PCI

E ❑ ISA

2 A Pentium computer is likely to have which expansion slots available? (Choose two.)

A ❑ VESA

B ❑ ISA

C ❑ PCI

D ❑ MCA

3 The IRQ commonly assigned to the primary hard disk controller is

A ○ IRQ3

B ○ IRQ5

C ○ IRQ10

D ○ IRQ14

4 A base I/O port address commonly used for network cards is

A ○ 270h

B ○ 2F8h

C ○ 300h

D ○ 3F8h

5 ODI/NDIS are acronyms for

A ○ Open Database Interface/Network Database Interface Specification

B ○ Open Data-Link Interface/Network Data-Link Interface Specification

C ○ Open Data-Link Interface/Network Device Interface Specification

D ○ Open Datagram Interface/Network Datagram Interface Specification

6 The RJ-45 connector is identified with

A ○ RG-56

B ○ 10BaseF

C ○ 10Base2

D ○ 10BaseT

7 The maximum segment distance of a cable medium is associated with

A ○ Collisions

B ○ Attenuation

C ○ Terminators

D ○ Continuance

8 The following devices are OSI model Physical layer devices. (Choose four.)

A ❑ Bridge

B ❑ Repeater

C ❑ Active hub

D ❑ Router

E ❑ Passive hub

F ❑ NIC

9 The maximum distance for 10BaseT cabling is

A ○ 100 meters

B ○ 185 meters

C ○ 500 meters

D ○ 660 meters

10 In an Ethernet 10BaseT network, a wiring closet is located 85 meters from the server. In the wiring closet, a passive hub connects into a patch panel using 2-meter-long patch cables. The patch panel is connected to a punch-down block with 1-meter-long patch cables. The punch-down block is connected through the ceilings and walls to a wall jack 20 meters away. A workstation is plugged into the wall jack with a 10-foot cable. The workstation is performing badly. What could be the problem?

A ○ The hub is faulty.

B ○ The hub should be replaced with an active hub.

C ○ The patch panel should be eliminated.

D ○ The NIC is probably intermittently faulty.

Answers

1 *A, C, D, and E.* Of these adapter types, PCI and ISA are by far the more common. EISA is used on some servers, and VESA on older hardware. *See "Getting a NIC without getting nicked."*

2 *B and C.* Most Pentium computers support both of these expansion bus types, and they commonly have several of each. *Review "Getting it in the right slot."*

3 *D.* For the Network+ test, you really don't need to memorize all the IRQs, but knowing them can help you eliminate some wrong answers. *Check out "Interrupt requests (IRQ)."*

4 *C.* Other common I/O addresses used for NICs are 280h and 310h. The "h" stands for hexadecimal number. *Take a look at "Base input/output (I/O) ports."*

5 *C.* ODI, a Novell standard, and NDIS, a Microsoft standard, are the device driver standards for network adapters. *Look over "Driving the NIC home."*

6 *D.* This connector, which resembles the smaller RJ-11 used with telephones, is the connector for twisted pair cable. *Glance over "Cables and Connectors."*

7 *B.* Attenuation is the distance point in the cable where the signal starts becoming unrecognizable. *Review "Can you repeat that?"*

8 *B, C, E, and F.* These devices, all concerned only with the movement of bits, are Physical layer devices. *See "Connectivity Devices."*

9 *A.* Because UTP cable does not have protection from electrical noise and radio interference, it does not have a very long attenuation point. *Check over "Can you repeat that?"*

10 *B.* The first thing that you must eliminate is the length of the UTP cabling that exceeds 100 meters. This is easily accomplished with an active hub. *Take a look at "The Physical Layer Connections."*

Chapter 9

The Data Link Layer

Exam Objectives

▶ Specifying the IEEE 802 standards

▶ Describing MAC addresses

▶ Describing the LLC sublayer

▶ Defining a bridge and its use

*T*he problem with networking — and testing your knowledge of its components, functions, and activities — is that you really cannot separate one subject area from another. This close association is especially true of the OSI model's layers. The actions of the layers are so interrelated that a prediction about the number of questions on any one part is virtually impossible.

The blueprint of the Network+ exam indicates that the four lowest OSI model layers make up about five percent of the test with either three or four questions on each layer, which may be good news, because if you don't quite grasp the Network layer, your risk is fairly small. However, I suggest you treat the OSI layers as one big topic — you can thank me after the exam.

The preceding announcement is intended to impress upon you the importance of the OSI model layers, especially the Data Link layer. The Data Link layer is where data is packaged for transmission by the Physical layer. This means that the Data Link layer must define both higher-level message formats and physical level formats, including two very important areas of network specifications: Media Access Control (MAC) addresses and the IEEE (Institute for Electric and Electronic Engineering) 802 specification.

Whatever you do preparation-wise, review this chapter! I hate to play favorites — the other layers can be so jealous — but the Data Link layer holds the key to understanding much of the testable stuff that follows: the other OSI layers, TCP/IP, and general network knowledge.

Quick Assessment

Specifying
the IEEE
802
standards

1 The IEEE _____ standard defines Ethernet and CSMA/CD.

2 High-speed networks are defined in the IEEE _____ standard.

3 The Data Link layer is divided into the _____ and the _____ sublayers.

Describing
MAC
addresses

4 The 48-bit unique identifying number assigned to each network device is also called its _____ address.

5 The method defined in IEEE 802.3 that is used to control access to the physical media of a network is _____.

Describing
the LLC
sublayer

6 _____ are used by network devices to transfer data to the upper layers of the OSI model.

7 _____ is the technique used to meter the flow of data between network devices that may be running at different speeds.

8 The two types of communications services employed at the LLC layer are _____ and _____.

Defining a
bridge and
its use

9 A bridge uses a _____ to determine the appropriate segment to which a message should be forwarded.

10 A bridge can be used to reduce or eliminate traffic _____ on a network.

Answers

1 *802.3.* See "IEEE Standards and the Data Link Layer."

2 *802.12.* Review "IEEE Standards and the Data Link Layer."

3 *LLC, MAC.* Check out "The sublayers of the Data Link layer."

4 *MAC or Media Access Control.* Look over "The media access control (MAC) sublayer."

5 *CSMA/CD.* See "Say, have you seen my CD?"

6 *SAPs (service access points).* Review "The logical link control (LLC) sublayer."

7 *Flow control.* Take a look at "The logical link control (LLC) sublayer."

8 *Connectionless, connection-oriented.* Check out "The logical link control (LLC) sublayer."

9 *Routing table.* Look over "Bridging the Difference."

10 *Bottlenecks.* Review "Using a bridge to eliminate a bottleneck."

IEEE 802 Standards and the Data Link Layer

Immediately after somebody connected two computers together to share files and send secret messages, the whole world recognized a Really Good Thing. As local area networks (LAN) began to proliferate and the future yielded possibility for these networks to grow very large and communicate with each other, an obvious need for some form of standards surfaced. So, the Institute for Electric and Electronic Engineering (IEEE), a well-known and highly respected organization, started a project in February 1980 to create a set of standards for LAN architectures, cabling, and data transmission. The date is important because it forms the name of the project (the 802 project — 80 for the year and 2 for the month) and the standards developed within the effort (IEEE 802).

The 802 project's goal was to define the Data Link layer, including the logical link control (LLC) and media access control (MAC) sublayers (I cover both of these acronymed items later in this chapter in "The logical link control (LLC) sublayer" and "The media access control (MAC) sublayer") and beyond. To date, the 802 project and its 12-plus subcommittees have produced a number of networking standards. I list standards that define the Data Link layer in Table 9-1. The standard's number represents the number of the subcommittee assigned to develop and define that specific subject. For example, the 802.3 standard is assigned to the 802.3 subcommittee. The logic is unparalleled.

Table 9-1	The IEEE 802 Standards	
Standard	*Name*	*Description*
802.1	Internetworking	Defines routing, bridging, and internetwork communications
802.2	Logical Link Control (LLC)	Enables Network layer protocols to link to Physical layer and MAC sublayer protocols
802.3	Ethernet	*THE* Ethernet standard; defines CSMA/CD
802.4	Physical bus	Defines physical token bus topology, media, and interfaces
802.5	Token ring	Defines logical ring topology, media, and interfaces
802.12	High-speed networks	Defines 100 Mbps technologies.

The IEEE 802 Standards You Don't Need to Know

The IEEE 802 subcommittees and standards beyond the Data Link layer are:

802.6 — Metropolitan Area Network (MAN) defines the Distributed Queue Dual Bus (DQDB) and MAN technologies, addressing, and services.

802.7 — The Broadband Technical Advisory Group defines broadband media, interfaces, and equipment.

802.8 — The Fiber-Optic Technical Advisory Group defines the use of fiber-optic cable and technologies in various networking types.

802.9 — Integrated/Voice Data Networks defines the integration of voice and data signals over a single network medium.

802.10 — Network security defines network access control, encryption, certification, and other security areas.

802.11 — Wireless networks defines wireless networking for many different broadcast frequencies and techniques.

The sublayers of the Data Link layer

The Data Link layer takes care of most of the activities used to communicate on a local area network (LAN). Communications beyond the LAN are handled on the Network layer (see Chapter 10). On the Data Link layer, outgoing messages from the upper layers of the OSI model are broken into frames for transmission on the Physical layer. Incoming messages are reassembled for processing at the higher layers.

The Data Link layer is divided into two sublayers by the 802 standards: the logical link control (LLC) and media access control (MAC) sublayers. The LLC sublayer is defined in IEEE 802.1 and 802.2, although some of 802.1 extends into the MAC sublayer as well. The MAC sublayer is defined in the 802.3, 802.4, 802.5, and 802.12 standards.

The logical link control (LLC) sublayer

The LLC sublayer is defined in the 802.2 standard to be topology (Ethernet, Token Ring, etc.) independent. Regardless of the type of network or media in use, the LLC sublayer allows the Network layer to interact with the Data Link layer, and its sublayers. Among other things the LLC sublayer does is provide an interface for the MAC sublayer and manage frames, which involves controlling, sequencing, and acknowledging frames being passed on to either the Physical or Network layers. It also performs some error control tasks at the same time.

LLC transfers data in two ways:

- ✔ **Connectionless services:** Messages are not acknowledged by the receiving device, which speeds up the processing. As unreliable as it may sound, this type of transfer is commonly used at this level because the upper OSI layers implement their own error-checking and control.

- ✔ **Connection-oriented services:** Because each message is acknowledged, this service is much slower than connectionless services, but it's much more reliable.

These two communications modes are normally associated with the Transport layer, but the LLC layer works within them to create and manage the communications links. Another service provided by the LLC sublayer is flow control. Flow control is used to meter the flow of data between network devices that may not be running at the same speeds. You can find more information on connectionless and connection-oriented communications and flow control in Chapter 11.

Another activity of the LLC sublayer is the calculation of the *cyclical redundancy check (CRC),* an important element in the error checking and error control functions. One or more bytes of the data is put through a mathematical calculation to create a single bit or byte profile (the CRC) of a message that is a part of the message when it is sent. The receiving end performs the same calculation and compares its result to the one in the message. If the two are not equal, the data is in error and thrown out. A request to resend the data is sent to the Transport layer (see Chapter 11).

The media access control (MAC) sublayer

The MAC sublayer of the Data Link layer identifies the devices attached to the network, defines the topology used on the network (but not the media), and controls network activity. By definition, a network involves more than one computer and often, more than two. With multiple computers competing for attention, the MAC layer controls access to the network by deciding who can speak, when, and for how long. Put your hand down, Client #3, you just went!

Another important job of the Data Link layer is addressing. The MAC sublayer carries the physical device address of each device on the network. Commonly called a device's MAC address, this 48-bit address is encoded on each device by its manufacturer. The address system works on the same principle as the individually numbered homes in your neighborhood — each domicile on your street has a unique address assigned to it by the postal service. It is the MAC address that is used by the Physical and Data Link layers to deliver data to nodes of the network.

Newer NICs (network interface cards) have their MAC addresses burned into the cards, but some older cards require that you use jumpers or DIP switches to manually configure a unique address (see Chapter 8).

Ethernet and the mighty 802.3

The IEEE 802.3 is *the* Ethernet standard today. Based on the original DIX (Digital-Intel-Xerox) Ethernet standard, 802.3 is by far the Ethernet networking standard of choice. The 802.3 standard defines the bus topology, media (10BaseT), and functions of the Ethernet network. The media defined in 802.3 is twisted pair wiring and this standard defines its support for a data rate of 10 Mbps over baseband communications. In addition to defining the media, protocols, and formats of Ethernet networks, 802.3 also defines the tools used by the MAC sublayer of the Data Link layer.

The primary tool defined in 802.3 for use in the Data Link layer, and actually by the MAC sublayer, to be precise, is CSMA/CD (Carrier Sense Multiple Access/ Collision Detection). These 15 fine syllables represent a method of controlling access to the physical media by network nodes. As can be inferred from its name, CSMA/CD (say it ten times fast to lock it away in your brain) tries to keep network devices from interfering with each other's communications. When they do, this tool also detects and deals with the *collision* that occurs.

To avoid collisions, CSMA/CD devices listen to the network backbone before sending a message over the network. If the network is quiet, meaning that it's not in use, the device can send a message. Otherwise, the device waits until the network is not in use. However, two devices may both act on the inviting sound of quiet, and their transmitted messages may collide on the network. When this happens, the device that detected the collision sends out an alert to all network devices that a collision has occurred. Each and all devices quit transmitting for a random amount of time to clear the line. After a brief, preset amount of time, and using some mysterious algorithm to determine just whose turn it is, one of the devices will once again begin trying to transmit its message while the contending nodes wait. Pretty civilized, what?

The other 802s

The standard defined in IEEE 802.4 is not a commonly used network standard. On the other hand, 802.5 defines the Data Link layer for token ring networks.

With the growing popularity of higher-speed networks (100 Mbps and higher), newer standards have been developed to deal with them. The 802.3u and 802.12 standards are fast becoming very important. The 802.12 standard, which is also called the Demand Priority standard, defines the 100BaseVG and 100BaseVG-AnyLAN networks. 802.12 networks can be either Ethernet or

Token Ring. Demand Priority is the network access method used for high-speed networks arranged in a star arrangement (using hubs). The 802.3u standard defines Fast Ethernet (also 100Mbps) networks as a derivitive of the 10Mbps 802.3 network.

Bridging the Difference

I devote this section to talk about routing tables. In Chapter 10, I cover something completely different — routing tables. Like many words or phrases in the English language, these two seemingly similar terms have completely different meanings. So, when confronted with the term *routing table* on the test, be sure that you know the context of the question (bridge versus router). See "The bridge routing table," later in this section for more information on the routing functions of a bridge.

You use a bridge to connect segments of a single network or to connect two small networks. A bridge is used to reduce network traffic and to move data from one network segment to another, but because a bridge has the abilities beyond the physical movement of the data, it operates at the Data Link layer. In some ways, a bridge works like a router. It filters network traffic and routes packets to the appropriate network segment. However, unlike a router it performs routing within the confines of a single network, which is why it is not on the Network layer.

A bridge is capable of accomplishing the following on a network:

- Extend the scope and distance of a network
- Increase the number of nodes on a LAN
- Eliminate network traffic bottlenecks
- Connect two different network media types
- Connect two dissimilar network segments

Crossing the MAC Bridge

No, the hamburger folks aren't in the networking business now. Bridges are commonly referred to as MAC layer bridges because they operate on the Media Access Control (MAC) sublayer of the Data Link layer. Each network device has a uniquely assigned identification number (MAC address) that identifies the device at the MAC layer. A bridge uses the MAC address to perform its tasks, including the following:

- ✔ Monitoring network traffic

- ✔ Identifying the destination and source addresses of a message

- ✔ Creating a routing table that identifies MAC addresses to the network segment on which they're located

- ✔ Sending messages to only the network segment on which its destination MAC address is located

Taking the bridge route

A bridge builds up its routing table by cataloging the network nodes that send out messages. In effect, a bridge looks to see where a message originated by examining the message source's MAC address. If the MAC address is new to the bridge, the bridge adds it to the routing table along with the network segment of the message. The bridge's RAM stores the routing table; the RAM is dynamic, just like a PC's RAM — when the power goes off, it goes away. When you restore the power, the bridge rebuilds the table. Because most network nodes send and receive packets continuously, the bridge can completely rebuild the routing table in no time flat.

Using a bridge to eliminate a bottleneck

Bridges forward network packets using the following rules:

- ✔ Messages with the same source and destination segment are thrown out. The assumption: The destination mode received the message before the message arrived at the bridge.

- ✔ A message with its destination address listed in the routing table is forwarded to the appropriate segment.

- ✔ A message with a destination address not listed in the routing table is forwarded to all segments except the one on which it originated.

Using these rules, a bridge can help reduce or eliminate network traffic bottlenecks by reducing the number of messages that are broadcast to the entire network.

The bridge with the split personality

One device that spans two layers of the OSI model is a *brouter*. To be honest, I first saw the word brouter on a practice test. The term showed up as a wrong answer, and I remember thinking at the time, "What a dumb and obvious attempt to make up trick answers!" Only later did I discover that a brouter, while it may be a dumb word, is actually a networking device that serves as both a bridge and a router.

A brouter operates on both the Data Link and the Network layers of the OSI Model. The brouter acts like a router with routable protocols and acts like a bridge for nonroutable protocols. Aren't you glad it's not called a "bridgter" or the like?

Prep Test

1 Which of the IEEE 802 standards defines CSMA/CD?

- A ○ 802.2
- B ○ 802.3
- C ○ 802.5
- D ○ 802.12

2 The Data Link layer functions primarily in which two sublayers? (Choose two.)

- A ❑ LLC
- B ❑ SAP
- C ❑ MAC
- D ❑ DQDB

3 The 48-bit identification number that identifies each device attached to a network is its _____ address.

- A ○ Logical link control
- B ○ Device identity control
- C ○ Logical device access control
- D ○ Media access control

4 The IEEE 802.5 standard defines

- A ○ Internetworking
- B ○ Token ring
- C ○ LLC
- D ○ High-speed networks

5 The LLC sublayer creates _____, which are used by network devices to pass data to the upper OSI Model layers.

- A ○ Service access points
- B ○ Media access points
- C ○ Link access points
- D ○ Multiple access points

6 The type of LLC sublayer connection that sends packets without waiting for an acknowledgment is

- A ○ Connection-oriented
- B ○ Connectionless
- C ○ Media-centered
- D ○ Directly-connected

7 Which of the following devices operate on the Data Link layer? (Choose two.)

A ❑ Router

B ❑ Repeater

C ❑ Brouter

D ❑ Bridge

8 Which of the following IEEE 802 standards define LLC sublayer operations? (Choose two.)

A ❑ 802.1

B ❑ 802.2

C ❑ 802.3

D ❑ 802.5

9 Which of the following IEEE 802 standards define 100Mbps networks? (Choose two.)

A ❑ 802.11

B ❑ 802.12

C ❑ 802.3u

D ❑ 802.1Q

10 The technique used on the LLC sublayer to meter the flow of data between computers is

A ◯ Flow control

B ◯ Logical link control

C ◯ Media access control

D ◯ Service access control

Answers

1 *B.* For the Data Link layer, the Ethernet standard (IEEE 802.3) defines Carrier Sense Multiple Access/Collision Detection (CSMA/CD), which is used to control access to the network media. *See "Ethernet and the mighty 802.3."*

2 *A and C.* The logical link control (LLC) and the media access control (MAC) are the two sublayers of the Data Link layer. *Review "The sublayers of the Data Link layer."*

3 *D.* The media access control (MAC) address is usually burned into the device by the manufacturer; the address can also be set manually, if need be. *Check out "The media access control (MAC) sublayer."*

4 *B.* Ethernet and token ring networks are the primary focus of the Project 802 subcommittees. 802.4 does define token-passing bus networks, but it is rarely used. *Look over "IEEE 802 Standards and the Data Link Layer."*

5 *A.* Service access points (SAPs) are interfaces between layers of the OSI model through which a device operating at one layer can provide services to a process in a higher layer. *Take a look at "Service access points (SAPs)."*

6 *B.* Because no acknowledgement is expected, or sent, for that matter, a formal connection is not required or maintained, creating a connectionless communication service. *Review "The logical link control (LLC) sublayer."*

7 *C and D.* Trick question? Not really! The brouter can operate at the Data Link layer using its built-in bridge capabilities. Of course, a bridge is a Data Link device. *See "The bridge with the split personality."*

8 *A and B.* LLC operations are defined by the 802.1 and 802.2 standards. *Check out "The sublayers of the Data Link layer."*

9 *B and C.* IEEE 802.3u defines Fast Ethernet networks and 802.12 defines the 100BaseVG and 100BaseVG-AnyLAN networks. *Take a look at "The other 802s."*

10 *A.* Flow control is used to control data flow between devices with different data speeds. *Look over "The logical link control (LLC) sublayer."*

Chapter 10

The Network Layer

Exam Objectives

▶ Defining routing

▶ Describing the functions of routers and brouters

▶ Differentiating static and dynamic routing

▶ Differentiating routable and nonroutable protocols

• •

*A*lthough you probably don't consider the option too much anymore, I'm sure you still remember how to send a snail mail letter. You know, the kind you print out, stuff into an envelope, affix a stamp to, and place in the big blue mailbox? Some are even written out by hand, can you believe it? Anyway, when you mail a letter to Aunt Sally, the postal service uses a system of forwarding stations to move your letter to its destination. Mail is sorted using destination postal codes (ZIP codes in the United States), starting with the first two digits of the code, and then more of the numbers as it nears its destination.

From an overview-at-20,000-feet perspective, this is how "routing" works. Routing is the process by which a network packet travels from its source network to its destination network. In this chapter, I describe how each packet has a kind of ZIP code that serves two purposes: determining the proper path to a destination and routing the packet accordingly. The whole process is much like the mechanism used to land your letter in Aunt Sally's appreciative hands.

The Network layer, which is where routing occurs, represents five percent of the test. However, like the other three OSI layers included on the exam (Physical layer — see Chapter 8; Data Link layer — see Chapter 9; and Chapter 11 — the Transport layer), the concepts from the Network layer are an integral part of the background knowledge you need for the whole test.

Quick Assessment

Defining routing

1 Routing is the process of transferring packets across an _____ using the most efficient path.

2 True or False: The routing table used by a bridge is the same as that used by a router.

3 Routing _____ are measurements indicating a preference of one route over others.

Describing the functions of routers and brouters

4 _____ are used to create multiple paths through network segments.

5 Routers are effective in helping to solve _____ storms on networks.

6 A _____ combines the advantages of a bridge and a router.

7 The three types of routing algorithm protocols are _____, _____, and _____.

Differentiating static and dynamic routing

8 _____ routing table entries must be created manually.

Differentiating routable and non-routable protocols

9 NetBEUI is a _____ protocol.

10 A _____ protocol cannot see beyond its LAN.

Answers

1   *Internetwork.* See "Routing on the Network Layer."

2   *False.* (The Network+ test does have True/False questions.) Review "Router routing tables."

3   *Metrics.* Check out "Routing metrics."

4   *Routers.* Take a look at "Everything You Ever Wanted to Know About Routers, and Then Some."

5   *Broadcast.* Look over "Smart router tricks."

6   *Brouter.* See "It's a bridge; it's a router; it's a brouter!"

7   *Link-state (OSPF), distance-vector protocol (RIP), IS-IS protocol (NLSP).* Review "Calculating the best route."

8   *Static.* Check out "Static versus dynamic routing."

9   *Nonroutable.* Take a look at "To route or not to route."

10   *Nonroutable.* Look over "To route or not to route."

Routing on the Network Layer

When a packet passes through the Data Link layer, the network node (MAC or media access control) address of the source and destination nodes are placed into the packet. If the packet is addressed to a device on the same segment or LAN (local area network) as the source node, a Data Link layer device, such as a bridge, is able to use these addresses to deliver the packet to its destination. However, if the destination is not on the LAN, another layer of addressing and network interconnection are required: the Network layer and routing. A packet on the Network layer uses network addresses that can include locations beyond the local network.

Semantics 101 is now in session. The Network+ test treats the term *network address* as synonymous with IP address, and the exam uses the terms node address and MAC address interchangeably. So, lock those pairs away as equals: network address = IP address; node address = MAC address.

Routing is the process of transferring data packets across an internetwork from its source to its destination. Routing also involves determining the best and most efficient path for the packet to take through the internetwork to its destination. As I cover in more detail later in this chapter in the "Routing metrics" section, calculating the best route involves the use of *metrics* (hop counts, etc.) and the maintenance of a routing table. Routing on the network layer is accomplished through the use of a *router*.

Before I venture too far into routing, I need to lay down a foundation and offer up a bit of background information.

Everything You Ever Wanted to Know About Routers, and Then Some

A *bridge*, which operates at the MAC sublayer of the Data Link layer, connects two network segments or dissimilar network media within a single network. On the other hand, a *router*, on the Network layer, connects separate physical networks to form *internetworks*. Routers work similarly to bridges to join network segments and filter traffic. However, they're also handy for building very complex networks, something a bridge cannot do. Routers are used to provide multiple paths through network segments.

In effect, a router is a very smart bridge. A router can do all the stuff a bridge does, but it can also analyze each message to see its content type, determine the best available route to its destination, and send the message on its way. In addition, a router communicates with other routers to assist them to determine the most efficient route to or from itself. Table 10-1 contrasts the advantages of bridges and routers.

Table 10-1	Comparison of Bridge and Router Advantages
Device	*Advantages*
Bridge	Extends network segment distances; filters traffic to ease network bottlenecks; connects networks using different media
Router	Connects networks of different media and architectures; determines the best path through an internetwork; does not forward broadcast or corrupted packets

Smart router tricks

Routers talk only to other routers, because only routers talk router. However, just what a router is or can be varies quite a bit. Many companies make devices (Cisco, Cabletron, and so on) specifically called routers that are designed to perform only routing services. However, any computer with more than one network interface card (NIC) and some special routing software can serve as a router. In fact, Novell NetWare includes software that enables it to work as the router for its network.

Routers are particularly effective in helping to solve *broadcast storms*. This network condition occurs when network devices must broadcast a message to the network because they do not know the destination device's address. The purpose of the broadcast is to spur a device to reveal its address so that the message can wind up in the right place. This is like asking, "Will the Node with the Parts database please identify yourself." Too much of this type of traffic creates a bottleneck caused by the mass of ineffective messages flooding the network. Placing a router between two or more subnets filters network traffic by routing messages to specific subnets (see "A little ditty on internetworks" later in the chapter) and not to the whole network.

It's a bridge; it's a router; it's a brouter!

A *brouter* combines the advantages of both a bridge and a router into a single networking device. It operates on both the Data Link and the Network OSI model layers. A brouter acts like a bridge for nonroutable protocols and like a router for routable protocols. What are routable and nonroutable protocols? Funny you should ask. I explain both of these LAN-related terms in the "To route or not to route," section later in this chapter.

The advantage of a brouter is that a network can solve nearly all its connection needs with a single device. This option is not only cost-effective but can also provide for a more manageable network, and the name really impresses nontechnical administrators.

A little ditty on internetworks

The best known internetwork is, of course, the Internet. As a part of an inter-network, a network segment is also known as a subnetwork, or *subnet*, each of which is assigned a network address (IP address). An internetwork results when two (or more) independent networks are connected. The separate networks continue to function independently, but the users on each network can access and share resources on the other network(s). I deal with these concepts and subnet addressing more completely in Chapter 13.

 The Internet, by far the most common internetwork, comprises a huge number of independent, smaller networks that can be connected in myriad ways to form an infinite number of internetworks. The mechanisms that make this limitless interconnection possible are the router and IP (Internet protocol) — or network — addresses.

Routing: Beyond the Basics

The way that the postal service routes the mail is a commonly used parallel for how internetwork routing works. The postal (ZIP) code on a letter or package can be used to route it to its destination. The first couple of digits represent a region, and each of the succeeding digits represent areas, streets, and locations within the region. Routing works essentially the same way, using a packet's IP address. A packet's IP address is much like the postal codes used throughout the world.

Router routing tables

The routing table used by a router is much different than the one used by a bridge. In fact, the only similarity is in the name. A router's routing table stores network addresses (as opposed to node addresses) to determine proper forwarding of packets. When a packet arrives at the router, the information in the routing table is used to identify the network (meaning the router) to which the packet should be sent.

Routing tables (also known as routing information tables) contain network numbers, routes to particular destinations, and *metrics* associated with each route. Routers use this information to determine the best route for a packet to trek to its destination. Figure 10-1 shows the Windows 98 routing table.

Figure 10-1:
The
Windows 98
routing
table.

Static versus dynamic routing

Static routing and dynamic routing refer to how the routing table is created and not to any action applied to network packets. A static router requires the network administrator to build his or her routing table by manually entering the network addresses, routing metrics (see "Routing metrics" later in this section), and other route information. On the other hand, a dynamic router uses the *discovery process* to build its routing table entries. The discovery process automatically identifies ("discovers") all the possible routes to a destination and then decides which is best. However, even a dynamic router needs its first entry created manually.

Table 10-2 summaries the difference between static and dynamic routers.

Table 10-2	Static versus Dynamic Routers	
Action	*Static Router*	*Dynamic Router*
Configuration	Manual	Automatic after first manual entry
Routing	Uses prescribed route	Route chosen using route metrics
Efficiency	Route may not be most efficient	Most efficient route dynamically chosen
Security	More secure due to predictability	Routing may include unsecured paths

Routing metrics

Routing metrics are quantified measurements that indicate a preference for one route over another to get to the same destination. Two commonly used routing metrics are

- **Maximum Transmission Units (MTUs):** The largest packet size in bytes that can be sent over a physical medium or network. For example, the MTU for Ethernet is 1,500.

- **Hop count:** The number of routers or other network devices a packet must pass through to reach its destination. One hop is one packet passing through one router. TCP/IP allows a maximum of 15 hops for a packet to reach its destination.

Other metrics used are communication costs, reliability, delay, bandwidth, and load.

Choosing the high road versus the low road

Routers attempt to untangle the web created by the multiple paths between points on an internetwork. A router's role includes deciding between two (or more) alternate routes to the same destination at any given time. The router uses what are called *routing algorithms* to calculate the most efficient or least expensive route.

Routers use several different algorithms to calculate the best route. The following three protocols are the most common types of routing algorithms:

- **OSPF (Open Shortest Path First):** A link-state protocol, which means it broadcasts status reports on its packets to provide information to other routers on its internetwork.

- **RIP (Routing Information Protocol):** A distance-vector protocol, which means it uses attributes of the route (such as hops) to determine the best route to use.

- **NLSP (Novell NetWare Link-Service Protocol):** This is an IS-IS protocol. No, I'm not stuttering. IS-IS means Intermediate-System-to-Intermediate-System, which is a link-state protocol that transfers information about routes between routers, including connectivity, costs, IPX network information, and media types.

To route or not to route

You find essentially two types of protocols on local area networks: routable and nonroutable. Most protocols are routable, but some aren't. The difference between the two are as follows:

- ✔ **Routable protocols:** Routers see networks and internetworks the same way that they are perceived by the protocol and as a result can route packets to their destinations.

- ✔ **Nonroutable protocols:** These protocols cannot perceive of a world beyond their LAN and cannot be routed. Their lives are obviously limited and boring.

Table 10-3 lists routable and nonroutable protocols. Know these for the test!

Table 10-3	Routable and Non-Routable Protocols
Protocol	_Routable/Nonroutable_
AppleTalk	Routable
IP	Routable
IPX	Routable
NetBEUI	NONROUTABLE
SNA	Routable

If you study Table 10-3 carefully, you may notice the fact that the NetBEUI protocol is nonroutable. Remember this fact! You can expect the exam to ask you about NetBEUI's routeability.

Prep Test

1 Packets on the Network layer are addressed using

- A ○ Network address
- B ○ Node address
- C ○ MAC address
- D ○ WINS address

2 Which of the following are advantages of a router? (Choose three.)

- A ❑ Connects networks of different media and architectures
- B ❑ Extends network segment distances
- C ❑ Helps eliminate broadcast storms
- D ❑ Determines the most efficient path through the internetwork

3 A brouter operates on which OSI Model layers? (Choose two.)

- A ❑ Physical
- B ❑ Network
- C ❑ Data Link
- D ❑ Transport

4 Which two mechanisms make internetworks possible? (Choose two.)

- A ❑ Bridges
- B ❑ MAC addressing
- C ❑ Routers
- D ❑ IP (network) addressing

5 Which of the following is not included in a routing table?

- A ○ Network addresses
- B ○ Routing metrics
- C ○ Interface information
- D ○ Remote network administrator e-mail address

6 The number of routers or routable network devices a packet must pass through to reach its destination is called the

- A ○ MTUs
- B ○ Hit count
- C ○ Hop count
- D ○ OSPF

7 What is the common distance-vector routing algorithm that uses route attributes to determine route efficiencies?

A ○ OSPF

B ○ RIP

C ○ NLSP

D ○ SNA

8 Which of the following protocols are routable? (Choose three.)

A ❑ AppleTalk

B ❑ IP

C ❑ IPX

D ❑ NetBEUI

9 A dynamic router uses the _____ process to create and update its routing table.

A ○ Discovery

B ○ Broadcast

C ○ Metrics

D ○ ARP

10 A protocol that sees networks and internetworks the same way they are perceived by a router is a _____ protocol.

A ○ Nonroutable

B ○ Routable

C ○ Either routable or nonroutable

D ○ Neither routable nor nonroutable

Answers

1 *A.* Network (IP) addresses are used to reference locations beyond the local network. *See "Routing on the Network Layer."*

2 *A, C, and D.* Bridges and repeaters can be used to extend network segment distances, but routers cannot perform the same service. *Review "Everything You Ever Wanted to Know About Routers, and Then Some."*

3 *B and C.* A brouter combines the best of a bridge, which operates on the Data Link layer, and a router, from the Network layer. *Check out "It's a bridge; it's a router; it's a brouter!"*

4 *C and D.* Routers and IP network addressing create and designate *internetworks. Take a look at "A little ditty on internetworks."*

5 *D.* Just about everything else is in there, but not this information. *Look over "Router routing tables."*

6 *C.* One hop is one packet passing through one router. *Review "Routing metrics."*

7 *B.* RIP (routing information protocol) uses route attributes to determine which route is best at a given instance for a packet. *See "Calculating the best route."*

8 *A, B, and C.* For some reason, the Network+ test makes a big deal out of the fact that NetBEUI is nonroutable, especially in the context of routers. *Check over "To route or not to route."*

9 *A.* The discovery process enables the dynamic router to continuously examine routes to discover the best route at a given time. *Look at "Static versus dynamic routing."*

10 *B.* A network protocol that shares the view of the network (especially an internetwork) is a routable protocol and its packets can be forwarded beyond the network. *See "To route or not to route."*

Chapter 11

The Transport Layer

● ●

Exam Objectives

▶ Differentiating connectionless and connection-oriented protocols

▶ Describing flow control and error handling

▶ Defining name resolution

● ●

*T*he OSI model's Transport layer is where data packets are formatted and transported between local or remote network nodes. If you think of the OSI model as a sort of production-chain for network data payloads, then the Transport layer is the equivalent of the transportation dispatcher and the shipping and receiving department. It repackages the goods for shipment, arranges for transportation, and then monitors progress of the cargo.

Large packets are broken into smaller parcels to fit the physical carrier (media) and the operations of the lower layers. The Transport layer also packs in some error checking to make sure that each package reaches its destination intact and error-free. On the receiving end of the process, the Transport layer checks incoming parcels for errors or problems and then reassembles the smaller packet segments into the original packet before sending it on to the OSI model's upper layers.

The Transport layer also monitors the transportation of network packets. It acknowledges those that arrive successfully and makes certain that undelivered or incorrect packets are resent. A packet may not reach its destination because a circuit crashes, a router along the way may be malfunctioning, or the packet contains an erroneous address or may contain errors that prevent it from being properly handled or interpreted. Regardless, the Transport layer ensures a message reaches its destination competely and without error.

At least for this layer, you have no specific hardware, hardware attributes, or lists of numbers to memorize, but you really do need to focus on these Transport layer concepts: the connection types used to transport data, error checking, flow control, and name resolution terms and functions.

Quick Assessment

Differentia-
ting connec-
tionless and
connection-
oriented
protocols

1   A _____ includes the prescribed rules, procedures, and processes that govern a type of communication.

2   When a group of protocols work cooperatively to accomplish a common objective, they form a _____.

3   The type of protocol that requires a direct connection between two computers is a _____ protocol.

4   Connectionless protocols send and receive packets called _____.

5   A _____ protocol is referred to as a best-effort protocol.

Describing
flow control
and error
handling

6   _____ is used when one communications device is faster than the other.

7   Three basic types of error checking are _____, _____, and _____.

8   _____ and _____ are the two general types of flow control.

Defining
name
resolution

9   Name resolution is used to translate between _____ and _____.

10 _____ is the standard syntax used to specify the path to a network resource.

Answers

1   *Protocol.* See "Protocols refresher."

2   *Protocol stack or protocol suite.* Review "Will that be a short stack?"

3   *Connection-oriented.* Check out "Making the connection."

4   *Datagrams.* Take a look at "Making the connection."

5   *Connectionless.* Look over "Two important protocol points."

6   *Flow control.* Review "Going with the Flow Control and Watching Out for Snags."

7   *Parity bit, checksum, CRC (cyclical redundancy check).* See "Error checking and handling."

8   *Software, hardware.* Take a look at "Flow control."

9   *Host or NetBIOS (network) names, logical IP (node) addresses.* Check out "Name Resolution."

10   *UNC (universal naming convention).* Review "Name resolution terms you need to know."

Understanding That It's All a Matter of Protocols

The Transport layer accepts data from the Session layer (the next higher layer), breaks the packet into smaller pieces, if necessary, and then insures its (their) error-free delivery to the destination. The Transport layer also provides connection-management services between a source computer to a destination computer and data-transfer services between the two Transport layer protocols.

Perhaps the biggest part of the Transport layer's work is recognizing the type of protocol and media in use on the network. The Transport layer is primarily concerned with organizing the data packet to conform to the appropriate protocols and type of network media.

The most commonly used Transport layer protocols are

- ✔ **TCP (Transmission Control Protocol):** Responsible for reliable delivery of packets.
- ✔ **UDP (User Datagram Protocol):** A TCP/IP protocol that does not acknowledge the receipt of a message
- ✔ **SPX (Sequenced Packet Exchange):** The Novell protocol that guarantees data delivery.
- ✔ **NWLink (NetWare Link):** The Microsoft version of IPX/SPX.
- ✔ **ATP/NBP (AppleTalk Transaction Protocol/Name Binding Protocol):** AppleTalk's data transport protocols.
- ✔ **NetBIOS/NetBEUI (Network Basic Input/Output System/NetBIOS Extended User Interface):** Microsoft network protocols that work together to manage communications (NetBIOS) and provide data transport services (NetBEUI).

For more information on these and other protocols and their relationship to the OSI model, see Chapter 7.

Making the connection

The protocols that networks use to communicate are either connection-oriented or connectionless. Any particular protocol either establishes and manages a linking connection between two computers in order to transfer data or it doesn't.

✔ **Connection-oriented protocols:** This type of protocol requires a direct connection between only two computers before data transfer begins. Packets are transferred using a prescribed sequence of actions that includes an acknowledgement when a packet arrives, and resending the packet if errors occur. This method is very reliable, and of course much slower than connectionless protocols. Using a modem to transfer data is a good example of a connection-oriented protocol.

✔ **Connectionless protocols:** This protocol is largely based on your faith in the technology. Packets are sent over the network without regard to whether they actually arrive at their destinations. Don't expect acknowledgements or guarantees with these protocols, but you can send a *datagram*, which is the name for connectionless protocol packets, to many different destinations at the same time. Connectionless protocols are fast because no time is used up establishing and tearing down connections. A fair analogy is mailing a first-class letter with the postal service. You have to have faith it will be delivered, and the carrier provides no immediate feedback that it has in fact done so.

Two important protocol points

Connectionless protocols are also referred to as *best-effort* protocols. This type of delivery system is common to protocols that do not include some form of acknowledgement system to guarantee the delivery of information.

You need to understand the primary difference between connection-oriented and connectionless protocols, but more importantly, you need to know the type for each of the common protocols. Table 11-1 lists common protocols and whether they are connection-oriented or connectionless.

Table 11-1   Connection-Oriented and Connectionless Protocols

Protocol	Type
IP (Internet Protocol)	Connectionless
IPX (Internetwork Packet Exchange)	Connectionless
TCP (Transmission Control Protocol)	Connection-oriented
UDP (User Datagram Protocol)	Connectionless
SPX (Sequenced Packet Exchange)	Connection-oriented

Going with the Flow Control and Watching Out for Snags

In addition to managing the transport of data over the network, the Transport layer performs two important services that are aimed at insuring data reaches its destination in a timely and error-free manner. These services are

- **Flow control:** This is the process used to manage the rate at which data is transmitted between two network devices. An optimal transmission speed that minimizes network congestion is determined through a process called flow-control negotiation. Flow control is commonly used in situations where one of the communicating devices is faster than the other.

- **Error handling:** This is the process used to deal with errors that occur in data transmission. In general terms, error handling also encompasses error control and error detection and correction. The whole ball of wax is devoted to ensuring that the received transmission matches the sent transmission.

Flow control

Flow control is most commonly discussed in connection with modems, but the same concepts apply to networks as well. In situations where one of the communicating devices has either faster or slower capabilities than the other device, some form of control is necessary to meter the flow of data between the devices. Flow control prevents the slower device from being swamped, and, more importantly, prevents data from being lost or garbled. The process works by pausing the faster device to enable the slower device to catch up. Table 11-2 details the two general types of flow control.

Table 11-2		Flow Control
Category	*Method*	*Description*
Software	XON/XOFF	Roughly translated, this stands for transmission on/transmission off. When the slower device wants to pause the faster device, it sends a control character (usually CTRL+S) that indicates it needs the faster device to wait a moment. When the slower device is ready to go, it sends another control signal (typically CTRL+Q) to the faster device indicating it's ready to go.

Category	Method	Description
Hardware	RTS/CTS	Ready To Send/Clear to Send. Two wires in the modem cable are designated as RTS and CTS. The sending device uses the RTS signal to indicate when it is ready to send. The receiving device uses the CTS to indicate that it's ready to receive. When either is turned off, the flow is interrupted.

Error checking and handling

Here's a small dose of reality for you: Errors can and do happen in transmitting data across a network, especially an internetwork. I'm sorry to be so blunt, but you'll thank me later. When a transmission error occurs, the receiving end is likely to be blessed with corrupted, useless data. Sounds pretty pitiful, huh?

Error checking is one part of the error-handling process used to prevent the loss of data. In the OSI model, error checking is used at many different levels, but primarily on the Transport and Data Link layers. Error checking is applied in three basic ways:

- ✓ **Parity bit:** The number of bits in the transmission is counted and then another bit is used to ensure the number of bits is an odd number. The receiving end recounts and verifies that an odd number of bits arrived. If not, a request to resend the packet is sent back.

- ✓ **Checksum:** The number of bits in the transmission is counted and the total is sent along as a part of the packet. The receiving end recounts and checks its count to the sum in the packet. If they are not equal, a request to resend the packet is sent.

- ✓ **Cyclical redundancy check (CRC):** This is actually a Data Link layer activity (see Chapter 9) in which one or more bytes of the data is put through a mathematical calculation to create a single bit or byte profile (the CRC) of a message that is a part of the message when it is sent. The receiving end performs the same calculation and compares its result to the one in the message. If the two are not equal, the data is in error and thrown out. A request to resend the data is sent.

In connection-oriented communications, error checking and handling is performed at each step of the process. However, connectionless transmissions assume the sending and receiving software are performing this task.

Error handling on the Transport layer includes the following activities:

✔ Acknowledges successful and unsuccessful transmissions

✔ Processes requests for retransmissions because of errors in the data detected through the following error checking methods:

- parity bit

- checksum

- CRC

✔ Uses a time-out mechanism to determine when packets have failed to arrive and need to be retransmitted. One of the more common time-out methods is TTL (time-to-live) which determines the length of time a transmitted message is allowed to reach its destination before being considered MIA (missing-in-action).

Playing the Name Resolution Game

You can expect at least a couple of questions on the Network+ exam about name resolution, the process used to translate between the logical names assigned to network devices (host names, NetBIOS names, or network names) and the physical network (node or MAC) addresses. The node address requires conversion to a human-friendly name, or vice versa, depending on whether a packet is inbound or outbound.

It is far easier for the human element of any network to use human-friendly names than it is to use the physical machine-friendly codes used by the non-human (or should that be inhuman?) elements of the network. I don't know about you, but it is far easier for me to remember SERVER1 than it is 050306669399.

Aunt Sally considers you her favorite relative, and she calls you by name. However, to the postal service, you are 111 Main Street in Yourtown, Yourstate, within your postal code. Your name is equivalent to the name assigned to devices on a network. Instead of John Smith, a device may be /MAIN_SERVER, and instead of your address, a network device uses its 48-bit MAC (media access control) address. Name resolution is being performed when Aunt Sally addresses and mails your birthday card and when a packet is forwarded to a particular device on a network.

For the Network+ exam, you need to know not only the different methods used for name resolution, but also the terminology involved. Study Chapters 12 and 13 for more in-depth information on name resolution, but first be sure you understand the following terminology:

- ✔ **DNS (Domain Naming System):** A service used to translate human-friendly domain names (such as www.dummies.com) into their numeric logical IP address (for example, 234.253.213.22).

- ✔ **Domain Name Server:** An Internet computer that translates Internet domain names into their IP address equivalents.

- ✔ **FQDN (Fully Qualified Domain Name):** The full name of a computer on the Internet that includes its hostname and domain server.

- ✔ **HOSTfile (a.k.a. host table):** A list of the TCP/IP hosts on a network, along with their network (IP) addresses.

- ✔ **Hostname:** The Internet term for a computer's name.

- ✔ **LMHOSTS file:** A Microsoft utility that relates network addresses to NetBIOS node names.

- ✔ **Naming service:** Most network operating systems include this function, which enables you to assign names to network resources.

- ✔ **UNC (Universal Naming Convention):** A standard syntax used to specify a path to a network resource. For example, the public area on the main server is specified as \\MAIN_SERVER\PUBLIC using the syntax \\servername\sharename

- ✔ **WINS (Windows Internet Naming Service):** A Microsoft service that translates NetBIOS node names to network addresses.

Remember that UNC slashes are backward slashes on Windows systems. Look forward to at least one question on the Network+ test that asks you to identify a UNC name from a choice of options. Something along the lines of \\MAIN_SERVER\PUBLIC is the answer.

Prep Test

1 Which of the following are Transport layer protocols? (Choose two.)

A ❑ IPX

B ❑ SPX

C ❑ UDP

D ❑ IP

2 A communications type that establishes and manages a direct connection between the communicating computers is

A ○ Connectionless

B ○ Connection-oriented

C ○ Flow control

D ○ RTS/CTS

3 A best-effort protocol is

A ○ Connectionless

B ○ Connection-oriented

C ○ Both A and B

D ○ Neither A nor B

4 Which of the following are connection-oriented protocols? (Choose two.)

A ❑ IP

B ❑ IPX

C ❑ TCP

D ❑ SPX

5 The process that enables faster devices to communicate with slower devices without the loss of data is

A ○ Error handling

B ○ Low control

C ○ CRC

D ○ Parity

6 Which two of the following are common implementations of flow control? (Choose two.)

A ❑ Parity bit

B ❑ XON/XOFF

C ❑ Checksum

D ❑ RTS/CTS

7 The service used to translate domain names into IP addresses is

A ○ FQDN

B ○ Flow control

C ○ DNS

D ○ LHHOSTS

8 WINS is a Microsoft service that

A ○ Translates NetBIOS node names to their network addresses

B ○ Replaces DNS to translate IP addresses and domain names

C ○ Provides connectionless TCP communications

D ○ Performs flow control on Transport layer communications

9 The standard naming convention used to specify a path to a network resource is

A ○ Naming services

B ○ FQDN

C ○ DNS

D ○ UNC

10 Which of the following are activities of error handling on the Transport layer? (Choose three.)

A ❑ Acknowledging successful and unsuccessful packet transmissions

B ❑ Processing requests for packet retransmissions

C ❑ Providing CRC error checking

D ❑ Determining when packets have failed to arrive at their destinations

Answers

1 *B, C.* SPX and UDP are Transport layer protocols. IPX and IP are Network layer protocols. You should remember which protocols operate on which levels for the Network+ test. *Check out "Understanding It's All a Matter of Protocols."*

2 *B.* Connection-oriented protocols must establish a connection that is used to manage the integrity of the data being transmitted. *See "Making the connection."*

3 *A.* Although it seems somewhat contradictory that a best-effort involves none of the control and process of the connection-oriented protocols, connection-less protocols are known as best-effort protocols. *Review "Two important protocol points."*

4 *C and D.* TCP and SPX are both connection-oriented protocols that formally guarantee the error-free and timely transmission of data. *Take a look at "Two important protocol points."*

5 *B.* Flow control uses signals between two devices to pause one while the other catches up. *See "Going with the Flow Control and Watching Out for Snags."*

6 *B and D.* XON/XOFF uses control characters, also called control indicators, to stop and start the data flow. RTS/CTS, common to modems, uses designated wires to communicate between the devices. *Review "Flow control."*

7 *C.* DNS (domain naming system) is a distributed service that is used to translate human-friendly domain names into their IP address equivalents. *Take a look at "Name Resolution."*

8 *A.* WINS shows up on the Network+ exam a number of times. You need to understand both DNS and WINS for the test. I cover both in more detail in Chapters 12 and 13. *See "Name Resolution."*

9 *D.* UNC (universal naming convention) is used as a standard for creating path-names for network devices. *Check out "Name Resolution."*

10 *A, B, and D.* This is what the Transport layer does. Remember that CRC is a Data Link layer function. *Review "Error Checking and Handling."*

Part IV
Working with TCP/IP

The 5th Wave   By Rich Tennant

"It's a wonderful idea, Ralph. But do you really think 'AnnoyPersonTP' and 'DumbMemoTP' will work as protocols on our TCP/IP suite?"

In this part . . .

*I*n my opinion, if you boil down the Network+ exam, it essentially measures a network technician's ability to configure, install, and maintain a TCP/IP client on a working network. So, it stands to reason that the exam must include a part to measure your knowledge of TCP/IP and its protocol suite.

Questions relating directly to TCP/IP represent at least 28 percent of the Network+ exam. I would venture to guess that you can add another 8 to 12 percent on top of that for questions that relate to TCP/IP indirectly. Given that TCP/IP may represent as much as 40 percent of the exam, it should be obvious to you that this is a very important part of the book, as well as a must-see stop on your study tour.

Chapter 12

TCP/IP Protocols and Addressing Basics

● ●

Exam Objectives

▶ Listing the main protocols in the TCP/IP protocol suite

▶ Identifying the OSI model layers of the TCP/IP protocols

▶ Describing the purpose and use of DNS, WINS, and host files

▶ Explaining the IP default gateway

● ●

*F*or the Network+ exam, you don't need to know the history of TCP/IP or the Internet, but you have to understand the virtually universal acceptance and support for TCP/IP in all forms of networking. You also need to know that TCP/IP is not just one or two protocols, but rather a suite of protocols that work together to enable Internet, intranet, and networking communications over local and wide area networks. You must know the use and function of each of the major protocols in the TCP/IP protocol suite. In addition, you really ought to be familiar with the layers of the OSI model on which each of the TCP/IP protocols operate.

Before you become too overwhelmed by the enormity of this task, take a deep breath, let it out slowly, and relax. Chances are that you are already using many of these protocols frequently, if not every day. When asked, you have no problem explaining the function and use of each. Inherent in understanding how the protocols work together is knowing how a message gets from point A to point B over the Internet and how Internet addressing works. This process involves important items such as default gateways, DNS, WINS, and other client- and server-based tools and resources.

If you know and understand all the ins and outs of TCP/IP fundamentals and protocols, which I cover in this chapter, you can look forward to conquering TCP/IP exam questions quickly and completely.

Quick Assessment

Listing the main protocols in the TCP/IP protocol suite

1 _____ is the primary transport protocol of the TCP/IP protocol suite.

2 The TCP/IP protocol that provides for source and destination addressing is _____.

3 The two most commonly used e-mail client protocols are _____ and _____.

4 The _____ TCP/IP utility is used to check the validity of a remote IP address.

5 TCP is a _____ communications protocol.

Identifying the OSI model layers of the TCP/IP protocols

6 The Internet Protocol operates on the OSI model's _____ layer.

7 TCP and UDP are _____ layer protocols.

Describing the purpose and use of DNS, WINS, and host files

8 The _____ is used to resolve an FQDN to its IP address.

9 The dynamic Windows-based service used to resolve NetBIOS names into their IP addresses is _____.

Explaining the IP default gateway

10 The _____ is the NIC installed on the network router.

Answers

1   *TCP (Transmission Control Protocol).* See "Transmission Control Protocol (TCP)."

2   *IP (Internet Protocol).* Review "Internet Protocol."

3   *POP3 (Post Office Protocol), IMAP (Interactive Mail Access Protocol).* Check out "Simple Mail Transport Protocol (SMTP)."

4   *PING (Packet Internet Groper).* Take a look at "TCP/IP Utilities."

5   *Connection-oriented.* Examine "Transmission Control Protocol (TCP)."

6   *Network.* See "TCP/IP and the OSI Model."

7   *Transport.* Review "TCP/IP and the OSI Model."

8   *DNS (Domain Name System).* Take a look at "Domain Name System (DNS)."

9   *WINS (Windows Internet Name Service).* Check out "Windows Internet Name Service (WINS)."

10   *IP default gateway.* Look over "Shooting out of the IP gateway."

TCP/IP: World Famous and Accepted Everywhere

The Transmission Control Protocol/Internet Protocol (TCP/IP) protocol suite, also known as simply the Internet Protocol suite, serves communications at both the global and local levels. From its conception, TCP/IP evolved with a definite emphasis on portability and universal support. Its adaptability and open structure are important reasons for its rapid and widespread growth.

Some of the characteristics that contribute to the popularity of TCP/IP are as follows:

✔ **Open protocol:** TCP/IP is not based on or tied to any particular operating system, making it an open standard that developers can base new systems on and be assured of interoperability.

✔ **Universal interconnectivity:** TCP/IP is the conduit through which two different operating systems or processes running on separate computers can directly communicate.

✔ **Conformity (modularity):** Even though it preceded the emergence of the OSI model by nearly a decade, TCP/IP conforms to the modularity of the OSI model. TCP/IP protocols communicate only with the layers immediately below and above the layers on which they operate. This creates a modularity easily adapted to any system.

✔ **Internet addressing:** TCP/IP supports a 32-bit (4-octet) addressing scheme that enables it to address over 4 billion Internet hosts. This address is used to identify both the network and the host. See Chapter 13 for more information on TCP/IP addressing.

In addition to the above characteristics, the protocols that make up the TCP/IP protocol suite also provide a wide range of functionality, versatility, and interoperatability (the famous Lity triplets) options to networked users.

The TCP/IP Protocols

I just can't stop saying it: TCP/IP is actually a suite of protocols that work together to provide for reliable and efficient data communications across an internetwork.

The major protocols of the TCP/IP protocol suite are

✔ Transmission Control Protocol (TCP)
✔ User Datagram Protocol (UDP)

✔ Domain Name System (DNS)

✔ Internet Protocol (IP)

✔ Address Resolution Protocol (ARP)

✔ File Transfer Protocol (FTP)

✔ Simple Mail Transport Protocol (SMTP)

✔ Post Office Protocol (POP3)

✔ Interactive Mail Access Protocol (IMAP)

✔ Internet Control Message Protocol (ICMP)

✔ Routing Information Protocol (RIP)

✔ Open Shortest Path First (OSPF)

✔ Hypertext Transfer Protocol (HTTP)

✔ TCP/IP Utilities (PING, Telnet, IPCONFIG, ARP, and more). See Chapter 14.

Don't waste time memorizing all the protocols in the TCP/IP protocol suite. Look over the preceding list and mentally note the first six or seven. Knowing the individual functions of these protocols is more important than memorizing this list.

Transmission Control Protocol (TCP)

TCP (Transmission Control Protocol) is one of the namesake and foundation protocols of the TCP/IP protocol suite. TCP accepts variable-length messages from the upper-layer OSI model protocols, fragments them for transmission, and then directs the transport of the data to the TCP layer of the destination network.

TCP has the following characteristics and features:

✔ **Connection-oriented:** It establishes and manages a direct connection to the remote network.

✔ **Reliable:** TCP guarantees the delivery of message packets to their destination by acknowledging those that arrive and requesting retransmission of late or erroneous packets.

✔ **Packet handling:** TCP performs message fragmentation, sequencing, and reassembly.

✔ **Error-checking:** It uses a checksum to ensure that packets are reassembled in the correct order.

TCP is the primary transport protocol of the TCP/IP protocol suite. TCP is a connection-oriented, reliable, delivery protocol that ensures internetwork packets will arrive at their destinations error-free.

User Datagram Protocol (UDP)

The User Datagram Protocol (UDP) is TCP's evil twin. UDP is a connection-less, unreliable message delivery protocol that makes no guarantees about whether packets will arrive at all, and if they do, that they will be in the correct sequence. It even uses a different name, *datagrams*, for the packets it sends.

UDP is generally used in situations where the message packet does not need to be fragmented and where the speed of the delivery is more important than the overhead required to ensure the delivery. UDP is often used with SNMP; see "Simple Network Management Protocol" later in this section.

Domain Name System (DNS)

I talk about this protocol, which is the name-to-address resolution service of the TCP/IP protocol suite, in detail in Chapter 13. In summary, DNS uses a distributed database of system names and their related IP addresses to enable Internet users to work with the human-friendly system names, such as www.dummies.com, rather than their less friendly IP addresses, such as 206.175.162.18 (the Dummies IP address).

Internet Protocol (IP)

The Internet Protocol (IP) provides for source and destination addressing and the routing of the packets across the internetwork. In contrast to TCP, IP is connectionless and unreliable, but it is fast. IP, like all connectionless protocols, is called a *best effort* protocol and relies on other protocols to handle reliability and other delivery issues. I offer up IP and IP addressing details in Chapter 13.

Address Resolution Protocol (ARP)

When delivering an IP packet on a network, the Address Resolution Protocol (ARP) picks up where DNS leaves off. DNS resolves the text domain name of a destination to its numeric IP address (see "Domain Name System" earlier in this section). ARP then resolves the IP address to the physical MAC (media access control) address of the destination.

ARP broadcasts a request packet to the network with the destination's IP address. The workstation or device that matches the IP address is expected to identify itself by sending back an ARP reply packet that contains its MAC address. The reply is stored in the ARP cache table, which is completely refreshed every two minutes.

File Transfer Protocol (FTP)

Of all the protocols that can possibly pop up on the Network+ test, FTP was the last one I expected to see — but appear it did, complete with a question fully devoted to the FTP topic. You can use the File Transfer Protocol (FTP) to transfer files from one Internet computer to another, which you've probably done sometime in your networking life. It is now commonly supported in virtually every network operating system, and as a built-in part of most World Wide Web browsers. If you wish to transfer files independent of your Web browser, a variety of FTP shareware and freeware clients are available.

When you transfer a file from your computer to a remote computer using FTP, you are _uploading_ the file. _Downloading_ a file is the reverse action — the file originates at the remote computer and copies to your computer. FTP clients, the software running on your computer, communicate with the FTP server (the software running on the remote host) to perform a variety of file management actions in addition to file transfers.

Simple Mail Transport Protocol (SMTP)

The Simple Mail Transport Protocol (SMTP) is the protocol that provides the foundation services for e-mail transfer across the Internet. SMTP makes sure that e-mail messages are delivered from the sender's server to the addressee's server. It does not deal with delivery to the addressee's mailbox, leaving that task to other protocols. SMTP is more like the postal service's trucks and airplanes that move mail from post office to post office, where those letters from Aunt Sally can then be sorted and delivered to the addressee by other services.

SMTP transfers e-mail across the Internet and your mail server holds the mail for you in your mailbox. What happens to your e-mail from this point on depends on the type of mail client you are using.

Post Office Protocol (POP3)

If you are using the Post Office Protocol (POP3) e-mail protocol, when you log ino your mailbox, POP3 downloads your mail to your computer. The number 3 in POP3 refers to the latest version of this popular e-mail protocol.

POP mail stores your e-mail until you log on, at which time your mail moves to your client computer and off the server. POP works well in situations where users log on from the same permanently assigned workstation.

Interactive Mail Access Protocol (IMAP)

If you are using the Interactive Mail Access Protocol (IMAP), your e-mail remains on the server regardless of what you do with it on your client computer. Your e-mail is stored on the server indefinitely — until you decide to remove it. IMAP e-mail works very well in situations where clients regularly access their mail from different locations on the network.

Internet Control Message Protocol (ICMP)

The Internet Control Message Protocol (ICMP) acts as a sort of intercom system for the TCP/IP protocol suite. ICMP carries control, status, and error messages between systems. ICMP messages are encapsulated inside of IP datagrams for transport over the network. For example, gateways and Internet hosts use the ICMP to transmit datagram problem reports back to the message source. Internet utilities, such as PING and TRACERT (see Chapter 14), send ICMP echo requests and wait for ICMP echo responses to time and trace the route to a remote location (see "TCP/IP utilities" later in this section").

Routing Information Protocol (RIP) and Open Shortest Path First (OSPF)

Routers work at maintaining the more efficient route to a remote destination at any given moment. To do this, they must communicate with one another and manage statistics (called *metrics*) about the number of hops and other route information that is used to calculate the best path for a packet to take. The Routing Information Protocol (RIP) and the Open Shortest Path First (OSPF) protocols perform this job.

Routing Information Protocol (RIP)

The Routing Information Protocol (RIP) counts the number of routers and network devices (called hops) a packet must pass through to reach its destination. The number of hops is then used to calculate the best and most efficient path available to a packet. The least number of hops is considered the best path.

Open Shortest Path First (OSPF)

The Open Shortest Path First (OSPF) protocol uses other factors in addition to the number of hops to determine the best path, including the speed of the network between hops and the amount of network traffic on each segment.

Hypertext Transfer Protocol (HTTP)

No doubt you're keenly aware of this protocol, but have you considered that it's one of the TCP/IP protocols? You look to the Hypertext Transfer Protocol (HTTP) for transferring documents encoded in the Hypertext Markup Language (HTML) over the World Wide Web (WWW). This protocol is the underlying protocol of WWW browser software.

TCP/IP utilities

Chapter 14 includes explanations and a few labs to help you understand the purpose and functions of the utilities included in the TCP/IP protocol suite. In short, the TCP/IP utilities are used to access, troubleshoot, and analyze TCP/IP operations. The most common of these utilities and their uses are as follows:

- ✔ **PING (Packet Internet Groper):** Checks validity of a remote IP address.

- ✔ **ARP (Address Resolution Protocol):** Serves to display and edit the ARP cache on a computer.

- ✔ **NETSTAT (Network Statistics):** Displays information on current TCP/IP connections.

- ✔ **NBTSTAT (NetBIOS over TCP/IP Statistics):** Displays the contents of the NetBIOS over TCP/IP name cache on a computer and to repair the contents of the hosts file (see "Using hosts files" later in this chapter).

- ✔ **IPCONFIG (IP Configuration):** Displays the entire TCP/IP configuration of a computer and renews DHCP (Dynamic Host Control Protocol) IP address leases (see Chapter 13 for more information on DHCP). Windows 95 has a unique version of this protocol named WINIPCFG (see Lab 12-1 later in the chapter).

- ✔ **TRACERT (Trace Route):** Traces the route a packet uses to reach a destination on the internetwork.

- ✔ **ROUTE:** Displays, configures, and maintains network routing tables.

- ✔ **NSLOOKUP (Name System Lookup):** Troubleshoots DNS problems and displays the DNS entry for a certain IP address or DNS name.

With Windows NT growing in popularity, the lines between what is pure TCP/IP and what is Microsoft's contribution to the TCP/IP world are becoming blurred. ARP, NETSTAT, IPCONFIG, and NBTSTAT are actually Microsoft TCP/IP protocols. However, you can expect to see them on the Network+ exam without regard to their origin.

TCP/IP and the OSI Model

Although TCP/IP has been around much longer than the OSI model, its protocols match up very nicely with the OSI model. Or should I say that the OSI model's layers match very well with TCP/IP protocols? Regardless, they make a nice couple.

Do yourself a favor: Know the OSI model layer for each of the most important TCP/IP protocols. Table 12-1 lists the protocols and the layers on which they operate. Pound this information into your memory!

Table 12-1	TCP/IP Protocols and Their OSI Model Layers
TCP/IP Protocol	*OSI Model Layer*
TCP	Transport
UDP	Transport
IP	Network
ICMP	Network
ARP	Data Link

Names and Addresses

Networked computers, like people, must have some identity by which other computers can refer to them. "Hey, you," just doesn't work any better on a network than it does in a group of people. Each computer must have a unique identifier assigned to it. Depending on the protocol or process communicating with a computer, the ID may have a number, a "friendly" name, or an address. Just like I have a government-assigned Social Security number, my given name, and a home address, a computer has a MAC address, an IP address, and perhaps a sharename.

MAC addresses

The Media Access Control sublayer of the Data Link layer uses MAC (media access control) addresses to physically address network devices, usually network interface cards (NICs). MAC addresses, also called Ethernet addresses, are assigned by manufacturers, and burned into the electronics. A MAC address is a 6-byte (48-bit) hexadecimal number in the form of six 2-digit numbers separated by colons or dashes, for example 00-11-22-33-44-55. Each digit of the MAC address can be in the range of the hexadecimal values 0-F.

The first 24 bits (3 bytes) of the MAC address contain a code for the manufacturer. The last 3 bytes (24 bits) contain a unique serialized station ID number. The IEEE (Institute for Electrical and Electronic Engineering) globally assigns and administers MAC manufacturer codes.

Labs 12-1 and 12-2 step you through the process of obtaining the MAC address for your computer on a Windows-based workstation or a Novell-based workstation, respectively.

Lab 12-1   Getting Your MAC Address on a Windows 95/98 Computer

1. **Select Run from the Start menu.**

2. **In the Run box, enter** winipcfg **and press Enter.**

   The box you see in Figure 12-1 appears. In addition to your Adapter address (the address of your NIC — your MAC address), this box shows your IP address, the subnet mask (see Chapter 13), and the default gateway (check out "The IP Gateway" later in this chapter).

MAC address manufacturer codes you don't need to know

The first three bytes of a MAC address contain a hexadecimal manufacturer code. The following are examples of IEEE assigned MAC address manufacturer codes and the manufacturer it identifies:

00 00 03 Standard Microsystems

00 00 0C Cisco Systems

00 00 11 Tektronix

00 00 1B Novell / Eagle

00 00 1D Cabletron

00 00 2A TRW

00 00 3D AT&T

00 01 E3 Xircom

00 55 00 Intel

00 DD 00 Ungermann-Bass

08 00 5A IBM

10 00 D8 DG

40 00 14 TI Texas Instruments

40 00 65 Network General

40 00 AA Xerox

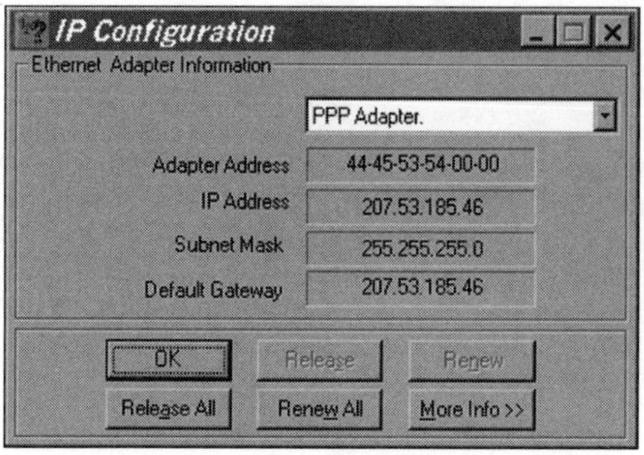

IP Configuration

Ethernet Adapter Information

PPP Adapter.

Adapter Address	44-45-53-54-00-00
IP Address	207.53.185.46
Subnet Mask	255.255.255.0
Default Gateway	207.53.185.46

OK   Release   Renew

Release All   Renew All   More Info >>

Figure 12-1:
The Windows IP configuration window.

Lab 12-2   Getting a MAC Address on a Novell Workstation

1. **Log on to a NetWare server.**

2. **Open an MS-DOS prompt window and enter the command line** nlist user=accountname.

   Your network configuration data appears, including your MAC address.

UNC names

REMEMBER

The Universal Naming Convention (UNC) is not pronounced like a short-form of uncle, its initials are spelled out. UNC is the generally accepted network naming syntax used to reference network resources. UNC names take the form of:

```
\\SERVER_NAME\SHARE_NAME or PATH
```

where the computer name and the share name are names that have been assigned by the network administrator or the users who own a shared resource. For example, in the Windows UNC name

```
\\MAGOO\OPTICIANS
```

Magoo is the network, or "friendly," name for the computer, the name used by the network to refer to that device, and "opticians" is a shared folder name on that computer. Users on other computers can request access to both the computer and its resources using the UNC name format.

You can expect the Network+ exam to ask specifically about UNC names. In fact, you're likely to encounter a list of sample names from which to pick the one that conforms to UNC (NetBIOS) syntax. Remember which way the slashes go (Windows uses backward slashes and UNIX uses forward slashes) and that two of them appear in front.

NetBIOS and NDS names

Every computer in a Microsoft network has a NetBIOS name assigned to it. The computer name is also a NetBIOS name. NetBIOS is the standard network basic input/output system used by Windows NT and Windows 98.

Likewise, every resource that you want to reference on a NetWare 4.x and NetWare 5.x network must have an NDS name. NDS (NetWare Directory Services) is a database that contains all the users, devices, and computers of the network and the NDS name for each.

NetBIOS names follow the UNC format I describe in the previous section, but NetWare names are slightly different. For example, the format that Microsoft Windows uses is

```
\\SERVER\FOLDER
```

under Novell's NDS, this name is

```
\\SERVER\VOLUME\DIRECTORY\SUB-DIRECTORY
```

IP addresses

An IP (Internet Protocol) address consists of four numbers connected (or separated, depending on how you look at it) by periods (a.k.a. dots). For example, the IP address for the fine folks at Dummies Books is 206.175.162.18. (The last dot is the period at the end of the sentence.) Chapter 13 presents the meaning of each separate number in the IP address.

Comparing names and addresses

The examples in Table 12-2 summarize and contrast UNC names (made up of server names and share names), MAC addresses (device physical addresses), and IP (Internet Protocol) addresses.

Table 12-2 Examples of UNC Names and MAC and IP Addresses

Actual Name	UNC Name	MAC Address	IP Address
Primary network server	\\SERVER1	00.00.0C.33.56.01	10.0.100.1
Susan's workstation in Accounting	\\SERVER1\ ACCTG_SUSAN	00.00.1D.78.21.09	10.0.100.22
The Documents folder on Susan's computer	\\SERVER1\ ACCTG_SUSAN\ DOCUMENTS	00.00.1D.78.21.09	10.0.100.22

Table 12-2 illustrates the following three principles of network naming and addressing:

- ✔ The UNC format used to designate servers and network shared resources.

- ✔ No relationship exists between MAC and IP addresses.

- ✔ MAC and IP addresses are assigned to the device, and moving deeper on a device does not change these values.

Host and domain names

Every device on a TCP/IP network has two pieces of identification: an IP address and a Fully Qualified Domain Name (FQDN), which consists of a hostname and a domain name. The network administrator assigns a *hostname* to uniquely identify the device, usually a computer, on the network. The InterNIC, the company that assigns domain names on the Internet, assigns the *domain name* to the network (server) by the InterNIC. For example, for the FQDN www.dummies.com, the network administrator assigned the clever and unique name www to the network host, and Network Solutions blessed, ordained, and registered the domain name dummies.com to the network server's assigned IP address. Together, www.dummies.com, the host name, and the domain name create the fully qualified domain name for this Internet site.

DNS and WINS: What's in a Name?

FQDNs are registered in the DNS (Domain Name System) database that is distributed around the Internet and used to look up a domain name and convert it into its IP address. The DNS database literally contains all the FQDNs and their IP addresses for the entire Internet, a collection of information that requires frequent updating. However, the file is considered to be a static database because its updates are manually entered periodically by the InterNIC agency.

You can use the DNS database to look up names on any TCP/IP network, including a local area network (LAN) using TCP/IP, but DNS comes into play mostly for finding names on a wide area network (WAN). As I talk about later in this section, DNS is not necessarily the best tool for LAN use.

Domain Name System (DNS)

If the host to which you want to connect is on a remote network, you must know the host's IP address in order to properly route your data over the Internet. This is where name resolution and the Domain Name System (DNS) come in. DNS can search through its database to find the FQDN you are looking to reach and supply its IP address to your system.

The effect of name resolution is as follows: If you enter the command

```
telnet www.dummies.com (before name resolution)
```

the name changes to

```
telnet 206.175.162.18 (after name resolution).
```

In this example, the FQDN www.dummies.com is converted into its IP address. (Just for the record, you don't need to know the Dummies IP address for the Network+ exam.)

DNS database architecture

The DNS database is actually a series of interconnected files, each representing a group of local host names and IP addresses. Each of the local host databases is connected to parent, or *root*, servers above them in the DNS hierarchy.

The DNS structure begins at the top with root domains. Six root domains are commonplace in the United States:

- ✔ **.COM:** This domain, which has the commercial, for-profit companies on the Internet, is the largest domain in terms of the number of entries.
- ✔ **.EDU:** This domain contains educational institutions.
- ✔ **.GOV:** The branches of the United States federal, state, county, and city governments are located in this domain.

- ✔ **.MIL:** The branches of the United States military are in this domain.

- ✔ **.NET:** This domain contains networking organizations, such as the `internic.net`, and Internet service providers, such as `internetnw.net`.

- ✔ **.ORG:** This domain contains nonprofit, noncommercial, charitable, or publicly owned organizations, such as `redcross.org` and `mariners.org`.

Memorize these six root DNS domains. Don't bother memorizing country domains, just know that they exist. Country domains are easy to recognize on the exam.

Outside the United States, and for a growing number of miscellaneous hosts inside as well, a two-letter abbreviation or representation of a country identifies the root domain. For example, `.uk` signifies the United Kingdom, `.br` identifies Brazil, `.ch` relates to Switzerland (it's a long story, but it comes from a former name of the country), `.ca` covers Canada, and `.us` says it all for the United States. Visit `www.networksolutions.com` for a complete list.

Resolving a domain name

When a host at `husky.uwashington.edu` needs to access `www.lotus.com` (see Figure 12-2), a number of small requests are generated. The first request goes to `uwashington.edu`, an address that `husky.uwashington.edu` already has. The primary DNS server at `uwashington.edu` tries to solve the request locally from its own database, but failing that, the request is passed up the hierarchy to the .edu server, which looks in its local databases. If the .edu server cannot find an entry for `www.lotus.com`, it passes the request to the .com server, which then searches down its hierarchy until the IP address shows up (or is found to not exist). If the URL cannot be resolved, for example you may have entered it incompletely or misspelled it and then you get an error message that says the domain name cannot be found. Try entering your name as www.your_name_here.com to see this error. That is of course, assuming you haven't generated your own commercial site using your name.

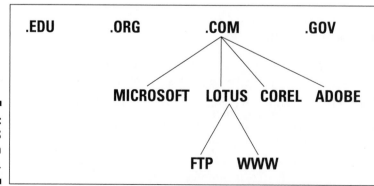

Figure 12-2: The DNS domain hierarchy.

Don't worry about recanting exactly how a DNS name lookup proceeds — the exam isn't going to ask. But you do need a reasonable understanding of how the process works. Chapter 13 provides more information on this topic.

Some systems use local files and services in place of the DNS database. These local files provide an abridged and more relevant database of names-to-IP-address and names-to-MAC-address conversions. Generically, these files are called *hosts files* because they contain a list of network hosts and their corresponding addresses. The most commonly used local name resolution service is WINS (Windows Internet Name Service).

Windows Internet Name Service (WINS)

The Windows Internet Name Service (WINS) is a dynamic service used to resolve NetBIOS computer names to their IP addresses on Windows-based networks. Whenever a network client computer boots up, it registers its name, IP address, the account name of its user, and whatever network services it's using with the WINS server. Note the word Windows in the name of this service. It tells you that this is a Microsoft product, and that other network operating systems (UNIX, Netware, etc.) do not support its use.

A WINS server is any Windows server on a TCP/IP network. It processes requests from client computers to register or look up IP addresses.

Another hosts file associated with NetBIOS name lookup is the LMHOSTS file. This static file, which requires manual maintenance, was essentially replaced by the WINS service, but many administrators use LMHOSTS as a backup name resolution technique. The LM in its name stands for LAN Manager, which may give you some insight into its age. The LMHOSTS file is also used to map NetBIOS names to their IP addresses.

The steps used to perform name lookup on a WINS system are

1. The local NetBIOS name cache is searched, and if the name is found, the process ends.

2. If the local NetBIOS cache does not contain the name, the client makes a request of the WINS server for the IP address associated with the computer name.

3. If found, the WINS server returns the IP address to the client, and the process stops.

4. If the address isn't found, and a secondary WINS server is in use, the request is forwarded to that server.

5. If the name cannot be resolved by a WINS server, the computer name for the needed IP address is broadcasted to the network in the hope that it responds with its IP address.

The IP Gateway

A gateway is a mechanism used to connect two dissimilar networks that operate independently of one another, such as a LAN and the Internet WAN. The gateway is also the demarcation point of routing over the Internet.

The primary protocol of a network may or not be TCP/IP. Even if the protocol is TCP/IP, each NOS (network operating system) functions slightly differently from good old regular TCP/IP. Regardless, the LAN and the Internet are separate networks that do operate independently of each other. However, on occasion they do need to interconnect.

The network needs a static IP address in order to have a gateway to or from the Internet. The address is important because other Internet hosts may want to access the network host (to deliver e-mail, for example), and they will probably use DNS to do it. So, the gateway must maintain a static, permanent identity.

To the clients on a LAN, the *default gateway* is the IP address of the router to another physical or logical network. This is the real connection to the Internet at the Physical layer and the addressable device to which the IP address is actually assigned and mapped.

These two addressing concepts may help you understand the workings of an IP gateway:

- **Static IP address:** This is an IP address that is permanently assigned to a computer, server, or device. Usually network servers supporting TCP/IP are assigned a static IP address, making them a stationary target for the rest of the Internet.

- **Dynamic IP address:** On many networks, workstation IP addresses are dynamically assigned to workstations as they identify and register themselves to the network. A great deal of flexibility is built into this scheme, supported by the Dynamic Host Configuration Protocol (DHCP). But this plan, if used for servers, would make them moving targets and potentially unreachable. See Chapter 13 for more information on DHCP.

Static and dynamic IP addressing appear throughout the Network+ exam in several different scenarios and contexts. Be sure you fully understand these two IP address assignment methods and when to use one or the other. See Chapter 13 for more information on both.

Prep Test

1 TCP/IP is the acronym for

A ○ Transport Control Program/Internet Program

B ○ Transmission Control Program/Internet Protocol

C ○ Transport Control Protocol/Internet Protocol

D ○ Transmission Control Protocol/Internet Protocol

2 Which of the following is not a characteristic or function of TCP?

A ○ Connectionless

B ○ Error-checking

C ○ Message fragmentation

D ○ Guarantees packet delivery

3 The TCP/IP protocol used to transfer files between Internet computers is

A ○ SMTP

B ○ IP

C ○ FTP

D ○ TCP

4 The TCP/IP utility used to display the entire TCP/IP configuration of a Windows NT computer is

A ○ PING

B ○ ROUTE

C ○ NETSTAT

D ○ IPCONFIG

5 Which of the following is a valid MAC address?

A ○ 000-123-456

B ○ 00.00.0D.11.22.33

C ○ HK.11.22.33.44

D ○ ABC123456

6 Which of the following is a valid UNC name?

A ○ //COMPUTER_NAME/SERVER_NAME

B ○ \\COMPUTER_NAME\SERVER_NAME

C ○ //SERVER_NAME/COMPUTER_NAME

D ○ \\SERVER_NAME\COMPUTER_NAME

7 An Internet name that contains a domain name and a host name is called a

A ○ FQDN

B ○ URL

C ○ DNS address

D ○ Locator name

8 Which of the following are valid DNS root domains? (Choose four.)

A ❑ .ORG

B ❑ .EDU

C ❑ .BUS

D ❑ .NET

E ❑ .MIL

F ❑ .ISP

9 The Windows-based TCP/IP service that processes requests from client work-stations to dynamically register or look up IP addresses and NetBIOS names is

A ○ DNS

B ○ WINS

C ○ LMHOSTS

D ○ MAC

10 To clients on a LAN, the IP address assigned to a router used to access another physical or logical network is designated as the default

A ○ DNS server

B ○ HCP server

C ○ IP gateway

D ○ WINS server

Answers

1 *D.* Many people take an incorrect clue from the fact that TCP operates on the Transport layer. Remember that TCP is the Transmission Control Protocol. *See "The TCP/IP Protocols."*

2 *A.* TCP is a connection-oriented protocol that makes possible guaranteed packet delivery. TCP also performs error-checking and control and fragments variable-length messages to an appropriate length for transmission. *Review "Transmission Control Protocol (TCP)."*

3 *C.* Just remember that FTP stands for File Transfer Protocol, and you're not likely to have problems with any questions like this one. *Take a look at "File Transfer Protocol (FTP)."*

4 *D.* There are versions of the TCP/IP utility IPCONFIG for different clients, as demonstrated in Labs 12-1 and 12-2. *Check out "TCP/IP utilities."*

5 *B.* A MAC or Ethernet or adapter address is made up of six 2-digit numbers connected by periods or dashes. The first three 2-digit numbers identify the manufacturer and the remaining numbers represent a serialized unique ID assigned by the manufacturer to each NIC. *Examine "MAC addresses."*

6 *D.* Expect to see a question like this on the Network+ exam. Remember that UNC slashes are backward slashes and the server precedes the share name. *See "UNC names."*

7 *A.* A fully qualified domain name (FQDN) is made up of the host name, such as www, and a domain name, such as dummies.com. *Review "Host and domain names."*

8 *A, B, D, and E.* Memorize the six top-level domains for the test. *Check out "DNS database architecture."*

9 *B.* The trick to this question is the word "dynamic." DNS and HOSTS name resolutions are static systems where WINS is a dynamic service. *Take a look at "Windows Internet Name Service (WINS)."*

10 *C.* The gateway server houses the default IP gateway. Understand that the IP address is tied to the MAC address of the NIC that serves as the gateway. *Review "The IP Gateway."*

Chapter 13

TCP/IP Addressing and Configuration

- -

Exam Objectives

▶ Defining Class A, B, and C IP addresses

▶ Developing subnet masks for IP addresses

▶ Describing the use of DHCP

▶ Identifying the port numbers assigned to TCP/IP services

▶ Explaining the purpose and use of an IP proxy

▶ Setting the TCP/IP configuring of a workstation

- -

*T*his chapter, along with Chapter 12, focuses on TCP/IP fundamentals that make up 12 percent of the Network+ exam. Chapter 12 covers the functions of TCP/IP, and this chapter explains IP addressing schemes, subnet masking, and configuring a workstation to work with TCP/IP.

IP addressing schemes are a popular topic on the Network+ exam. You are expected to know the address ranges for IP Class A, B, and C addresses, as well as how subnet masks are derived for each and then applied to identify the host or the server of an IP address. Piece of cake!

If you are preparing for your first certification in networking, TCP/IP addressing and configuration may be new to you. However, if you have taken any of the MCSE (Microsoft Certified Systems Engineer) certifications, especially the exams for TCP/IP or Windows NT in the Enterprise, you've seen all of this before. Regardless, don't underestimate the importance of TCP/IP addressing and configuration on the Network+ exam. By all means, don't overestimate your knowledge of it. Review TCP/IP addressing until you are absolutely sure you know it and then study it some more. One more time for emphasis: Absolutely include TCP/IP in your last-minute study session. I say this not as a ploy to get you to read this chapter, but if it works, so much the better. Though TCP/IP directly accounts for only about 20 percent of the Network+ test, a thorough knowledge of its underlying fundamentals and addressing is essential to success in well over half of the entire Network+ exam.

Quick Assessment

Defining Class A, B, and C IP addresses

1 The IP address range for a Class A network address is _____ to _____.

2 _____ IP addresses are assigned to small networks.

3 Special network addresses are those that are all _____, all _____, and those that begin with _____.

Developing subnet masks for IP addresses

4 A common subnet mask for a Class C network is _____.

5 The Class B subnet mask 255.255.192.0 allows for _____ subnets and _____ nodes per subnet.

6 _____ and _____ are the two types of IP addresses (in terms of how they are assigned) that can be assigned to a client workstation.

Describing the use of DHCP

7 IP address, subnet mask, default gateway, lease time, DNS server, WINS server, and node type are configuration elements that are assigned to a client by a _____.

Identifying the port numbers assigned to TCP/IP services

8 The well-known TCP/IP port 80 is used for _____.

Explaining the purpose and use of an IP proxy

9 A proxy server can also provide _____ services to an intranet.

Setting the TCP/IP configuring of a workstation

10 You can configure a Windows client with either a _____ or _____ IP address.

Answers

1   *1.xxx.xxx.xxx to 126.xxx.xxx.xxx.* Review "Class A IP addresses."

2   *Class C.* Check out "Class C IP addresses."

3   *0s, 1s, 127.* Take a look at "Special network addresses."

4   *255.255.255.0.* Check out "Separating networks from hosts."

5   *2 and 16,382.* Review "Subnet masks for Class B and Class C networks."

6   *Static, dynamic.* See "Assigning IP Addresses Dynamically."

7   *DHCP Server.* Check out "To DHCP or not to DHCP."

8   *HTTP.* Take a look at "TCP/IP Ports and Protocols."

9   *Firewall.* See "Using an Internet Proxy Server."

10 *Dynamic (or DHCP) or static.* Review "Configuring a Workstation for TCP/IP."

Dissecting the IP Class System

First of all, don't confuse IP network address classes with the class certifications issued by the Federal Communications Commission (FCC). The FCC issues certificates for computer systems certifying their conformity to standards for information technology and digital equipment. IP address classes have nothing to do with FCC certificates.

IP addresses are divided into five classes, each of which is designated with the alphabetic letters A to E. As you read about the different IP address classes, bear in mind that the inventors of this class system expected the Internet to remain a fairly small and exclusive club.

IP addressing refresher

Here is some IP address Gatorade:

- ✔ The Network Solutions organization (www.networksolutions.net) is responsible for registering domain names and assigning and tracking network IDs for use on the Internet. Another agency, ARIN (American Registry for Internet Numbers — www.arin.net) allocates IP addresses according to organizational need and size. The class of network address assigned is dependent on the number of networks needed by the organization. Generally, this means that larger organizations, those that have a need to identify more networks and hosts, are assigned the higher classes of IP addresses.
- ✔ IP addresses are made up of four decimal numbers connected by periods.
- ✔ IP addresses are 32 bits in length, with each of the four numbers using 8 bits.
- ✔ Each of the 8-bit numbers is called an *octet*.
- ✔ What each octet means is dependent on the class of the address and the corresponding subnet mask used.
- ✔ The IP address for the URL www.dummies.com is 206.175.162.18. This is an example of an IP address. You really don't need to know this address, the human-friendly URL (Uniform Resource Locator) will work, but using either connects you to an excellent site for buying outstanding certification study guides. I'm so shameless!

Memorize the ranges of the Class A, B, and C IP addresses. You're asked to pick a Class A or B address from a list. Watch out for trick answer choices that are in the overall range of a Class but are set aside for a special purpose. (See "Special network addresses" later in the chapter.)

Class A IP addresses

If you don't count sheep in binary numbers to go to sleep at night or use binary numbers to balance your check book, then you may want to take a quick look ath the information on binary numbers in Chapter 2 before wading into the discussion on IP addresses, the IP address classes, and subnet masks.

Class A IP addresses are awarded to large networks. These addresses range from 1.hhh.hhh.hhh to 126.hhh.hhh.hhh, where all of the hhh's are used to identify a host computer by its unique address. Fifty percent of all IP addresses are Class A addresses.

Class A addresses use 8 bits to identify up to 126 Class A networks. Each network can address as many as 16 million network nodes. There are 128 network (0 to 127) values available, but the network addresses with all zeros or ones and network address 127 are reserved as special network addresses (see "Special network addresses" later in this section).

Class B IP addresses

Class B IP addresses are assigned to medium-sized networks. Twenty-five percent of all available IP addresses are in this class. A Class B address uses 16 bits to identify the network, which limits it to 16,000 networks using the range of 128.0.hhh.hhh (hhh represents the host address) to 191.255.hhh.hhh. Each Class B network can address more than 65,000 IP addresses.

Class C IP addresses

Class C networks are relatively small networks. Class C addresses account for 12.5 percent of all available IP addresses. Class C addresses use 24 bits to identify the network, enabling identification of more than 2 million networks in the range of 192.0.0.hhh to 223.255.255.hhh. Eight bits are used to identify the host computer, but host addresses with all zeros or ones are special host addresses (see "Special network addresses" later in this section). Each Class C network can address a maximum of 254 IP addresses.

Classes D and E addresses

Class D is set aside especially for network multicasting. Class D addresses account for 6.25 percent of all available IP addresses. Class D addresses are used for IP multicasting and do not have network or host address parts. *IP multicasting* sends datagrams to a group of hosts, which may be located on many separate networks. Class D addresses are in the range of 224.hhh.hhh.hhh.hhh to 239.hhh.hhh.hhh. Address 224.0.0.0 is reserved and cannot be used, and address 224.0.0.1 is reserved for addressing all hosts participating in an IP multicast.

Class E addresses are reserved for future use. A little over 3 percent of all IP addresses are in the range from 240.0.0.0 to 247.255.255.255.

Yes, I know that the percentages in the above IP address classes do not add up to 100 percent. Don't worry about why. In fact, don't worry about these percentages at all. I include them to give you a sense of scale. But, since you asked, the remaining addresses are special IP addresses or unassigned addresses.

Memorize the information in Table 13-1, especially the address range for each IP address class. Table 13-1 summarizes the characteristics of the IP address classes.

Table 13-1		Characteristics of the IP Address Classes			
Class	*Bits in Network ID*	*Number of Networks*	*Bits in Host ID*	*Number of Hosts/Network*	*Address Range*
A	8	126	24	4,000,000	1.0.0.0 to 126.255.255.255
B	16	16,384	16	65,536	128.0.0.0 to 191.255.255.255
C	24	2,000,000	8	65,536	192.0.0.0 to 223.255.255.255
D	0	0	28	268,400,000	224.0.0.0.0 to 239.255.255.255
E	Class E addresses are reserved for future use				

Assigning host IDs

Network Solutions may assign network IDs, but the local network administrator assigns host IDs. The host ID identifies any device on the local network that has an IP address, which includes almost any addressable entity on the network — computers, printers, routers, and so forth.

A commonly accepted practice is to assign host IDs in groups based on the host types and to give routers the lowest range of numbers. For example, in a a commonly used scheme, host IDs are assigned as follows:

- ✔ a.b.c.1 through a.b.c.10 — routers and servers
- ✔ a.b.c.11 through a.b.c.204 — workstations
- ✔ a.b.c.241 through a.b.c.254 — UNIX hosts

Special network addresses

Network addresses that are all binary zeros, all binary ones, and network addresses beginning with 127 are special network addresses. These set aside IP addresses are used by networks as shortcut addresses to specific locations, such as the current host or a nearby host computer, to broadcast to a LAN or WAN, or to perform testing. Table 13-2 offers a list of special network addresses:

Table 13-2		Special Addresses	
Network Part	**Host Part**	**Example**	**Description**
0s	0s	0.0.0.0	This host
0s	host address	0.0.0.34	Host on this network
1s	1s	255.255.255.255	Broadcast to local network
Network address	1s	197.21.12.255	Broadcast to network
127	1s or 0s	127.0.0.1	Loopback testing

Intranet network IDs

Ranges of numbers are set aside for network managers to use on internal networks, intranets not connected to the Internet, or networks that are connected to the Internet but sit behind a firewall. These addresses are in three ranges:

- ✔ 10.0.0.0 through 10.255.255.255
- ✔ 172.16.0.0 through 172.31.255.255
- ✔ 192.168.0.0 through 192.168.255.255

Who Was That Subnet Masked Man?

IP addresses contain information on both the network ID and the host ID. To pull this information out of an IP address, a filter mechanism is applied to mask out the unneeded bits and highlight the needed address portion. This mechanism is the subnet mask, which you can also call the subnetwork address mask.

The basic function of a subnet mask is to determine if an IP address exists on the local network or if it exists outside on a remote network. The subnet mask is used to extract the network ID from a message's destination address. It is then compared to the local network ID. If they match, the host ID must be on the local network. Otherwise, the message requires routing outside of the local network. The process used to apply the subnet mask uses the properties of Boolean algebra to filter out nonmatching bits to identify the network ID.

Separating networks from hosts

The subnet mask is the mechanism applied to an IP address to determine if the address' network (NETID) is the local network and to extract the host address (HOSTID) of the node referenced in the address. Remember that an IP address can represent either the source or the destination of a message. Table 13-3 lists the commonly used subnet masks for each IP address class. It is a good idea for you to take the time to memorize these.

Table 13-3	Default Subnet Masks
IP Address Class	*Subnet Mask*
Class A	255.0.0.0
Class B	255.255.0.0
Class C	255.255.255.0

Here's how the the subnet mask is applied:

1. On the Dummies Class C network, an IP address is 206.175.162.18 and it's the binary equivalent of this address is 11001110 10101111 10100010 00010010. See Chapter 2 if you need to review binary numbers.

2. The common Class C subnet mask is 255.255.255.0, and its binary equivalent is 11111111 11111111 11111111 00000000.

3. These two binary numbers (the IP address and the subnet mask) are combined using Boolean algebra yielding the network ID of the destination:

```
Address: 206.175.162.18     11001110 10101111 10100010 00010010

Subnet mask: 255.255.255.0 11111111 11111111 11111111 00000000

Network ID: 206.175.162.0  11001110 10101111 10100010 00000000
```

4. The resulting ID is the IP address of the network, which means the message is for a node on the local network.

If you think that there has to be a simpler way, you're pretty bright, because there is! All of the ones in a subnet mask extract the NETID and the zeros yield the HOSTID.

Subnet masks apply only to Class A, B, or C IP addresses.

Subnetting a network

Unfortunately, the founding mothers and fathers of the Internet and the IP protocol had a much smaller Internet in mind than the one that has emerged. Companies that have only one network address assigned now may have need for multiple networks, which creates an addressing problem. The solution to this problem is subnetting.

Subnetting a network can manage many network problems, such as reduced network traffic, better network throughput, improved WAN performance, and others, but the best reason of all is simplified management of the network. Breaking the network into smaller pieces helps deliver the promise of "less is more." However, subnetting a network introduces the problem of IP addressing and subnet routing, which is the real challenge in developing and applying a subnet mask.

Developing a subnet mask

The trick to developing a subnet mask that can identify subnets in addition to networks and hosts is to borrow enough bits from the host ID so that you can address the subnets while still addressing all the host IDs. The 32-bit IP address is a fixed-length entity — you don't have any more bits to use. You can only borrow bits from the part that you, as the network administrator, control — the host ID portion of the IP address.

Subnetting a Class A network

The default subnet mask for a Class A network is 255.0.0.0, which allows for over 16 million hosts on a single network. The Class A subnet mask uses only 8 bits, leaving 24 bits for host addressing. If you want to subnet a Class A network, you need to borrow enough bits from the host ID portion of the mask to allow the number of subnets you plan to create, now and in the future.

For example, if you need to create 2 subnets with over 4 millions hosts per subnet, you must borrow two bits from the second octet and use 10 masked (value equals one) bits for the subnet mask (11111111 11000000) or 255.192 in decimal.

For a Class A network that needs a maximum of 254 subnets with 65,534 hosts on each subnet, you must borrow 8-bits from the host ID, creating a subnet mask with 16 masked bits, 255.255.0.0.

Table 13-4 includes a sampling of subnet mask options available for Class A addresses.

Table 13-4		Class A Subnet Masks	
Subnet Mask	*Number of Bits in Mask*	*Number of Usable Subnets*	*Number of Hosts per Subnet*
255.0.0.0	8	1	16,777,214
255.192.0.0	10	2	4,194,302
255.240.0.0	12	14	1,048,574
255.255.0.0	16	254	65,534
255.255.128.0	17	510	32,766
255.255.240.0	20	4,094	4,094
255.255.255.128	25	131,070	126
255.255.255.240	28	1,048,574	14
255.255.255.252	30	4,192,302	2

A subnet mask cannot be more than 30 bits in length. Also remember that you cannot use addresses that have all ones and all zeros because they have special meanings (see "Special network addresses" earlier in this section).

You can see a pattern (a bit pattern actually) in Table 13-4. As more bits are taken from the host ID and used in the subnet mask to identify subnets, more subnets are possible — but at the cost of a few number of hosts per subnet. You can see a similar pattern in Tables 13-5 and 13-6, which show subnet masks available for Class B and Class C IP addresses, respectively.

Subnet masks for Class B and Class C networks

The pattern presented in the previous section continues with Class B and Class C IP addresses and subnet masks. The only differences are that you have few options (because of the fewer number of bits available) and that you are much more likely to work with these networks in real life. Table 13-5 lists a sampling of the subnet masks available for Class B networks, and Table 13-6 lists all of the subnet masks available for Class C networks.

Table 13-5	Class B Subnet Masks		
Subnet Mask	*Number of Bits in Mask*	*Number of Usable Subnets*	*Number of Hosts per Subnet*
255.255.0.0	16	1	65,534
255.255.192.0	18	2	16,382
255.255.240.0	20	14	4,094
255.255.255.0	24	254	254
255.255.255.240	28	4,094	14
255.255.255.252	30	16,382	2

Table 13-6	Class C Subnet Masks		
Subnet Mask	*Number of Bits in Mask*	*Number of Usable Subnets*	*Number of Hosts per Subnet*
255.255.255.0	24	1	254
255.255.255.192	26	2	62
255.255.255.224	27	6	30
255.255.255.240	28	14	14
255.255.255.248	29	30	6
255.255.255.252	30	62	2

Assigning IP Addresses Dynamically

Every client workstation on a TCP/IP network must be assigned an IP address in order for it to send and receive Internet packets during an Internet session. IP addresses can be assigned to a client computer in one of two ways: manually, by the network administrator, or automatically, by a server. A manually assigned IP address is also called a *static* address. An automatically assigned IP address is more commonly called a *dynamic* address. In this section, I focus on the dynamic addresses.

For the Network+ exam, you need to thoroughly understand the terminology and processes of DHCP (Dynamic Host Control Protocol). Know why to use DHCP and how it works.

To DHCP or not to DHCP

If you are the administrator of a fairly small network that has an ample number of IP addresses for its workstations and devices, assigning each node its own static IP address is probably not a problem. However, if you must configure a network with 50, 100, 200, or more workstations, or you don't have quite enough IP addresses available to permanently assign the IP addresses to each node, then you consider using the Dynamic Host Control Protocol (DHCP).

The use of DHCP is fairly common for just about any network, large or small. DHCP provides you, the network administrator, with a number of benefits, including

✔ **Automatic configuration:** At minimum, a DHCP server provides a client with its IP address, subnet mask, and normally the default gateway option when the client identifies itself during logon.

✔ **Configuration control:** DHCP assignments are defined by a *DHCP scope*, which is an administrative tool that enables you to set the range, value, and exceptions for client configurations. The DHCP scope usually defines a range of available IP addresses, the subnet mask, and gives the option to configure the default gateway (router) for a range of addresses, and any IP addresses that have been set aside or reserved for other devices. Other values that can be configured into a scope for its IP addresses are

  • DNS server

  • WINS server

  • Lease time

  • Renewal time

✔ **Length of use:** DHCP IP address assignments are called *leases*. When a client receives assignment of an IP address, the length of time that the client can use that particular address is also set. A three-day time period is a common default lease period. The length of the lease is a configurable value controlled by the network administrator.

How DHCP works

Don't sweat the details, but do review the sequence of events that the DHCP uses to control IP address assignments on its clients. The DHCP process is divided into four phases: initializing, selecting, requesting, and binding. The following describes the actions of each phase:

- **Initializing:** The DHCP client boots up with a null IP address and broadcasts a discover message, containing its MAC address and computer name, to its server. The source address of the discover message is 0.0.0.0 and its destination is 255.255.255.255, which are reserved IP addresses (see "Special network addresses" earlier in this chapter).

- **Selecting:** The DHCP server receives the discover message and, if it has a valid configuration available for the client, responds with an offer message that contains the client's MAC address (for delivery purposes) and the offered IP address, subnet mask, gateway, the address of the DHCP server, and the length of the lease. If the server does not have an IP address available to the client, the client nags the server 4 times in the next 5 minutes. If it still doesn't have one, it waits 5 minutes, and then repeats the discover cycle.

- **Requesting:** To accept the IP address offered to it, the client responds with a request message. Some networks can have multiple DHCP servers all of which may have made offers to the client. The request message is a broadcast message, so that all DHCP servers know to withdraw their offers.

- **Binding:** This phase is also called the *bound* phase. The DHCP server that had its offer accepted politely sends a request message that includes an acknowledgement of the client's acceptance. When the client receives this acknowledgement, it proceeds with its initialization of TCP/IP and becomes a bound DHCP client.

Renewing your lease

Once the DHCP lease expires, the client will not have an IP address. To prevent that sad state of affairs, the client uses a renewal process. The renewal process involves the client sending the same type of request message it used to get its lease in the first place to the server that issued the lease. The renewal request message is first sent when the lease is 50 percent expired. If the server can renew the lease, it does. However, if the lease is not renewed at the 50 percent point, the request message is sent out again at the 87.5 percent point. If the lease is not renewed, the client reverts to the initializing phase and begins requesting an IP address to be assigned. The primary reason a lease would not be renewed is that there are more workstations than IP addresses available, which means there are workstations waiting to grab a lease the moment it expires.

Setting Sail for TCP/IP Ports and Protocols

The Internet Assigned Numbers Authority (IANA) registers service ports for use by the various TCP/IP protocols. Ports are used for interprocess communications between two connection points. Port numbers and keywords are used to designate the ends of the logical connections created when protocols, such as TCP (remember that TCP is a connection-oriented protocol), connect over the Internet for long-term interaction. Ports are especially handy for providing services to unknown callers, such as during an anonymous FTP session.

Ports are numbered and assigned keywords for easy reference. Some of the more common TCP/IP ports are port 80 (HTTP), ports 20 and 21 (FTP), and port 23 (SMTP). The port number assigned to a service by IANA is usually the server-side contact port, also called the "well-known" port.

IANA divides port numbers into three groups:

- ✔ **Well-known ports:** These are the most commonly used TCP/IP ports. These ports are in the range of 0 through 1023. These ports can be used only by system processes or privileged programs. Well-known ports are TCP ports, but are usually registered to UDP services as well.

- ✔ **Registered ports:** The ports in the range of 1024 through 49151. On most systems, user programs use registered ports to create and control logical connections between proprietary programs.

- ✔ **Dynamic (private) ports:** Ports in the range of 49152 through 65535. These ports are unregistered and can be used dynamically for private connections.

Have you noticed ports in use in the location bar (navigation bar) of your World Wide Web (WWW) browser? A URL of something like the following:

```
http://www.dummies.com:80
```

may appear as you are navigating forward or backward on some sites. The 80 indicates that this port is being used to track the connection to a remote site.

Prepare yourself: The Network+ exam is bound to ask you to identify the port assignment of several common TCP/IP protocols. If you know the ports listed in Table 13-7, you'll definitely know more than you need for the test. Table 13-7 lists most of the commonly used port assignments.

Table 13-7	TCP/IP Well-Known Port Assignments
Port Number	*Assignment*
20	FTP data transfer
21	FTP (File Transfer Protocol) control
23	Telnet
25	SMTP (Simple Mail Transfer Protocol)
53	DNS (Domain Name System)
70	Gopher
80	HTTP (Hypertext Transfer Protocol)
110	POP3 (Post Office Protocol)
119	NNTP (Network News Transfer Protocol)
137	NetBIOS name service

A network operating system uses the port number to identify the service to which an incoming or outgoing packet should be passed.

Using an Internet Proxy Server

A proxy server placed on a local network often acts in place of the Web server for the network's clients, but the real benefit of a proxy server is what it adds to network security. Proxy servers also provide a form of firewall protection. A firewall is a network service used to control access to the internal network from the outside. A proxy server acts as a logical barrier between your local network users and the rest of the Internet.

A couple of generic Internet proxy server types exist. The first is the all-in-one approach that can include gateway, proxy, firewall, and Internet server capabilities that support POP, FTP, Telnet, SSL tunneling, HTTP caching and site access blocking services, such as Cyborg (www.cyborg.com) and WinGate (www.wingate.net). The second type involves products that provide some firewall protection in roles as proxy servers, such as Microsoft Proxy Server (www.microsoft.com) and NetGuard's Guardian (www.ntguard.com).

I'm sorry, but you're not on the list

Proxy servers, and firewalls for that matter, maintain access control lists. These lists, which you manually create and maintain, include sites on the Web or Internet that network clients are blocked from visiting. The access control list on a proxy server may also contain IP addresses from which requests for information are not accepted.

The proxy servers intercept all IP-based WWW requests from network clients. If a request is for an allowed Web page that was previously visited, the page is provided from the proxy server's cache. However, if the requested Web page is not in the proxy server's cache and is not on the access control list, the request is processed normally and the Web page is passed on to the requesting client. If the requested page or site is on the access control list, the requesting user receives a message indicating that the site is not authorized or accessible. Unauthorized incoming requests receive the same responses.

Putting up the proxy

You have three reasons to implement a proxy server (firewall):

- ✔ A dial-up connection gives you Internet access. Proxy servers can handle multiple phone lines, providing an avenue to a single Internet access point.

- ✔ You have only one connection point to the wide, wild world of the Internet (versus separate connection points). This limits your exposure to unauthorized entry to your network and enables you to protect your network from the sites of evildoers.

- ✔ You can enjoy the benefits of shared caching. Frequently visited sites may be in the cache, perhaps eliminating connection to the Internet service altogether. Proxy servers often cache FTP and Gopher data, as well as HTTP pages.

Configuring a Workstation for TCP/IP

The first rule of setting up a workstation is plain and simple: Have an operating system that is compatible with the network operating system (NOS). With either Windows NT or NetWare, you usually have no problem with any of the more common client operating systems, such as DOS or any of the Windows panes. But, these aren't the only client systems, so before using any nonmainstream operating system on a network, check it out.

You can expect to see at least one or two questions on the Network+ exam regarding the process and settings used to configure a network client for the TCP/IP protocol. Be familiar with the steps used to configure the following settings on a Windows client:

✔ Choosing the TCP/IP redirector

✔ Static or dynamic (DHCP) IP address

✔ DNS and/or WINS server

✔ Default gateway address

✔ Host and domain name

Lab 13-1 details the steps that you take to configure a Windows workstation for these settings.

Lab 13-1   Installing the TCP/IP Client on a Windows Workstation

1. **Choose Start⇨Settings⇨Control Panel.**

2. **Double-click the Networks icon to open the Network Properties window, shown in Figure 13-1.**

   If TCP/IP is not installed, you're likely to see only the Dialup adapter listed.

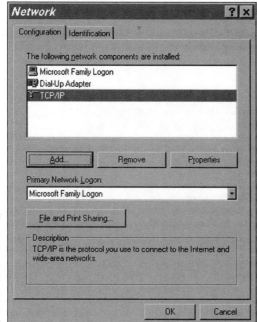

Figure 13-1:
A config-
ured
Network
Properties
window.

3. **Click on the Add button to open the Select Network Component Type window. Choose Protocol and click Add.**

   The Select Network Protocol window displays.

4. **Find and click on Microsoft in the list of supported protocol families and then click on TCP/IP in the list on the right-hand side of the window. See Figure 13-2.**

   The Network Properties window reappears, with Microsoft Family Logon and TCP/IP added to the list of network components that are now installed.

5. **Click on TCP/IP in the protocols list and then click the Properties button.**

   The TCP/IP Properties window displays. You use the tabs across the top of the window to access each of the properties types to be configured (see Figure 13-3).

6. **Click on the IP Address tab.**

   In most situations, you choose Obtain An IP Address Automatically. In those situations where a static IP address is assigned, click the indicator for an assigned (static) IP address and enter it in the box provided.

7. **Click on the DNS Configuration tab.**

   If you want to use DNS lookup on the network, click on the adjacent radio button to indicate that choice and then enter the host ID, the domain ID, and IP address of the DNS server. You can enter more than one DNS server, and you can set an order of access.

8. **Click on the Gateway tab. Enter the IP address of the gateways on the network. You can set the access order for gateways; the first one listed is the default gateway.**

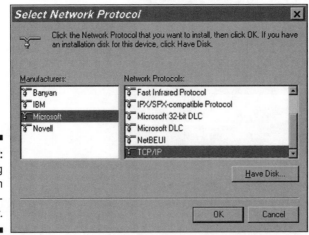

Figure 13-2:
Choosing
TCP/IP from
the proto-
cols list.

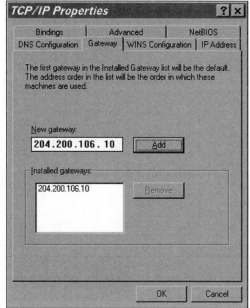

Figure 13-3:
Setting
TCP/IP
properties
for a
Windows
client.

9. **Click on the WINS Configuration tab.**

The WINS Configuration tab is strictly a Microsoft thing. It is used to indicate whether or not the network supports WINS services. If so, you must enter a WINS service ID.

Prep Test

1 Which of the following is a Class A IP address? (Choose two.)

A ❑ 204.134.2.0

B ❑ 195.115.6.24

C ❑ 125.2.45.123

D ❑ 10.0.1.0

2 IP addresses in the range of 128.0.0.0 to 191.255.0.0 are in which class of IP addresses?

A ○ Class A

B ○ Class B

C ○ Class C

D ○ Special IP addresses

3 Which of the following characterizes a Class C IP address? (Choose all that apply.)

A ❑ Assigned to relatively small networks

B ❑ Account for 25 percent of all available IP addresses

C ❑ Addresses range from 192.0.0.0 to 223.255.255.255

D ❑ 16-bits are used to identify the host address

4 Which of the following IP addresses is not reserved for special use?

A ○ 000.000.000.000

B ○ 127.0.223.10

C ○ 10.0.100.1

D ○ 200.204.0.1

5 The basic function of a subnet mask is to determine which of the following?

A ○ If an IP address is valid before forwarding packets to it

B ○ If an IP address is reachable in less than 30 hops

C ○ If an IP address exists on the local network or on a remote network

D ○ If an IP address requires protocol translation

6 The subnet mask 255.255.255.0 is a default subnet mask for which class of IP address?

A ○ Class A

B ○ Class B

C ○ Class C

D ○ This is not a valid subnet mask.

7 If you require a network of 12 subnets with at least 2,500 nodes per subnet, which of the following subnet masks must be used?

A ○ 255.255.192.0

B ○ 255.255.240.0

C ○ 255.255.255.240

D ○ 255.192.0.0

8 What is the TCP/IP protocol that is used to automatically assign IP addresses and other configuration information to network clients?

A ○ SNMP

B ○ ICMP

C ○ DHCP

D ○ IPCONFIG

9 The well-known TCP/IP port assigned to HTTP is

A ○ 20

B ○ 25

C ○ 80

D ○ 110

10 Which of the following is a network mechanism, either hardware or software, that acts as a logical barrier between local network users and the Internet and sometimes between remote users and the local network?

A ○ Gateway

B ○ Proxy server

C ○ Router

D ○ ARP cache

Answers

1 *C and D.* Class A IP addresses are in the range of 1.0.0.0 to 126.255.255.255. 10.x.x.x is a Class A address. Yes, it is reserved for firewall and internal network purposes, but it is still a Class A IP address. *See "Class A IP addresses."*

2 *B.* Class B IP addresses use 14 bits to identify the network, which enables it 16,384 networks with over 65,536 nodes in each network. *Review "Class B IP addresses."*

3 *A, and C.* Class C IP addresses account for only 12.5 percent of all IP addresses, and use only 8 bits to define the network. *See "Class C IP addresses."*

4 *D.* This address is not a special purpose address. Each of the other addresses listed is included in the group of IP addresses set aside for special purposes. *Check out "Special network addresses."*

5 *C.* The subnet mask combined with the IP address using Boolean algebra to expose the IP address of the network. *Take a look at "Who Was That Subnet Masked Man?"*

6 *C.* One way to remember this for the exam is to focus on the fact that Class A default subnet masks use one octet of 255 (255.0.0.0), Class B subnet masks use two (255.255.0.0), and Class C subnet masks use three (255.255.255.0). *Review "Separating networks from hosts."*

7 *B.* You can expect to see at least one question like this on the exam. If you are really intent on getting a perfect score, then study how the increasing binary values in the octets yield increasing subnets while yielding a declining number of nodes. Otherwise, forget it and focus on the rest of what you expect on the test. *See "Developing a subnet mask."*

8 *C.* The Dynamic Host Control Protocol (DHCP) is used to automatically configure TCP/IP clients as they log on to a network. *Check out "To DHCP or not to DHCP."*

9 *C.* TCP/IP ports are used to designate the ends of a logical connection and enable interprocess communications between the connecting processes. *Take a look at "TCP/IP Ports and Protocols."*

10 *B.* Proxy servers provide a form of firewall protection to the local network as well as reduce traffic beyond the network. *See "Using an Internet Proxy Server."*

Chapter 14

TCP/IP Utilities

Exam Objectives

▶ Describing SNMP operations

▶ Managing networks with TCP/IP utilities

▶ Verifying the IP network with TCP/IP utilities

▶ Troubleshooting with TCP/IP utilities

▶ Transferring files with FTP

*T*o some people, the fact that TCP/IP utilities account for 8 percent of the Network+ test may seem something of an overkill. To others, however, the fact that these tools are the virtual toolkit for diagnosing, troubleshooting, validating, and testing an IP connection is very significant and should be emphasized. Because the Network+ test certifies that you have the knowledge and skills of a networking technician with around two years of experience, you should have a good working knowledge of the more common utilities in the TCP/IP protocol suite.

The best part about these utilities is that they're largely available for free on any system supporting TCP/IP. So a good part of your tools are already waiting for you when you work on the local network, go to a customer site, or do the cyber-repair thing and remotely troubleshoot a problem.

The TCP/IP utilities perform address checking, a remote system connection, network-status checking, configuration verification, and file-transfer services. Some of these utilities perform similar and overlapping activities, but each has a unique function for which it is best applied, as explained in this chapter. For the Network+ test, you need to know when to use the different utilities, how to run them, and, when applicable, how to interpret the information that they display.

After you familiarize yourself with each of the TCP/IP utilities in this chapter, I recommend that you spend some time using them to really get to know them and what they do. Work with network SNMP and IP data that you know and can predict the results of, as well as some off-the-wall stuff.

Quick Assessment

Describing SNMP operations

1 SNMP works at two levels: _____ and _____.

2 An SNMP agent is _____.

3 Every SNMP device has a _____ that contains information on what the device can do.

Managing networks with TCP/IP utilities

4 You use the _____ command to display a network client's routing information.

Verifying the IP network with TCP/IP utilities

5 The TCP/IP utility that verifies the connectivity of an IP host is _____.

6 The utility that displays the IP configuration of a Windows NT TCP/IP workstation is _____.

7 The Windows 95-based utility that displays the IP information of a client is _____.

Troubleshooting with TCP/IP utilities

8 The _____ utility displays the route packets used to move from one IP location to another, as well as timing information.

9 To display statistics on an active network, use the _____.

Transferring files with FTP

10 The FTP utility is used to transfer _____ from one Internet computer to another.

Answers

1   *Central management system, management information base (MIB).* See "SNMP levels, agents, and communities."

2   *Any device running SNMP agent software.* Review "SNMP agents."

3   *MIB.* Take a look at "Management information bases (MIBs)."

4   *ROUTE.* Check out "Other maintenance utilities."

5   *PING.* Look over "PING, are you there?"

6   *IPCONFIG.* See "Using the IPCONFIG utility."

7   *WINIPCFG.* Review "The Windows WINIPCFG utility."

8   *TRACERT.* Check out "TCP/IP Troubleshooting Utilities."

9   *NETSTAT.* Take a look at "TCP/IP Troubleshooting Utilities."

10   *Files.* Review "The File Transfer Protocol."

Arranging Your TCP/IP Toolkit

You can group TCP/IP's utilities into three categories: management, validation, and troubleshooting. You use management utilities, such as the Simple Network Management Protocol (SNMP) and the Address Resolution Protocol (ARP), to remotely manage networks and network-related tables and files. Validation utilities, such as PING and IPCONFIG, enable you to verify network actions and addresses or reset network activities. Troubleshooting utilities, such as TRACERT and NETSTAT, display network statistics and determine IP network trouble spots. Together, the three TCP/IP utility types create quite a toolkit for working with TCP/IP-based systems.

Using SNMP to Manage a Network

Simple Network Management Protocol (SNMP) lets your fingers do the walking when you're managing an IP network. SNMP saves network administrators time and effort in performing network configuration and maintenance tasks. Any network administrator who has ever had to configure a router, bridge, or switch in another part of a building, campus, town, state, or country — and has wasted a goodly amount of time getting to it — can fully appreciate the benefits of SNMP.

SNMP is an Internet standard protocol that provides a method for remotely managing network devices, including a hub, a router, or even a program running on a server. SNMP provides a client/server environment for network management and monitoring and is endorsed and supported by virtually every network equipment manufacturer and software provider.

SNMP levels, agents, and communities

SNMP works at two levels: the central management system and the management information base (MIB). The central management system is located on the central server, and the MIB is located on each managed device.

The SNMP structure includes a manager, agents, and communities:

> ✔ **The SNMP manager** collects messages from SNMP agents and enables administrators to view and configure network devices from a central location.

✔ **SNMP agents** monitor and communicate the activities of network devices. SNMP agents respond to requests from the central management system and report any errors or problems. SNMP uses a mechanism called a *trap* to capture and send information back to the management system. An SNMP agent is any network device running SNMP agent software. (See "SNMP agents" for more information.)

✔ **SNMP communities** are logical groups of managers and agents formed to serve the needs of an individual network. An SNMP community groups certain managers with certain agents, which limits the number of managers to which the agent must send its traps. SNMP communities are often created as a security precaution, because they can limit SNMP access to a network segment.

The SNMP management system

An SNMP management system is any computer running the SNMP management software. Most SNMP management systems collect data on network devices, which can be viewed as text or graphics. SNMP management data is collected from SNMP agents using a set of three commands:

✔ **Get:** Used to request a specific fixed or variable value, such as the number of maximum users or the current CPU utilization rate.

✔ **Get-next:** Used immediately after a get command to retrieve the next value in sequence following the get command.

✔ **Set:** Used to send a configuration value to a managed device.

SNMP agents

An SNMP agent is any device running SNMP agent software, such as a server, router, hub, switch, or bridge. SNMP agents respond to SNMP manager's get, get-next, and set commands. An SNMP agent has only one command of its own: trap.

The SNMP trap command captures errors and problems that occur on managed devices and reports them back to the SNMP management system. Traps can also be issued for security or network connectivity issues as well.

It takes a community to raise an SNMP

A network administrator may want to cluster certain SNMP managers and agents for any or all of the following reasons:

✔ To limit the number of managers to which agents must respond.

✔ To limit the number of agents that a manager or managers control.

✔ To restrict the SNMP access points to a system compared to the public SNMP community created by default.

Management information bases (MIBs)

Every SNMP-managed device has a table that contains information on what that device can do. This table is called a management information base (MIB), and it contains the network management information and objects used by SNMP to manage, configure, and interact with the device.

Different systems support different MIBs. Several standard MIBs found on Windows-based systems are as follows:

✔ **Internet II MIB:** This standard Internet MIB contains a standard set of objects used for fault-tolerance and system management in an Internet environment.

✔ **DHCP MIB:** This standard MIB manages and monitors Dynamic Host Control Protocol (DHCP) activities.

✔ **WINS MIB:** Windows NT enables an SNMP management system to monitor the Windows Internet Name Server service.

Other maintenance utilities

Two other TCP/IP utilities that maintain the network are ARP (Address Resolution Protocol) and the ROUTE command. These tools enable the administrator to display and edit routing information used by the network to send messages beyond the subnet of a client as follows:

✔ **ARP (Address Resolution Protocol):** You use ARP to display, add, change, or delete ARP address entries from a computer's ARP cache.

✔ **ROUTE:** You use the ROUTE command to display the routing information of a network client. As shown in Figure 14-1, the ROUTE command, which is a Microsoft Windows command, is executed from the command prompt in Windows NT or from the Run box in Windows 9x.

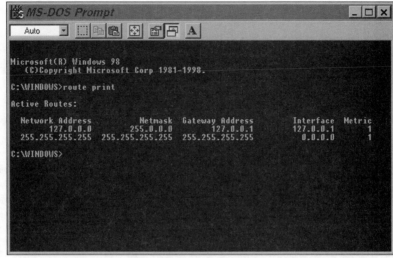

Figure 14-1:
The ROUTE
command
display.

Validating the Network

On occasion, a particular IP address doesn't respond or a network workstation is having trouble connecting to either the internal network or the Internet or both. Included in the TCP/IP suite are protocols to help you determine the cause in either case, Standard TCP/IP protocols — such as PING, IPCONFIG, and NBTSTAT — can validate the configuration of an IP network. These tools can tell you whether an address is a good address or display a computer's current network configuration.

PING, are you there?

You use PING (Packet Internet Groper) to verify that an IP address is a good address and that it can be reached from a workstation on the local network. PING can also test the connection to a local or remote network. PING is executed either from the command line of the NOS (network operating system) or in the Windows Run box.

PING sends out an ICMP (Internet Command Message Protocol) echo request packet to a destination address. If the destination address is a good one, the destination computer device answers back with an ICMP echo response packet. If no answer returns, however, which means that the request times out, the address is either not valid or is not functioning. Figure 14-2 illustrates the display messages of the PING command.

```
MS-DOS Prompt

Auto

C:\WINDOWS>ping www.dummies.com

Pinging www.dummies.com [206.175.162.18] with 32 bytes of data:

Reply from 206.175.162.18: bytes=32 time=278ms TTL=110
Reply from 206.175.162.18: bytes=32 time=265ms TTL=110
Reply from 206.175.162.18: bytes=32 time=285ms TTL=110
Reply from 206.175.162.18: bytes=32 time=244ms TTL=110

Ping statistics for 206.175.162.18:
    Packets: Sent = 4, Received = 4, Lost = 0 (0% loss),
Approximate round trip times in milli-seconds:
    Minimum = 244ms, Maximum = 285ms, Average = 268ms

C:\WINDOWS>
```

Figure 14-2:
The PING
utility in
action.

Using the IPCONFIG utility

IPCONFIG (Internet Protocol Configuration) is a very useful utility that displays a Windows NT computer's TCP/IP configuration. IPCONFIG uses several command-line options, each of which provides varying levels of details on a computer's TCP/IP configuration, including its host name, DNS (Domain Name Server) servers, node type, MAC (Media Access Control) address, DHCP (Dynamic Host Control Protocol) status, IP address, subnet mask, and default IP gateway.

In addition to the information that it can display, IPCONFIG has a functional side as well. You can use it to renew a DHCP IP address lease. (See Chapter 13 for more information on DHCP.) IPCONFIG offers a wide variety of display options.

Several versions of IPCONFIG are available, all of which provide you with essentially the same information. (See Figure 14-3.) In Windows NT, the command IPCONFIG (the one on the Network+ test, by the way) is executed from the Windows NT command line. On a UNIX system, the command IFCONFIG is executed from the command line prompt, and in Windows 9x, the command WINIPCFG is started in the Start⇨Run command box.

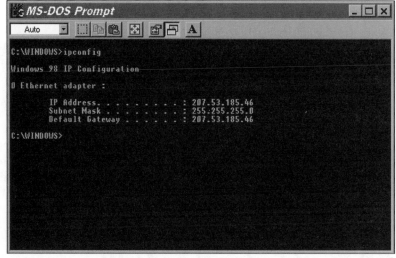

Figure 14-3:
The IPCON-
FIG utility's
display.

The Windows WINIPCFG utility

Microsoft Windows 95 and Windows 98-based systems also include
WINIPCFG, a Windows version of IPCONFIG. WINIPCFG provides you with IP-
address information for a client, including the IP address, its subnet mask,
and the default gateway, as shown in Figure 14-4.

Figure 14-4:
The
WINIPCFG
window.

Using NBTSTAT

NBTSTAT (NetBIOS over TCP/IP Statistics) is a Microsoft utility. You use it to display and verify the computer names cache created and used by NetBIOS for forwarding TCP/IP packets over the network. NBTSTAT also troubleshoots problems in the LMHOSTS (LAN Manager Hosts File) and other hosts files. Like nearly all the Microsoft TCP/IP utilities, NBTSTAT is executed on the Windows NT command line.

NBSTAT is used on Windows NT Server-based networks running TCP/IP to display identifying information of a workstation or server. It can be used to display the MAC address corresponding to an IP address, or vice versa, or it can be used to display the NetBIOS names that have been recorded into the name resolution services running on the network.

TCP/IP Troubleshooting Utilities

TCP/IP also includes utilities that can help determine whether and where a problem exists. Although you can troubleshoot with some of the utilities discussed earlier in this chapter (such as PING and NBTSTAT), some utilities specifically find and diagnose problems as the following list describes:

- ✔ **TRACERT (Trace Route):** This utility is most commonly used to pinpoint problems on a TCP/IP path. Like PING, it uses ICMP echo request packets to follow the route that packets would use to reach a certain destination. Although PING can tell you whether a destination address is good, TRACERT also displays the hops that a packet would make along with the TTL (Time-to-Live) values of each hop. Figure 14-5 shows an example of the display produced from a TRACERT command. Remember that not all network firewalls permit TRACERT (or PING) to trace through the firewall, and it may appear to dead-end there.

- ✔ **NETSTAT (Network Statistics):** The NETSTAT utility, available on both Windows and UNIX systems, includes a number of display options to list statistics on an active network. These options include active connections on a TCP/IP network, the status of Ethernet connections, and the current contents of the system's routing table.

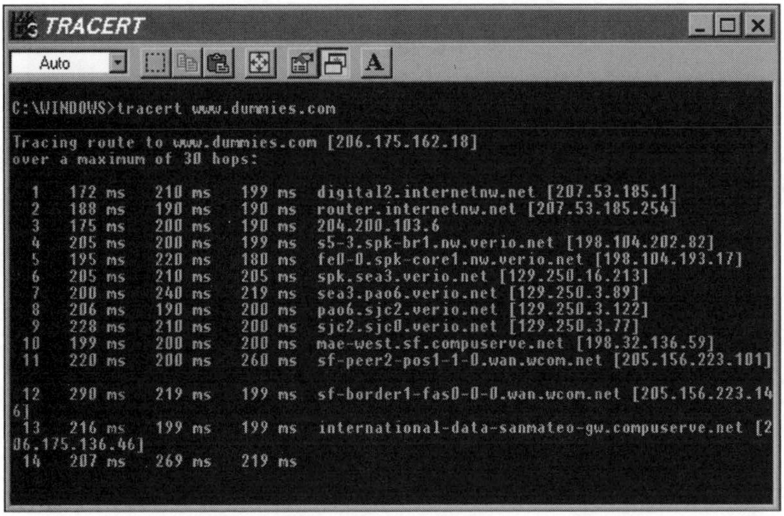

Figure 14-5:
The
TRACERT
command
traces the
route used
to reach a
destination.

The File Transfer Protocol

The File Transfer Protocol (FTP) is one protocol utility in the TCP/IP protocol suite that is not used to maintain, verify, or troubleshoot IP networks. This protocol is used exclusively to transfer files across the Internet from one computer to another.

FTP includes services to log you onto a remote server, to move between directories, and to manipulate files and directories on the remote site, as well as to segment files into packets, transfer them over the Internet, prevent and detect errors, and reassemble the file at the receiving end. You can use a wide variety of FTP clients, most of which are available in a demonstration or shareware form. Perhaps the most commonly used FTP clients, besides those built into Web browsers, are WS_FTP, Cute FTP, and Voyager FTP. A smaller-scale version of FTP that does not include logon services or directory access and manipulation services is the Trivial File Transfer Protocol (TFTP).

If you have no experience with an FTP client, visit Download.com (www.download.com) to download one to your desktop and practice transferring files. You can expect to see a question about FTP on the Network+ test.

Prep Test

1 The Internet protocol that provides a method for remotely managing network devices is

A ○ TCP/IP

B ○ NETSTAT

C ○ SNMP

D ○ SMTP

2 A network device that supports SNMP monitoring and has software to communicate its activity to an SNMP server is a

A ○ SNMP agent

B ○ SNMP manager

B ○ SNMP community

C ○ SNMP node

3 The three general-use SNMP commands are: (Choose three.)

A ❑ Get

B ❑ Push

C ❑ Get-next

D ❑ Set

E ❑ Request

F ❑ Discover

G ❑ Refresh

4 Every SNMP-managed device has a table of information called a(n)

A ○ SNMTable

B ○ DIB

C ○ SNMP directory

D ○ MIB

5 To verify that an IP address is a valid address and that it can be reached from a particular workstation, you use which TCP/IP utility?

A ○ TRACERT

B ○ PING

C ○ ROUTE

D ○ IPCONFIG

6 The Windows NT TCP/IP utility that is used to display a computer's host name, DNS server, MAC address, IP address, DHCP status, subnet mask, and other configuration details is

A ○ TRACERT

B ○ PING

C ○ ROUTE

D ○ IPCONFIG

7 Which TCP/IP utility is commonly used to locate path problems between a source and a destination IP address?

A ○ TRACERT

B ○ PING

C ○ ROUTE

D ○ IPCONFIG

8 Which of the following utilities and protocols are used on a TCP/IP network? (Choose four.)

A ❑ TRACERT

B ❑ REGEDIT

C ❑ PING

D ❑ WINIPCFG

E ❑ IPCONFIG

F ❑ ARP

9 Which TCP/IP protocol carries out the functions of the PING utility?

A ○ IP

B ○ TCP

C ○ UDP

D ○ ICMP

10 The TCP/IP suite protocol that is used to transfer data files from one Internet host to another is

A ○ ICMP

B ○ IP

C ○ UDP

D ○ FTP

Answers

1 *C.* SNMP enables the network administrator to remotely monitor and configure SNMP-capable network devices. *See "Using SNMP to Manage a Network."*

2 *A.* An SNMP agent is any network device running SNMP software that enables the device to maintain a management information base (MIB) about itself as well as report its activities to an SNMP server. *Review "SNMP levels, agents, and communities."*

3 *A, C, D.* These three commands are used to communicate between the SNMP managers and agents to report and collect device information. *Check out "The SNMP management system."*

4 *D.* Each SNMP maintains a Management Information Base (MIB) to store device management information and objects, which SNMP managers use to manage, configure, and interact with the device. *Take a look at "Management information bases (MIBs)."*

5 *B.* PING works like Internet SONAR, the underwater detection system used in all the submarine movies, to send a signal out so that it can bounce back from a remote location indicating it is there and operating. *See "PING, are you there?"*

6 *D.* IPCONFIG has a number of options and switches that can be used to alter its display, which can include virtually everything about a Windows NT computer's TCP/IP configuration. *Review "Using the IPCONFIG utility."*

7 *A.* TRACERT displays address and timing information about each hop that an ICMP packet passes through to reach the destination IP address entered on the command line. *Check out "TCP/IP Troubleshooting Utilities."*

8 *A, C, E, F.* REGEDIT is a Windows utility used to edit the Registry. WINIPCFG, a Windows-based version of IPCONFIG, may be included in the Microsoft version of TCP/IP, but don't consider it part of the standard protocol suite. *Take a look at "Arranging Your TCP/IP Toolkit."*

9 *D.* Several TCP/IP utilities use Internet Control Message Protocol (ICMP) to send out echo and request packets. *See "PING, are you there?"*

10 *D.* I just can't think of a way to make this a hard question, and apparently neither can the Network+ people. This question is almost verbatim of what you can expect to see on the test. *Review "The File Transfer Protocol."*

Part V

Remote Connectivity and Security

In this part . . .

Somewhere along the way, somebody discovered that computers and telephones can be used together, and the network technician's life became a living hell. Unfortunately, the Network+ exam, with about 6 percent of the test devoted to remote dial-up connectivity, only encourages this madness to continue. Approach this part of the exam with the attitude that the best offense is a good defense. The more you know about your enemies, the easier it is to combat them, and you can gather your intelligence using Chapter 15 in this part. You do need to know how to provide dial-up connectivity to a network, but it doesn't mean you have to like it!

Chapter 16 covers security. Letting users actually use your network really creates security problems. The network was created for people to use, so you must address and administer security issues on your network. If you have a good working knowledge of security modes, account policies, password procedures, data encryption, and other network security methods and devices, you'll have no problems with the 5 percent of the exam devoted to security.

Chapter 15

Remote Connectivity and Protocols

• •

Exam Objectives

▶ Describing the use and configuration of a modem

▶ Listing common modem standards

▶ Differentiating PPP and SLIP

▶ Defining PPTP and describing its use

▶ Explaining the advantages and disadvantages of ISDN and PSTN

• •

A growing number of people (which for sure includes me and very likely includes you) use remote connectivity to access a network. These people use dial-up services to access e-mail and other network resources, to browse the Internet and the World Wide Web, or to download or upload files. Whatever their reason, they are taking advantage of the fact that remote connectivity enables them to connect to a network wherever they happen to be. The services and technologies applied in a remote connection work together to turn their modems into network interface card work-alikes.

If you're like most frequent dialers, you take remote connectivity for granted. As you connect, you hum along to the haunting melody of the modem handshake, daydreaming of the wonders to see after the connection is finally completed. How many times have you given serious thought to what exactly is going on? Pay attention the next time you connect and really think about the process.

In general, remote connectivity includes a variety of protocols, standards, operating system services, and hardware. About 5 percent of the Network+ test deals specifically with these tools and how you apply them to make a connection and transmit data up and down the line. In addition, a significant portion of the test assumes that you know and understand data communications in general, as well as know how to configure and use a modem, what the various modem standards are, and what protocols and transmission modes are used in a remote transmission, in particular.

Quick Assessment

Describing the use and configuration of a modem

1 All modems communicate through a _____ port.

2 Modems _____ analog signals into digital signals and then _____ them at the receiving end.

Listing common modem standards

3 A(n) _____ modem is the most commonly used type of modem.

4 HDLC is a primary _____ protocol.

5 Many standards developed by the ITU/CCITT are designated by the letter _____.

Differentiating PPP and SLIP

6 PPP is short for _____.

7 The _____ protocol connects only to TCP/IP, provides no addressing, and relies on the communications hardware to perform error-checking.

Defining PPTP and describing its use

8 If one protocol is routed over another protocol so that two networks can communicate with their native protocol, this process is called _____.

Explaining the advantages and disadvantages of ISDN and PSTN

9 ISDN is available in two formats: _____ and _____.

10 _____ is the ISDN process used to combine B-channels to get higher data speeds.

Answers

1 *Serial.* See "Connecting a modem."

2 *Modulate, demodulate.* Review "Working with Modems."

3 *Asynchronous.* Check out "Asynchronous modems."

4 *Synchronous.* Take a look at "Synchronous modems."

5 *V.* Investigate "Modem standards."

6 *Point-to-point.* Review "Getting to the point."

7 *SLIP.* See "Giving it the SLIP."

8 *Tunneling.* Check out "PPTP, VPN, ABC, NBC, and Other Networks."

9 *BRI, PRI.* Take a look at "ISDN: It Should Do Networking."

10 *Inverse multiplexing.* Check out "Inverse multiplexing."

Working with Modems

The term *modem* is formed from the words *mo*dulate and *dem*odulate, the two actions that this device performs. A modem modulates the computer's digital signal into an analog signal that can be sent over the Plain Old Telephone Service (POTS). POTS is the standard telephone system that is available just about everywhere in some form. The other half of the modem's action occurs at a receiving end of a transmission where the modem demodulates the POTS analog signal — converts it back into a digital signal — and sends it on to a computer.

Modems do not make up a large portion of the Network+ test. You should be familiar with the *V dot* standards, point-to-point protocols, and the AT command set, all of which are discussed in this chapter. However, don't skip over the rest of the discussions. Study each area marked with an icon carefully; this information may appear on the test in a different context.

Modem standards

Since the late 1980s, the International Telecommunications Union (ITU), formally known as CCITT (Consultative Committee for International Telegraphy and Telephony), has been producing the standards used for modems. The CCITT/ITU standards are the *V* standards that you've probably heard of. Table 15-1 lists the *V dot* modem standards that you're likely to see on the Network+ test.

Table 15-1	ITU Modem Standards
Standard	*Bits per Second (bps)*
V.32	9,600
V.32bis	14,400
V.34	28,800
V.34bis	33,600
V.42	57,600
V.90	56,000

The suffix *bis* means *second* in French, and it indicates the second version of a modem standard. Some standards also have *terbo,* for third versions.

Another common modem standard is the Microcom Networking Protocol (MNP), which is defined as a series of classes (Class 1 through Class 5) that offer differing levels of error detection and correction capabilities. MNP Class 5 protocol is common on modems because it includes data compression that effectively doubles the data transmission rate.

The V.90 standard is the latest modem standard. It transfers data to the modem by using a technology that lets the data bypass modulation at a speed of 56 Kbps. However, when sending data *up* the line, a V.90 modem transfers data at a speed of 33.6 Kbps, which must be modulated.

Asynchronous modems

An asynchronous (called *async* for short) modem is the most commonly used modem type largely because it's the most widely used communications type. Async data is transmitted in a serial stream, which has start and stop bits embedded in the stream to mark the beginning and end of each character.

Asynchronous communications are not controlled by a clocking device. Instead, the slower of the two computers controls the flow by interrupting the transmission whenever it needs to catch up. The sending computer just sends its data stream, and the receiving computer just receives it. The potential for error is present in async communications, so a parity bit and parity checking are used for error control.

In addition to the speeds listed earlier in Table 15-1, many of the V.*xx* standards also include error control and data compression techniques, which asynchronous communications apply. Often, a communications link to a local area network employs a number of protocols that incorporate several standards. For example, a typical LAN to LAN link using dial-up modems may employ V.32bis signaling, V.42 error checking, and V.42bis data compression techniques.

Synchronous modems

A synchronous modem uses a timing scheme that coordinates the transmission between the two computers. Data is grouped in blocks of characters, called frames, and synchronizing characters precede each frame. If the sync characters arrive at the correct point, no problem occurs. Otherwise, the frame is retransmitted.

Synchronous communications use a number of primary protocols. Following are the ones that you should know:

- ✔ **SDLC (synchronous data link control):** A versatile point-to-point and multipoint protocol that designates one station as the controlling node and the other station(s) as the controlled node(s).

- ✔ **HDLC (high-level Data Link control):** A high-level, bit-oriented protocol that sends messages in frames of variable sizes.

- ✔ **BSC (binary synchronous communications):** Also known as *bisync,* a protocol in which the communicating devices are synchronized before data transmission begins. The data frame includes a header and trailer for synchronization.

Connecting a modem

Modems connect to a computer either internally, in the form of an expansion card, or externally through a serial port. In either case, you use an RJ-11 plug — which is a smaller look-alike of the RJ-45 connector used with 10BaseT media — to attach the modem to the telephone service.

Regardless of whether the modem is internal or external, it communicates through a serial port. The serial ports on most computers are COM1 and COM2. (*COM* refers to communication.) Some computers also have COM3 and COM4 as well.

The modem itself usually requires little in the way of configuration. Most modems are preset to the general communications standards. Some minor configuration settings may need adjusting, but generally most modems are good to go right out of the box. If the modem does need configuration, you can configure it by using software, AT commands, or DIP switches, depending on the modem.

Setting up a modem connection in Windows

Lab 15-1 provides you with some background and helps you internalize some of the terminology and processes that you use when setting up a modem connection. In this lab, you use Windows 95 or 98 tools to set up modem communications. You set up a modem connection in two phases: setting up the modem itself and configuring the dial-up networking properties.

Lab 15-1   Setting Up a Modem Connection

1. **To set up the modem, use the Modem Installation Wizard, shown in Figure 15-1, which you access from the Windows Control Panel and the Modems icon. The window that opens is the Modem Properties dialog box. To start the Modem Installation Wizard, click the Add button on the Modem Properties dialog box.**

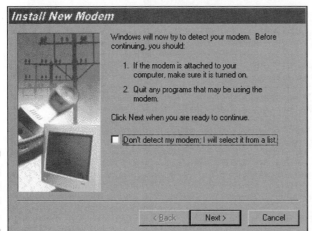

Figure 15-1:
The Modem
Installation
Wizard.

You have the choice of letting the Wizard detect the new modem (assuming that you've already installed the modem into an expansion slot or connected it to a serial port) or picking the modem from the list of supported modems (my recommendation), as shown in Figure 15-2.

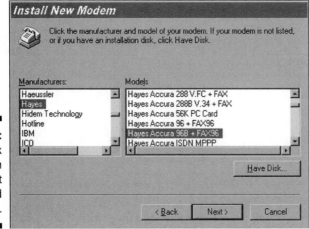

Figure 15-2:
You can pick
your modem
from the list
of supported
modems.

2. **On most newer systems, a modem is standard equipment and already installed and configured. In this case, check its configuration settings by clicking the Properties button on the Modems Properties window. Figure 15-3 shows the properties window for a specific modem.**

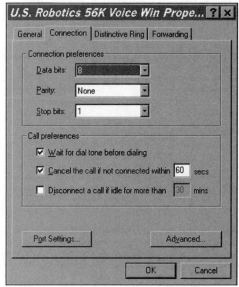

Figure 15-3:
The
connection
properties
of a modem.

3. **Configure a dial-up destination by clicking the Dial-Up Networking icon on the My Computer window, as shown in Figure 15-4. The My Computer window is opened from the My Computer icon on the Windows Desktop.**

   On the Dial-Up Networking window, you should see a New Connection icon and possibly some existing connections.

4. **Click the New Connection icon to open the Make New Connection Wizard, shown in Figure 15-5, which guides you through the creation of a new dial-up remote connection.**

Figure 15-4:
The Dial-Up Networking icon on My Computer.

Figure 15-5:
The Make New Connection Wizard.

AT commands

The AT command set is common to nearly all modems, although most users never come into contact with it. You may see a question or two on the Network+ exam that refers to AT commands indirectly.

Except for the special character commands, the code *AT*, which stands for attention, precedes each AT command. For example, the command to dial 555-1212 is ATDT5551212. Table 15-2 contains only a few of the more common AT commands but are the ones you may run into on the Network+ exam.

Table 15-2	AT Commands
Command	*Meaning*
, (comma)	Pause
*70	Turn off call-waiting feature on telephone line
AT	Attention command that precedes each command line (the source of the name *AT commands*)
DT	Dial using Touch-Tone mode
H	Hang up

Analog modems and digital codecs

You'll never guess which type of modem carries an analog signal. Ah, you peeked! Most modems in use are analog modems, because they connect to and modulate signals for the analog telephone system. Because the analog system uses sound waves to send data, any extra noise or interference on the line can corrupt the data that's being transmitted.

A digital signal, on the other hand, is far less affected by interference. To transmit digital data over digital lines, you don't really need a modem. However, sometimes you need the reverse of an analog modem — a device that encodes the analog signal into a digital signal. For example, you would need such a device — which is called a codec — to transmit an analog video image over digital lines. Like the word modem, *codec* is a contraction (of *co*der/*dec*oder).

The Network+ exam refers to all protocols, standards, and technologies only by their initials or abbreviations. So make sure that you know their initials or abbreviations as well as their names.

PPP versus SLIP

When you connect to a remote network (such as the Internet) by using a modem, you most commonly use PPP (Point-to-Point Protocol) or perhaps SLIP (Serial Line Internet Protocol). You can use these protocols over ISDN (see "ISDN: It Should Do Networking," later in this chapter) or on dedicated high-speed lines, as well as use them to connect some routers to other routers.

Getting to the point

PPP is the current standard protocol for point-to-point connections. It provides both Physical and Data Link layer connections to a variety of network protocols, including TCP/IP, NetBEUI, AppleTalk, and IPX. In effect, PPP enables your modem to act like a network adapter, seamlessly connecting you to a remote network protocol. PPP also inherently supports compression and error checking, making it very fast and reliable.

Giving it the SLIP

SLIP is an older, legacy protocol, common to UNIX systems, that operates only at the Physical layer. You use SLIP primarily to connect to the Internet via a modem. Because its only connection is to TCP/IP, SLIP provides no addressing and relies on the connecting hardware to provide any error-checking and correction performed in the transmission.

PPTP, VPN, ABC, NBC, and Other Networks

Tunneling a protocol means that one protocol, such as IPX or AppleTalk, is routed over another protocol, such as TCP/IP. This arrangement enables two networks to connect and communicate with their native protocol, such as AppleTalk, with their packets transmitted in a TCP/IP format.

The most common of the tunneling protocols is PPTP (Point-to-Point Tunneling Protocol). PPTP tunnels PPP over an IP network to create a network connection. In effect, PPTP uses the Internet as a network connection. PPTP enables you to encapsulate a variety of protocols (IP, IPX, or NetBEUI) inside of IP packets for transmission. As you would plain brown shipping paper, the receiving end discards the IP packet, and the original packet is forwarded on to its destination.

PPTP creates a virtual connection for remote users. The users perceive that they are directly connected to the network, as if they were local to it. This PPTP connection creates what is called a *virtual private network* (VPN). Although the connection is made over the public Internet, the connection is virtually private because data is essentially double-wrapped inside IP packets. PPTP itself does not create a connection. The connection is actually made by the carrying protocol, PPP or the like.

Analog and Digital Carrier Services

This chapter is probably the best place to discuss some of the data-communication carrier services that you may see on the Network+ exam. As discussed earlier in this chapter, the two basic communication types for data are analog and digital. Within a LAN, you use a digital signal, but when the LAN is expanded or attached to a WAN, a different type of digital carrier or, very commonly, an analog service may be necessary. Within each of these two communication types, you can use a number of carrier services.

Analog carrier services

In general, an analog carrier service is POTS, but it is also referred to as the *Public Switched Telephone Network* (PSTN). Actually, a few subtle differences exist between PSTN and POTS, besides the *N* and the *O,* but for the Network+ exam, they are essentially the same thing.

The telephone company typically provides analog carrier services, but some other companies offer data networking services called public data networks (PDNs). The most common type of analog carrier service, however, is a dial-up switched line. The public telephone system is a switched service to which you can connect by using a dial-up access. Switching occurs as the signal travels from your telephone connection to the central office — the central office uses the telephone number as an address to switch the call to its destination.

Digital carrier services

You are very likely to see the most common digital services referenced on the Network+ test. You aren't asked any questions directly about these items, but you can count on seeing them in a situational question or as part of a question's information.

The most common digital carriers are DDS (Digital Data Service) lines that provide a direct point-to-point synchronous connection. In general, these lines are all leased lines. A leased line is a dial-up line that is reserved for a single user or company for private use. This type of service is also called a *dedicated line.*

Because the DDS line is private and dedicated to connecting two points, you do not use a modem. Instead, you place a CSU/DSU (customer service unit/data service unit) at each end of the line. Leased lines use PPP (see "PPP versus SLIP," earlier in the chapter) and HDLC protocols.

T-carriers and DS levels

High-speed DDS lines are designated a couple of different ways, the most common of which are T-carriers (T1, T2, and so on) and DS-level specifications (DS-0, DS-1, DS-2, and so on). Generally, you use these two line designations interchangeably, where a T1 line is the equivalent of the DS-1 specification.

The most widely used high-speed digital service is the T1 line, which uses two pairs of wires to send signals at a maximum data rate of 1.544 Mbps. A T1 line is a full-duplex carrier that uses one pair of wires to send and the other pair to receive. It consists of 24 individual 64 Kbps channels that can be used individually or in groups to create what is called *fractional T1* service. Table 15-3 lists the five T-carrier categories in use.

Table 15-3	T-Carrier Categories		
Level	*Number of Channels*	*Number of T1s*	*Bandwidth*
T1	24	1	1.54 Mbps
T2	96	4	6.31 Mbps
T3	672	28	44.74 Mbps
T4	4,032	168	274.18 Mbps

Instead of memorizing Table 15-3, just remember the T1 line's characteristics and the number of T1 lines that each succeeding T-carrier level represents.

In Europe, DDS lines are categorized as E-series carriers. An E1 line is capable of 2.048 Mbps. The Network+ test may refer to the E-series lines in conjunction with T-carrier lines.

The DS (Data Signaling or Digital Service) scale categorizes DDS lines. The relationship to the T-carrier lines is that a DS-0 represents the data rate of a single T1 channel, and the data rate of the full T1 line (all 24 channels) is categorized as DS-1. Table 15-4 lists the DS specifications and their T-carrier equivalents.

Table 15-4	DS Specifications	
DS Level	T-Carrier	Data Rate
DS-0	N/A	64 Kbps
DS-1	T1	1.54 Mbps
DS-2	T2	6.31 Mbps
DS-3	T3	44.74 Mbps
DS-4	T4	274.18 Mbps

WANs and other digital services

You generally use each of the various types of DDS lines to extend a network. In many cases, you use digital data services to interconnect two or more local area networks to create a wide area network (WAN). If you connect to the Internet from your office or school, most likely you're connecting beyond the company's or school's LAN to the large Internet WAN using some form of DDS.

Other forms of digital data services that you use almost exclusively for connecting to a WAN are as follows:

✔ **Switched 56:** This is the low-end of DDS services. Switched 56 is a point-to-point service that is essentially an on-demand dial-up dedicated line using partial T1 service. When the service is accessed, a T1 channel switches to the user's link. Because most service providers also offer dedicated 56 Kbps lines, you often use Switched 56 as a backup service.

✔ **X.25:** Most commonly used to connect remote terminals to mainframes, this specification defines switched virtual circuits (SVC) networks. An SVC is a circuit that is established dynamically for the communications session and remains connected until its users shut it down.

✔ **Frame relay:** This is a point-to-point permanent virtual circuit (PVC), which is either a type of plastic used to make diskettes or a permanent communications path between two fixed points, such as a leased DDS line. Frame relay is a packet-switched networking protocol that uses a variable-length packet and achieves fast data throughput, because it doesn't apply error-checking.

✔ **ATM (Asynchronous Transfer Mode):** ATM is a high-speed packet-switching technology that uses a 53-byte fixed-length packet, called a cell, in which 20 percent of the bits are used for error-checking. ATM supports data transmission rates of 622 Mbps or higher.

✔ **SONET (Synchronous Optical Network):** Originally developed to bridge the Baby Bells to long-distance carriers, SONET is a WAN technology implemented on fiber-optic cabling. Its data rates are defined in OC (optical carrier) levels: OC-1 is rated at 51.84 Mbps, OC-3 is rated at 155.52 Mbps, and OC-24 at 622 Mbps.

✔ **SMDS (Switched Multimegabit Data Service):** SMDS is similar to ATM, using the same-sized cell; it applies no error-checking and offers 1.544 to 45 Mbps data speeds.

ISDN: It Should Do Networking

ISDN (Integrated Services Digital Network) is another digital data service that has been bursting onto the scene since 1984. It is a completely digital communications networking specification that is capable of carrying voice, data, images, video, or just about anything that can be digitized.

ISDN services are available in two formats:

✔ **BRI (Basic Rate Interface):** This service consists of two B-channels, each of which carries 64 Kbps, and one D-channel that carries control signals at 16 Kbps. You can use the two B-channels independently or multiplex them together to reach a 128 Kbps data speed.

✔ **PRI (Primary Rate Interface):** This ISDN type uses 23 B-channels and one D-channel. You can use the B-channels independently or combine them to attain the equivalent of a T1 service. You use the D-channel for control and signaling.

For the Network+ exam, remember the number and type of lines that make up each of the two ISDN types. Don't worry about speeds, but remember that ISDN PRI service is the rough equivalent of a T1 line.

Inverse multiplexing

The technology used to combine multiple ISDN B-channels to achieve data speeds higher than 64 Kbps is called *inverse multiplexing*. In general, you implement inverse multiplexing methods outside of the ISDN technology. You use the following three methods for inverse multiplexing:

- ✔ **BONDING (for Bandwidth On Demand Interoperability Group):** The most common method used, BONDING combines up to 63 56 Kbps or 64 Kbps B-channels.

- ✔ **Multilink PPP (Point-to-Point Protocol):** Routes IP over ISDN. A single logical connection is multiplexed across several physical connections.

- ✔ **Multirate service (also known as Nx64 service):** Normally included as a part of PRI service. The service provider, usually the telephone company, combines as many channels as needed to give you the speed required on demand (in multiples of 64Kbps) each time that you make a connection.

Advantages of ISDN

Some of the advantages of ISDN over using the PSTN are as follows:

- ✔ ISDN offers data speeds of two to four times faster than what is available on the PSTN using an analog modem.

- ✔ ISDN provides a relatively low-cost, moderately higher-speed service to home or small office/home office (SOHO) users.

- ✔ ISDN is cost-effective when used as a dial-up nondedicated WAN service.

- ✔ ISDN service is available on a per usage basis from most Internet service providers (ISPs).

Disadvantages of ISDN

A few disadvantages of ISDN when compared to the PSTN are as follows:

- ✔ ISDN data transmission speeds don't offer great improvements over those available on an analog modem and PSTN.

- ✔ ISDN dedicated services can cost much more than nondedicated services.

- ✔ ISDN requires a special adapter (called an inverse multiplexer) to translate between analog and digital signals.

Prep Test

1 Which of the following are commonly used ITU/CCITT V.xx standards? (Choose three.)

A ❑ V.10

B ❑ V.32

C ❑ V.34 bis

D ❑ V.90

E ❑ V.232

2 Which of the following are synchronous communications protocols? (Choose three.)

A ❑ BSC

B ❑ HDLC

C ❑ IPX

D ❑ NetBEUI

E ❑ SDLC

3 The command string used to dial the telephone number 555-8812 from a modem is

A ○ ADT5558812&F

B ○ ATX555,8812+++

C ○ ATDT5558812

D ○ +++AT,DT,5558812

4 The protocol that is most commonly used with dial-up connections is

A ○ SLIP

B ○ PPTP

C ○ ISDN

D ○ PPP

5 The protocol that tunnels point-to-point communications over an IP network is

A ○ SLIP

B ○ PPTP

C ○ ISDN

D ○ PPP

6 The bandwidth available on a T1/DS-1 service is

A ○ 64 Kbps

B ○ 1.54 Kbps

C ○ 1.54 Mbps

D ○ 44.74 Mbps

7 Which of the following is a form of digital data services? (Choose three.)

A ❑ X.25

B ❑ Frame relay

C ❑ SLIP

D ❑ ATM

8 ISDN BRI service provides

A ○ 23 B-channels and 1 D-channel

B ○ 2 D-channels and 1 B-channel

C ○ 23 D-channels and 1 B-channel

D ○ 2 B-channels and 1 D-channel

9 Which of the following is not an advantage of ISDN over PSTN?

A ○ Two to four times faster

B ○ Higher bandwidth available on demand

C ○ Less expensive

D ○ Dedicated service

10 The process used to combine multiple ISDN channels to achieve higher band-widths is called

A ○ Multiplexing

B ○ Inverse multiplexing

C ○ Rate services

D ○ Binding

Answers

1 *B, C, D.* Until very recently, most modems used either the V.32 (and V.32 bis) or V.34 (and V.34 bis) standards. The V.42 standards were mainly used for networking; the recently set V.90 standard allows for 56 Kbps modem communications. *See "Modem standards."*

2 *A, B, E.* These are the three commonly used synchronous protocols. IPX and NetBEUI are networking protocols. *Review "Synchronous modems."*

3 *C.* AT is the command for attention; DT stands for dial using Touch-Tone; and what follows is the telephone number. Don't worry too much about memorizing all the AT commands, but do be familiar with those included in this chapter. *Take a look at "AT commands."*

4 *D.* The Point-to-Point Protocol (PPP) is by far the most commonly used protocol for modem communications. The Network+ test refers to all protocols only by their initials or abbreviations. *Check out "Getting to the point."*

5 *B.* The Point-to-Point Tunneling Protocol (PPTP) enables you to encapsulate one protocol inside of IP packets so that you can use the Internet as a part of your network. *See "PPTP, VPN, ABC, NBC, and Other Networks."*

6 *C.* Watch that qualifier very carefully. Be absolutely sure that any specific data speeds that you choose for answers have the correct speed abbreviations on them. *Review "T-carriers and DS levels."*

7 *A, B, D.* SLIP is a dial-up analog protocol. You need to know which protocols are DDS and which are analog. *Check out "WANs and other digital services."*

8 *D.* BRI (Basic Rate Interface) is the most commonly available ISDN service, which naturally means it's the less capable of the ISDN formats. B-channels bear bytes, and D-channels carry directives. BRI has two Bs and one D. Just remember my high school report cards. *See "ISDN: It Should Do Networking."*

9 *C.* ISDN is definitely not less expensive than using the PSTN (POTS). In most cases, you're already paying for dial-up analog service, so in a way, it is free. ISDN, although not exactly costing a fortune (depending on the service), is definitely not free. *Review "Disadvantages of ISDN."*

10 *A.* Multiplexing involves combining multiple outbound lines onto a single line. Conversely, inverse multiplexing combines multiple inbound lines to connect to your computer. *Take a look at "Inverse multiplexing."*

Chapter 16

Security

Exam Objectives

▶ Choosing between user- and share-level security models

▶ Setting account policies

▶ Assigning permissions

▶ Describing standard password practices

▶ Employing data encryption

▶ Using a firewall

A number of recent studies show the danger of a variety of different threats to a network. What is somewhat remarkable, although somewhat predictable, is that the majority of network security threats come from within an organization. Although outside hackers, phreaks, and the like pose a real and serious danger, authorized network users or people associated with them perpetrate most of the theft, damage, and pranks.

So what's a poor, unsuspecting network administrator to do? Why can't users just be nice and respect each other's servers? Although I agree with these sentiments, having chanted them repeatedly while hugging my server protectively, they're just a bit naive. This is the real world, and mean and nasty evil-doers are out there with nothing better to do than to attack your network and its security.

The Network+ exam realistically recognizes the need for selecting and using a security plan that's appropriate to the network's size, scope, and usage. In fact, security issues comprise 6 percent of the Network+ exam. With so much ground to cover, this topic commands a relatively high percentage of questions.

Whether you're setting up your own network, administrating the company network, or installing and configuring networks for customers, network security is equal in importance to the hardware, network operating system, and cabling to correctly secure network operations. Keeping the bad, mean people out is a good and worthwhile thing to do.

Quick Assessment

Selecting between user- and share-level security models

1 You use _____ to restrict the user's access to specific network resources.

2 _____ sets up file permissions and access rights to individual users.

3 On a NetWare 4 system, you maintain user access rights through _____.

Setting account policies

4 A(n) _____ is a set of rules used to define the privileges of user accounts.

Describing standard password practices

5 Experts recommend that users change passwords every _____ days.

6 Passwords should be a minimum of _____ characters in length.

7 Users should use up to _____ passwords before reusing a password.

Employing data encryption

8 A(n) _____ encrypts plain-text data for transmission over a public network.

9 Popular encryption methods are _____ and _____.

Using a firewall

10 _____ is a firewall technique that screens packets looking for certain IP addresses or port numbers.

Answers

1 *Share-level security.* See "Share-level security model."

2 *User-level security.* Review "User-level security model."

3 *NDS or NetWare Directory Services.* Take a look at "Security models in the Novell NetWare realm."

4 *Account policy.* Check out "Account Policies."

5 *30 to 60 days.* Review "Practicing Safe Passwording."

6 *6 to 8.* See "Practicing Safe Passwording."

7 8. Look at "Practicing Safe Passwording."

8 *Encryption algorithm.* See "Encrypting Data to Keep Your Secrets."

9 *DES or RSA.* Review "The keys to encryption."

10 *Packet filter.* Check out "Hiding Safely Behind the Firewall."

Applying a Security Model

Few would argue that you must secure network resources from unauthorized access. Only those users authorized to access network devices and data should have access to them. Restricting access helps ensure that network resources are not corrupted or misused and remain available to network users. The two approaches, or models, to network security are as follows:

- ✔ Share-level security
- ✔ User-level security

Logon account authorization

Most network administrators agree that without users, their jobs would be a whole lot easier. Unfortunately, networks exist to enable users to share resources, and sharing inherently includes accessing. Access to a network most commonly involves using a logon account and password.

A logon account is usually a code word easily remembered by the user to whom it belongs. Logons can be just about anything the network administrator can get the users to accept. Users' logons are normally something like their initials, name, or both. (For example, at work, my logon account is *rgilster*.)

In general, a password is a code number, word, or phrase chosen by the user that uniquely identifies that user. The password tells the network that the users logging in are who they say they are. Anyone with a valid logon account and password combination gains access to the network. The person who successfully logs onto the network is assumed to be the actual account owner or someone trusted by the account owner. However, that person could also be someone who has stolen the account and password. I discuss passwords and password policies in more detail in "Practicing Safe Passwording," later in the chapter.

Share-level security model

In the same way that you verify the users' accounts and passwords before granting them access to the network in general, you use share-level security to restrict users' access to specific network resources. However, in the share-level security model, you assign passwords to the resources rather than the user. If the user knows the password for a shared network device or folder, he gains access to it on a shared basis. Share-level security is built on the concept that any network user with the knowledge of the password can access the resource.

Lab 16-1 demonstrates how to set up share-level security in Windows 98. The process used in this lab is very similar to what you use in Windows NT Server and Windows NT Workstation as well.

Although this lab demonstrates the creation of share-level security on a folder, the process is very similar to that used to set share-level security on printers, computers, and other network devices.

Lab 16-1   Share-Level Security in Windows 98

1. **Open Windows Explorer and browse to the folder that you want to share (for example, C:\TEMP).**

2. **Right-click the folder and choose Sharing from the short-cut menu that appears.**

   The properties window for the selected folder appears, as shown in Figure 16-1.

3. **Click the Sharing tab.**

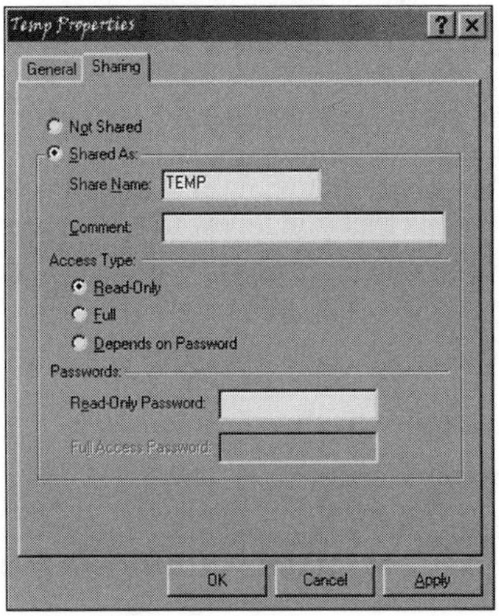

Figure 16-1:
The Sharing tab of the folder properties window.

4. **On the Sharing tab, you can choose to share the folder (and its contents, by the way), restrict the action that can be taken on the files in the folder (read, write, or full access), and set a share-level security password.**

5. **Click the Apply and OK buttons.**

   Now, any user other than the owner wanting to access this folder must enter the password.

User-level security model

User-level security is assigned individually to users wanting to gain access to a particular shared resource. On the peer-to-peer network, each workstation owner must grant the access right, but on a server-based network, user-level rights are administered centrally to the user's profile.

User-level security as it is used today was defined originally in the NetWare NOS. Windows NT, with its roots in peer-to-peer networks, and UNIX, with its multiprogramming environment, implement user-level security only slightly differently from one another. However, the final result is that individual users must be given the right and permission to access certain network resources.

In contrast to the process and results of Lab 16-1, user-level security sets up file permissions and access rights to individual users. For example, if you were to extend the process in Lab 16-1 to set user-level security for the shared folder TEMP, you could grant Uncle Harry full access rights and restrict Aunt Sally to read-only.

Applying the security model

On a NetWare or UNIX network, you have only the user-level security model to choose. However, in the Windows NT world, implementing the security model involves a choice. Implementing that choice is very straightforward. Lab 16-2 demonstrates the few steps that you follow to set the security model.

Lab 16-2   Implementing the Security Model in Windows 9x

1. **From the Control Panel, double-click the Network icon.**

   The Network properties window appears.

2. **Click the Access Control tab and then choose the security model that you want to use for your computer, as shown in Figure 16-2, by clicking its corresponding radio button.**

The primary difference between the share-level and user-level security models in the Windows environment is that the user-level option enables you to specify a file that contains all the users that may access shared resources.

Remember that much of the world still uses the Novell NetWare NOS. However, the Network+ exam reflects the growing popularity of the Windows NT operating systems.

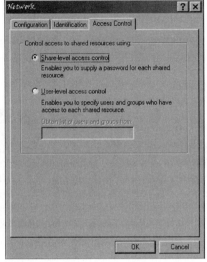

Figure 16-2:
The security
model
choices on
the Network
properties
window.

Account Policies

An *account policy* is a set of rules that defines which access rights are assigned to which users on a network. Windows NT has a formal mechanism (called of all things *Account Policies*) to set the default account policies for all user accounts. In Windows NT, account policies are one of the many system policies that the administrator sets.

As the network administrator, you can set up a series of user-account parameters that combine to create the account policy. The account policy is then applied to each account as it logs in. Account policies are restrictive. In other words, you are defining the parameters of acceptable behavior and allowable travel for users of the network: what they can do and where they can go.

The types of settings that you set and the questions you should ask to determine the correct setting to create an account policy are as follows:

- **Password restrictions:** Do passwords expire? How often can users change passwords? What is a password's minimum length? How many different passwords must you use before you can repeat one? Must you log in to change the password?

- **Account lockout:** How many tries does the user (or hacker) get to enter their password correctly before the account is locked out?

✔ **Lockout duration:** If an account gets locked out, must the administrator reset it or does it reset automatically after a certain period of time?

✔ **Forced disconnect:** Under Windows NT, system policies also set the network's login hours. After these hours expire, are users disconnected?

Assigning File and Directory Permissions

File and directory permissions are another part of the security policies for a network aimed at restricting the user and protecting data resources. Folders, directories, and files have attributes that restrict the actions that users can take on their contents (see Chapter 5). You can set the permissions on a file to read-only, which restricts users from writing or changing the file. Other permission settings that you can apply enable (or prohibit) others to change, share, purge, or copy the file.

Practicing Safe Passwording

Until such time that you can use retinal scanners, thumbprint verification, and saliva-sample DNA analysis (no chewing-tobacco, please) on network workstations, passwords are the gatekeepers of the networking world. Even after the real techie stuff becomes available, passwords are most likely to still play a very valuable part in network security policies.

Password policies do include the commonsense stuff, such as don't use your name, your birthday, your dog's name, your dog's birthday, and so on. For the Network+ exam, you should know the types of policies that a sound password security plan includes, which are as follows:

✔ **Changing passwords frequently:** Users should change passwords regularly to prevent the risk of discovery. However, users should not change passwords too often because users are prone to forgetting passwords that are changed frequently. Changing passwords every 30 to 60 days is usually sufficient.

✔ **Minimum password length:** A single-character password is only slightly more secure than no password at all. For each character in its length, a password becomes exponentially more difficult to guess. The flip side of this policy is that a password shouldn't be too long either, because longer passwords are harder to remember. If users can't remember their passwords, you have the ultimate security, but that's a bad thing, I'm told. The most recent Gilster poll says that four out of five experts agree that six characters is an acceptable minimum length for a password.

- ✔ **Password uniqueness:** Users should not reuse passwords too frequently. Many users want to recycle the same three or four passwords over and over. A determined, mean-and-nasty hacker can figure out the pattern of these passwords easily. Force your users to dream up new passwords and use them before you let them return to the safety of using *password* as their password again. Call it tough love, but it's for their own good. The experts in the Gilster poll say that eight is a safe number of passwords to use before repeating one.

- ✔ **Password protection:** Somebody with unauthorized access to your network can wreak havoc on you and your company's resources. Counsel users on protecting the secrecy of their passwords. They should know that taping their password to the monitor or the outside window is not the best way to keep it secret. You should also explain the dangers of sharing passwords with friends and coworkers.

Encrypting Data to Keep Your Secrets

Beyond restricting who can log into the network, you can also protect your network data resources by using a secret code. Encrypting data before transmitting makes its safe and secure arrival more likely. It may sound like something out of James Bond, but encrypting data is becoming very common, especially in networks carrying e-commerce (credit card numbers, bank accounts, and the like).

Data encryption, or *cryptography,* converts data into a secret code so that you can transmit it over a public network. Some private networks also use encryption but usually on specialized and highly secure systems only. You use an *encryption algorithm* to convert the plain-text data into a *cipher,* also called *cipher text.* The cipher text is transmitted, and at the receiving end, it is decrypted back into plain text by using an *encryption key,* the basis for the original encryption.

The keys to encryption

An encryption key is a 40- to 128-bit binary number. Plain text is encrypted mathematically by combining the encryption key with its bits. Decryption involves extracting the key from the cipher-text bits to return the data to its original form.

Two encryption methods are in use, as follows:

- ✔ **DES (Data-Encryption Standard):** Both the sender and receiver use the same key to encrypt and decrypt. This encryption method is the fastest and easiest method, but the key itself also must be transmitted.

⮕ **RSA (Rivest, Shamir, and Adleman):** This patented method, which is named for its creators, is also called the public-key algorithm. It uses both a private and a public key to encrypt and decrypt data. Each recipient holds a private and unique key that is used in conjunction with a published public key. The sender uses the recipient's public key to encrypt the message, and then the recipient uses his private key to decrypt the message.

Digital certificates

A digital certificate is your identity card on the Internet. You use it to supply your public encryption key to those to whom you send encrypted data. Certification authorities — such as Verisign, Inc. (www.verisign.com) — issue digital certificates, also called digital IDs. To have a digital certificate issued to you requires lots of documentation verifying who you are, such as a drivers license, a notarized statement, and fingerprints.

A digital certificate contains the following data: the certificate owner's name, the owner's company name and its address, the public key, the owner's certificate serial number, the certificate's validity dates, the ID code of the certifying authority, and the digital signature of the certifying authority.

For more information on encryption, visit the Electronic Frontier Foundation (www.eff.org).

Hiding Safely Behind the Firewall

The best way to keep a network secure is to make sure that only those authorized to share its resources have access to the network. Restricting access is an easy task if the network is only a LAN, but everything changes if you connect to the outside world. Opening a door for LAN users to exit also opens the door for others to enter.

One method for keeping your network secure is to implement a *firewall*. In general, a firewall — a set of programs running on your network's gateway server — monitors outgoing and incoming network traffic to allow authorized packets in or out. Commonly, you use firewalls to let users access the Internet and to securely separate a network's public Web server from the internal network. You can use a firewall to secure internal subnetworks from unauthorized internal users. In a nutshell, you use firewalls to keep unauthorized users out of the internal network and to block internal users from accessing unauthorized outside locations.

Following are some firewall techniques that you may run into on the Network+ exam:

- ✔ **Packet filter:** A packet filter, also called a screening router, screens packets looking for certain IP addresses or port numbers.

- ✔ **Proxy server:** In addition to caching Web pages for a LAN, a proxy server acts as a switch between the LAN and the WAN, breaking the connection if necessary to prevent access.

- ✔ **Network Address Translation (NAT):** NAT serves as a translator to convert and conceal all internal IP addresses into a single IP address that is publicized to the world.

- ✔ **Stateful inspection:** This process matches outgoing requests to incoming responses and blocks any incoming messages without a matching request.

Prep Test

1 Establishing a network security policy includes deciding on the appropriate security model to apply. Which of the following are network security models? (Choose two.)

A ❑ User-level security

B ❑ File permissions and rights

C ❑ Share-level security

D ❑ Firewall policies

2 In which security model are passwords assigned to the shared devices?

A ○ User-level security

B ○ File permissions and rights

C ○ Share-level security

D ○ Firewall policies

3 In which security model does a list of users indicate which users are allowed to access a shared device?

A ○ User-level security

B ○ File permissions and rights

C ○ Share-level security

D ○ Firewall policies

4 Which of the following are included in setting an account policy? (Choose three.)

A ❑ Password restriction policies

B ❑ Account lockout policy

C ❑ User account workstation location ID

D ❑ Account lockout duration policy

5 A good password policy should include: (Choose two.)

A ❑ Changing passwords frequently

B ❑ A maximum length for passwords

C ❑ A standard for password uniqueness

D ❑ A minimum reliance on passwords

6 A user calls complaining that she cannot log into the network. She tried to enter her login and password three times, and then the system would no longer let her login. What could be the reasons for this? (Choose two.)

- A ❑ A network error occured.
- B ❑ The user was entering an incorrect account name or password.
- C ❑ The user's workstation or network connection is faulty.
- D ❑ The user's account was locked out after three tries.
- E ❑ All of the above.

7 The process that converts plain text data into an unreadable form for transmission is called

- A ◯ Bit stripping
- B ◯ Data encryption
- C ◯ Data compression
- D ◯ Data encapsulation

8 Which of the following are commonly used encryption methods? (Choose two.)

- A ❑ NSA
- B ❑ DES
- C ❑ U812
- D ❑ RSA

9 Which of the following best compares user-level and share-level security?

- A ◯ More permission levels are available to users under share-level security.
- B ◯ More devices are available to users under user-level security.
- C ◯ More permission levels are available to users under user-level security.
- D ◯ No difference exists between user-level and share-level security.

10 A(n) _____ is a set of programs running on the network gateway server that filters incoming and outgoing mail for appropriate and allowable destinations. (Choose two.)

- A ❑ Proxy server
- B ❑ Packet filter
- C ❑ Default gateway
- D ❑ Router

Answers

1 *A and C.* You access network resources through either share-level or user-level rights and permissions. On a Windows NT system, you must decide which security model you want to implement. *See "Applying a Security Model."*

2 *C.* To share a device, you must know the share-level password for that resource. *Review "Share-level security model."*

3 *A.* Under user-level security, a list of authorized users indicates the users that have been granted access to a resource. *Check out "User-level security model."*

4 *A, B, and D.* Account policies apply to all network users globally. You do not need to identify individual workstations in the policy. *See "Account Policies."*

5 *A and C.* Some systems have password length maximums, but they aren't typically included in the password policy. *Take a look at "Practicing Safe Passwording."*

6 *B and D.* If an account policy has been established that limits account logins to three tries, the account lockout policy may have been engaged, locking the account to any additional tries. More than likely the account name is good, and the password is wrong. *Review "Account Policies."*

7 *B.* Data encryption uses encryption algorithms and encryption keys to alter transmitted data so that it cannot be intercepted and interpreted. *See "Encrypting Data to Keep Your Secrets."*

8 *B, D.* DES and RSA are commonly used encryption models that use different types of keys and codes to encrypt data transmitted over the Internet. *Check out "The keys to encryption"*

9 *C.* Because user permissions are assigned to individual users, different levels of security and access can be assigned to different users. *Review "User-level security model."*

10 *A and B.* Proxy servers and packet filters are types of firewall implementations. You use a firewall to screen incoming and outgoing messages to prevent unauthorized access to the local network and ensure that local users do not visit unauthorized sites. *See "Hiding Safely Behind the Firewall."*

Part VI
Networking Management

The 5th Wave   By Rich Tennant

"...and Bobby here found a way to extend our data transmission an additional 3000 meters using coax cable. How'd you do that, Bobby—repeaters?"

In this part . . .

To a true network technician, there is no greater enjoyment than designing and installing a new network or network segment. Okay, so there are some things that are more enjoyable, but none that you can do at work, legally. Most administrative duties are routine and repetitive, but working with the configuration, interconnectivity, cabling, and environmental issues of a new network can be challenging.

In this part you discover the actions you must take before you install a network, including hardware, software, and environmental considerations. You also discover the duties performed by the network administrator on an ongoing basis, including documentation, configuration control, network and workstation backups, and applying system upgrades.

Chapter 17

Installing a Network

• •

Exam Objectives

▶ Preparing to install a network

▶ Installing a NOS

▶ Configuring network services

▶ Identifying common peripheral ports and connectors

• •

*Y*ou really don't become a network administrator until you actually install your network. You can have the title and the business cards to prove your status to your friends, but until you prepare the hardware and install the software, what do you have? Nice business cards.

Most of the work installing a network comes before you even begin crimping connectors on the cables; plugging them into NICs, hubs, MAUs, switches, or servers; or even putting the CD-ROM in the drive to install the software. Most of the network installation work comes when you're planning the network, its configuration, components, and services. Every minute that you spend preparing, training, and planning saves you several minutes, perhaps hours, of frustration, troubleshooting, and starting over. In networking, no ingredient is more valuable than planning, except perhaps pizza.

Expect the Network+ test to have around four questions from this area. You should understand the elements of the network that are affected by planning, the basic services of a NOS, and the commonly used device connectors — all of which must be decided before you begin installing a network.

Quick Assessment

Preparing to install a network

1 _____ and _____ accounts, which are created automatically by the NOS, can be used for the initial testing of the network.

2 The _____ of the network is perhaps the most important pre-installation consideration.

3 The _____ and _____ of security are important pre-installation considerations.

4 _____, _____, _____ and _____ should be gathered together before you begin installing the NOS.

Installing a NOS

5 Among others, questions about file storage, virtual memory, and security are asked during installation of the _____.

Configuring network services

6 _____ connects the network protocol to network services and device drivers.

7 Printing services provide network users with access to _____ and _____ printers.

8 A shared folder can be accessed by a(n) _____ name assigned to it.

Identifying common peripheral ports and connectors

9 The three types of SCSI connectors are _____-pin high-density, _____-pin Centronics, and _____-pin DB.

10 The _____ connector is commonly used with UTP media.

Answers

1   *Administrator, user-level.* See "Gathering the facts."

2   *Purpose.* Review "Preparing to Install a Network: The Ultimate Reality Check."

3   *Level, type.* Check out "Preparing to Install a Network: The Ultimate Reality Check."

4   *Supervisor and user accounts, passwords, IP addresses, guidelines and procedures.* Take a look at "Preparing to Install a Network: The Ultimate Reality Check."

5   *NOS.* See "Installing an NOS."

6   *Binding.* Review "Hey, Can I Get Some Services Here?"

7   *Local, remote.* Check out "Hey, Can I Get Some Services Here?"

8   *UNC.* Take a look at "Hey, Can I Get Some Services Here?"

9   *68, 50, 25.* See "Getting Connected."

10   *RJ-45.* Review "Getting Connected."

Preparing to Install a Network: The Ultimate Reality Check

People don't just wake up one day and say to themselves, "What a great day! I think I'll just go install a network! What a great thing to do on such a wonderful day!" Well, at least I wouldn't do that. First of all, you'd need to find a network that needs to be installed, and secondly, you can't install a network on the spur of the moment. I don't mean to be a drag, but networks require some planning.

The network installation process has many important considerations that must be understood and then agreed on before any installation can begin. Some of the more important aspects of the network that must be considered before installation are as follows:

- ✔ **The purpose of the network.** Beyond the basic reason to have a network, what is the purpose of this network? Who does it serve and why? What is the budget? Does the network need to grow? These are the kinds of questions that you need to ask and answer so that your network is designed to serve its intended clients.

- ✔ **The overall size of the network.** Must you segregate departments on the network? Do you need more than one server? Are all the users in one location? How many users are to be connected? Perhaps you need to break up the network into segments and other subnetworks.

- ✔ **The network's topology.** Which type of topology best suits the needs of the organization and its employees? Some topologies are ill-suited for some physical layouts and networks beyond a certain size.

- ✔ **The file system.** How should data files be organized to best serve the needs of the network's users? Is most user access to be interactive or off-line? The file system may very well help answer the NOS questions.

- ✔ **The operating systems on the servers and the clients.** Based on what you know about the way the network is to function, which NOS and client operation system is best for the users' needs, expertise, and training levels? The operating system that is best for the network administrator may not always be best for the network's clients.

- ✔ **The naming convention.** What naming scheme can you use? Is a convention already in use in the company? Is this the time to change or establish the name conventions? Network resources and shared devices must be consistently named for reference purposes.

- ✔ **The level and type of fault tolerance.** How reliable must the network be? If the network is down, how critical is recovery? How long can the network be down before it affects the organization? What safeguards must you use to protect the network's data? Data backups? RAID? You must decide which methods to use to ensure high reliability of the system.

> ✔ **The type and level of security.** Certainly not last, and hardly least, are
> the security issues of the network. What password policies are you to
> use? Who has access to resources? Can outsiders access the network?
> You must work out security policies ahead of time so that they can be
> applied consistently as the network is installed.

Gathering the facts

In addition to the policy decisions that they must make prior to implementing
a network, network administrators must also plan for the testing of the network after it is installed. To plan for the testing of a newly installed network,
you must have an understanding of the key elements of the hardware and
software used to create the network, which are as follows:

> ✔ Administrative accounts and user-level accounts created automatically
> by the NOS. You can use these accounts for initial testing and for logging
> onto the network to perform other testing and to create other test
> accounts.
>
> ✔ The passwords associated with each of the accounts created on the
> system and the process used to add and change administrator, user, and
> guest accounts.
>
> ✔ The IP addresses of key network resources, such as servers, hubs,
> routers, gateways, and so on so that they can be PINGed for connectivity
> testing and tested for compatibility and interoperability.
>
> ✔ Any existing guidelines and operating procedures of the organization
> that prescribe network or system testing and how it is documented.
> Where none exist, creating some may be a good idea. Remember that
> you are likely to need to do all of this again in the future.

In short, you need to gather together everything that you need to test the
network before you install the network. The process that you use to test the
network should include some means to test that the network meets or
exceeds the policies and criteria defined in the planning stage of network
development.

What comes first? The hardware or the NOS?

Which part of the network you should install first is governed by Gilster's
Law of Network Planning: "You never can tell, and it all depends." You never
can tell which part of the network comes first, and you never can tell why it
happens that way. Whether you install all the hardware components of the

network first or install the NOS on the primary server and then add every-thing in a manner similar to decorating a Christmas tree, either way is as right as it is wrong.

My way is to lay out and connect as much of the network hardware as possi-ble so that I can test the cabling for continuity and the connections for compatibility and configure all the routers, switches, firewalls, and such beforehand. Then, when I install the NOS, everything should work like magic. On the other hand, installing the NOS on the primary server first does enable you to test each addition with the system that's driving it.

As I said, it really shouldn't matter which part you install first. What does matter, however, is that you have a plan and that your plan contains all the things you need to systematically install and test your network. Just as in baseball, there's no crying in networks. Planning ahead for your installation prevents that from happening.

Installing a NOS

After you complete planning the network and installing the hardware, installing the actual network software seems kind of anticlimactic. However, you may soon experience some excitement when inevitably one network seg-ment can't see or be seen by the server or, from the it-never-fails department, users scattered about the network cannot login.

During installation, the NOS asks you a number of questions on such diverse topics as file storage, virtual memory, security, and others. If you've prepared sufficiently, you ace this test with flying windows. Whether you're installing Windows NT, NetWare, or another NOS flavor, questions regarding file stor-age, virtual memory, security, and the like come up during the installation.

Before you can install the NOS, the computer hard disk must be prepared in much the same way that any computer is prepared before you install its oper-ating system. Preparing the hard disk involves partitioning and formatting it so that the operating system can use it.

Getting one NOS to talk to another

When installing a NOS, you must plan ahead for the clients to which it must interface — especially when the clients speak totally different protocols. Communication is particularly a problem when you install Windows clients into a Novell NetWare network. This is a problem for two reasons: The first reason is IPX, and the second reason is that it's on the Network+ test. For Windows to communicate with Novell NetWare IPX/SPX, the Client Service for NetWare or perhaps the Gateway Service for NetWare must be installed.

For a Windows client to communicate with NetWare, these protocols must be installed: the Client for Microsoft Networks or the Novell NetWare client, which some adminstrators prefer, and the IPX/SPX Compatible Protocol. Another common problem is that NetWare supports a number of frame types. Often, if a NetWare network is having difficulty communicating with another network, the problem may be incompatible frame types.

Hey, Can I Get Some Services Here?

Within a network operating system (NOS), a variety of network applications exists that on the whole are called the NOS. Without the basic services provided by these applications, a network cannot fulfill its basic purpose — to share resources — or provide the other services usually associated with a network. Two essential services that a NOS must have are printing and file-sharing services.

Following is a list of services and applications that are common in network operating systems:

- **Binding services:** Like the bookbinder adding the cover to a book and binding the pages so they don't fall out, network binding services tie the network's primary protocols to other network services and devices. In using binding services, the most frequently used protocol, such as TCP/IP, IPX, or NetBEUI, is assigned to network devices and drivers.

- **Printing services:** Network printing services enable network users to send documents to any printer on the network and provide spooling services to ensure that documents are printed in turn. Printing services also include printer management, which is comprised of such activities as granting (or restricting) access to printers, monitoring the print queue, and maintaining printer drivers for local and remote printers.

- **Modem and fax services:** Like printers, modems can be shared across the network. Modem services are a built-in component of virtually all NOSs, but fax services that create a shared fax server on the network require the addition of a third-party software application, such as Global Village's FaxWorks Pro or FACSys from Optus Software.

- **Directory sharing services:** Essential network services, directory sharing services enable network users to access and share data that is stored on computers and storage devices located throughout the network. You can share shared network directories — that's folders to you Windows 9x people — including subdirectories and folders. A directory or folder is the lowest structure that you can share. You cannot create a single document as a share. In addition to directories, you can create shares for printers, hard drives, CD-ROM drives, and any addressable device. You designate network shares in the following three ways:

- Mapping the shared directory, commonly called a directory share or just share, to an unused drive letter.

- Assigning a UNC (Universal Naming Convention) name to the share. UNC names are in the format \\COMPUTER\SHARE_NAME.

- Including the directory share in a list of shared resources.

Getting Connected

One of the easiest and yet more complex aspects of installing a network is making sure that you have the correct connectors in place for each of the various types of network ports, devices, and media. Which connectors and ports a particular network uses is subject to Gilster's Law, but nothing can be more frustrating than having your thinnet cabling pulled into place and ready to go and then find out that some idiot, and it wasn't me this time, ordered RJ-45 connectors.

Following is a refresher on the connector and ports that you can expect to see on the Network+ test:

- ✔ **AUI:** This port is a universal connector for Ethernet cabling most commonly used with coaxial cable.

- ✔ **BNC:** Also called a BNC-T connector, BNC is a common thinnet connector (see Figure 17-1).

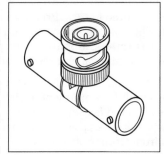

Figure 17-1:
The BNC-T connector is used with 10Base2 networks.

- ✔ **RJ-45:** An eight-wire (four-pair) connector and plug used with UTP (unshielded twisted pair) cabling.

- ✔ **SCSI:** Not really a type of connector or port, SCSI (small computer system interface) is an industry standard for interconnecting peripheral devices. SCSI uses four types of connections (this is on the test!):

  - 68-pin high-density connector (external)

- 50-pin ribbon cable (internal)
- 50-pin Centronics-style connector (external)
- 25-pin DB-25 connector (external)

See Chapter 6 for more detailed coverage of cabling, ports, and connector types.

Prep Test

1 Which of the following are considerations that should be addressed when planning a network (choose four)?

A ☐ Purpose of network

B ☐ User account names

C ☐ Network topology

D ☐ Network operating system

E ☐ Naming conventions

F ☐ Brand and model of user workstations

2 After completing the installation of Windows NT on a server that had been running NetWare, attempts to login to the domain from user workstations fail. What is most likely the cause of this problem?

A ○ The network cabling is incompatible.

B ○ The NIC is incompatible.

C ○ The workstations are not running the correct clients.

D ○ Windows NT is incompatible with the network.

3 Which of the following should be gathered together before you begin the installation of the NOS (choose two)?

A ☐ Supervisor and user level accounts and passwords

B ☐ Standard operating procedures

C ☐ User passwords

D ☐ Hardware MAC addresses

4 Which of the following are important issues that should be decided before the installation of the NOS (choose three)?

A ☐ The type and level of security

B ☐ The type and level of fault tolerance

C ☐ The owner of each user account

D ☐ The color of the Windows desktop wallpaper

5 When binding network protocols to network services, which protocol should be bound first?

A ○ TCP/IP

B ○ NetBIOS

C ○ The least-often-used protocol

D ○ The most-frequently used protocol

6 Which of the following is an example of a UNC share name?

A ○ \\MYCOMPUTER/myfile

B ○ //BOZO/sales/pending_sales

C ○ \\MINNIE\Boyfriends\MICKEY

D ○ $COMPUTER1::FILES

7 For which of the following can a network share be created? (Choose three.)

A ❑ Single documents

B ❑ Printers

C ❑ Disk drive file directory

D ❑ A CD-ROM drive on a remote server

8 The SCSI interface uses three types of connectors. They are: (Choose three)

A ❑ 36-pin Centronics connectors

B ❑ 25-pin DB-25 connectors

C ❑ 50-pin Centronics connectors

D ❑ 68-pin high-density connectors

9 The connector used with UTP Ethernet cabling is the

A ○ RJ-11

B ○ RG-58

C ○ RG-45

D ○ RJ-45

10 The service that assigns network protocols to network services and LAN drivers is

A ○ Binding services

B ○ Printer services

C ○ TCP/IP

D ○ Device management services

Answers

1 *A, C, D, E.* Although the policies that govern the creation of user names and passwords are a part of network preplanning, the actual user names and passwords can be put off until implementation. *See "Preparing to Install a Network: The Ultimate Reality Check."*

2 *C.* Whether NetWare or Windows NT is the NOS, the workstations on the network must have the appropriate clients to interact with the network. *Review "Getting one NOS to talk to another."*

3 *A, B.* To best properly plan the testing of the new system, user and supervisor (administrator) accounts and passwords along with any network operating procedures should be gathered. *Check out "Installing a NOS."*

4 *A, B.* These two considerations plus several others should be addressed before the NOS is installed. *Take a look at "Installing a NOS."*

5 *D.* Binding the most-frequently used protocol speeds up the network's connections. *See "Hey, Can I Get Some Services Here?"*

6 *C.* The Universal Naming Convention is the name of the server/computer and then the share name. Remember that those are backward slashes for Windows. *Review "Hey, Can I Get Some Services Here?"*

7 *B, C, D.* You cannot create network shares below the file directory (folder), but you can assign them to computers and any of their addressable devices. *Check out "Hey, Can I Get Some Services Here?"*

8 *B, C, D.* Remember that the 68-pin high-density connector is not a Centronics and that the 50-pin connector is. DB-25 is also a standard used with serial communications. *Take a look at "Getting Connected."*

9 *D.* You see RJ-11 as an answer choice any time that you see RJ-45; ignore it; RJ-11 is the telephone connector used throughout your home and office. *See "Getting Connected."*

10 *A.* Binding assigns a protocol to a device so that it knows which protocol to use for connections. *Review "Hey, Can I Get Some Services Here?"*

Chapter 18

The Network and the Environment

. . . .

Exam Objectives

▶ Identifying network environmental factors

▶ Avoiding power problems

*T*he computer is an essential tool for any job or task and, unfortunately, in any environment. To be of service, a computer must be readily accessible, no matter what the situation or conditions. You've probably heard or read horror stories about computers that have operated under some extreme conditions: the computer from the manufacturing floor filled with grease and gunk; the computer from the school classroom choked by chalk dust; and the computer that wore tennis shoes (oops, wrong problem!). Needless to say, a computer's environment can have a definite effect on how well the computer operates.

The worst kind of computer problem is one that is intermittent. Most environment-related problems are intermittent. Therefore, logic tells us that environment-related problems are the worst kind of problems. Okay, maybe they're not as bad as losing the entire RAID drive, but they are still serious problems to have on a network. With an intermittent problem, a computer works fine one minute, and the next minute it reboots itself, freezes up, or shuts down completely. Having a workstation on a network that has an intermittent problem can be a real headache, especially if the network is the host of some frequently accessed shared resources. Having a network server with an environmentally induced intermittent problem is sheer terror.

Electrical power is the cause of most environment-related computer problems. The challenge of every network technician and administrator is to ensure that a clean and constant source of power is available for network devices at all times.

So what do environment-related problems have to do with the Network+ test? Included on the test are at least three questions that directly relate to computer problems caused by the environment, as well as a smattering of other questions that reference power and power-conditioning-equipment terminology.

Quick Assessment

Identifying network environmental factors

1 The number-one environmental threat to networks is from _____.

2 _____ is caused by other electrical equipment and can be a problem for computers on the same circuit as *noisy* equipment.

3 You should keep the humidity around computer equipment at about _____ percent.

4 When the air is too dry, you face an increased threat of _____.

Avoiding power problems

5 An ESD of _____ volts can destroy a computer circuit.

6 A _____ absorbs electrical spikes by smoothing out EMI noise.

7 A device's capability to absorb energy is measured in _____.

8 A _____ filters the power stream to eliminate line noise.

9 The device that provides a constant power stream to equipment that's plugged into it is a(n) _____.

10 A(n) _____ provides power when none is available, but it does not provide line conditioning.

Answers

1 *Electrical power.* See "Pop machines, heaters, and other power monsters: A pop quiz."

2 *EMI (electromagnetic interference).* Review "Other electrical threats."

3 *50.* Check out "Striking a balance with nature."

4 *Static electricity or ESD (electrostatic discharge).* Take a look at "Don't give me any static."

5 *30.* Look over "Don't give me any static."

6 *Surge suppressor.* See "Suppressing the surge."

7 *Joules.* Review "Suppressing the surge."

8 *Line conditioner.* Check out "Conditioning the line."

9 *UPS (uninterruptable power supply).* Take a look at "May the flow be with you."

10 *SPS (standby power supply).* Look over "May the flow be with you."

Protecting the Network from the Environment

If you've been a network administrator for any time at all, you're likely to have become paranoid with all the threats your network faces physically and logically every minute of every day. Viruses, weather, construction, and users are just some of the threats you must grapple with every day.

Soda-pop machines, heaters, and other power monsters: A pop quiz

The Network+ test and I agree that power problems are probably the number-one environmental threat to networks. The very same people who depend on the network — the network users — create most of these problems. Most users never consider that their computers must have a smooth, eventless (free of spikes and brownouts) supply of electricity.

In the winter, every desk in the office suddenly has a small space heater under it, plugged carelessly into the same sockets as the network worksta-tions. In the summer, the heaters give way to oscillating fans or, worse, room-sized air conditioners. Perhaps I'm being too hard on the users. The problem could be that the building is just not wired very well. Consider each of the following scenarios:

1. A computer workstation works just fine during daylight hours when ample sunlight fills the room. However, in the late afternoon, when the room is in the shadows and the lights are turned on, the computer begins to lock up and frequently reboots itself.

2. A new lunchroom has been added to the building not far from the com-puter room in the Information Technology department, much to the delight of the IT personnel. Everyone is quite pleased with the newer and bigger vending machines, microwave ovens, and change machines placed in the new facility. About the time that the new lunchroom opened, the network administrator began experiencing a series of small problems, such as the alarm on the server's UPS sounding, especially on warmer days. Lately, larger problems, such as the server rebooting or locking up, are increasing in frequency.

3. Sally, in the billing department (which is located in the basement of the main building), called to report that her computer and those of her coworkers have started experiencing strange problems over the past week. Sometimes they lock up, other times they just restart themselves, and on still other occasions, they lose their network connections. The strange part is that the problems seem to occur only in the morning.

After lunch each day, the problems seem to go away. In the course of the conversation, Sally also joked about how cold it has been down in their "hole" and how everyone would be frozen stiff had they not brought in portable heaters. During your initial inspection of the area, you find that the heaters are all plugged into the surge-suppressor plug strips provided for the computers.

What do you suppose is the problem in each of these cases? Here's what I think is the problem (I have very special insight, because I made them all up):

1. When the room lights are turned on, the outlet that the computer is plugged into experiences a low-voltage situation, which shows up as problems on the computer. You should move the computer to a different electrical circuit, preferably one that it doesn't share with other devices. If moving the computer to a different circuit is not possible, protect the computer with a line-conditioning UPS (uninterruptable power supply — see "Protecting Against Power Evils," later in this chapter).

2. Very likely an error was made during construction, and some or all of the equipment in the new lunchroom is sharing the circuits used by the computer room. A single soda-pop vending machine alone can create a low-voltage problem or place a heap of EMI (electromagnetic interference) on the line or both, which gives any other electrical equipment, including the UPS and network server, serious power-related problems. You must isolate and correctly ground the power circuits for the computer room and install serious UPS protection.

3. It probably never occurred to the billing department folks that those heaters are voltage hogs, especially when they're plugged into the same outlets as computers. The employees are probably using the computers only in the mornings, which explains the strangeness of when the problems are happening. The real problem may be with the heating and ventilation system. If you can't correct that, you must install some form of power conditioning. Have you ever noticed how old buildings and computers don't mix?

Other electrical threats

Any electrical equipment that you place on the same circuit as your network equipment poses a potential problem. This equipment includes such innocent items as radios, pencil sharpeners, clocks, lava lamps, beer signs, or other electrical stuff that you may have in your work area. Although these devices use voltage and can cause a low-voltage condition, the real threat is from EMI (electromagnetic interference). Most electrical devices produce EMI, also called line noise, in one form or another. I remember what my mom's vacuum cleaner would do to the television when I was a kid and what the power lines did to the AM radio in my dad's DeSoto.

The electrical power lines can carry EMI, and a computer receives EMI as a spike or voltage drop. One such incident probably doesn't hurt the computer, but a constant bombardment of EMI eventually takes its toll. Each EMI incident probably does only a small amount of damage to the computer's electrical circuits (power supply, motherboard, expansion cards, and so on). However, in time, these small dings amount to a major dong, and your computer begins to have intermittent problems or the nearly-impossible-to-find kind.

The safest thing to do, if possible, is to isolate the computers and other devices of the network on separate and unshared electrical circuits that are all grounded straight into the earth. If the building in which the network is located can accommodate this setup, and few can, you should have few power-related problems. I discuss other ways to protect your network later in "Protecting Against Power Evils."

It isn't the heat; it's the humidity

Computers and humans can tolerate about the same temperatures and humidity levels, although computers prefer colder temperatures a little more than most humans do. The rule of thumb is that if *you* can stand it, the computer is usually very comfortable.

On the other hand, humidity, combined with the air temperature, can pose a threat to a computer or other networking devices. Too much humidity or too little humidity can both be problems. Too much humidity — even a light fog — can cause water, which conducts electricity, to condense on electronic components and play electrical havoc with them. Hard disk drives are especially susceptible to high humidity. However, if the air is too dry, and the air is also warm, your system faces an increased threat of damage due to electrostatic discharge (ESD).

If you can't see the computer from across the room, or if a blue bolt of ESD shoots up your arm when you touch the door knob, you probably need to take steps to control the environment in the computer's room. The goal is to keep the humidity and temperature in balance. The humidity should be around 50 percent, and the temperature should be as much on the cool side as the humans can stand.

Don't give me any static!

Static electricity is what makes your hair stand on end when you rub a balloon against your head. Of course, this explanation assumes that you have hair — and that you'd have occasion to rub a balloon against your head. Static electricity may occur when you walk across a carpet that has not been treated to be nonstatic. Static electricity is a natural phenomenon that can develop when the temperature is warm and the humidity is low. These conditions are also favorable for electrical storms and thunderstorms, which can also increase the static-electricity levels around the network.

Static electricity by itself isn't a problem; it's a fact of nature. The potential damage caused by its discharge is where problems lurk. You know — when you reach for the doorknob and zap! A blue spark as big as a anchor chain jumps from your finger to the metal. Although it may seem harmless (other than the pain), that spark can cause serious damage to a computer.

Following are some ESD facts:

- Most of the computer's electronic components use from 3 to 5 volts of electricity.
- A 30-volt ESD shock can destroy a computer circuit.
- An ESD shock that you can *feel,* such as on a doorknob, has around 3,000 volts.
- An ESD shock that you can *see* carries about 20,000 volts.

You can avoid static electricity. Good environmental preventative measures that help to eliminate, or at least reduce, static electricity are as follows:

- **Treat carpeting inexpensively with antistatic chemicals to reduce static buildup.** You can find these chemicals in aerosol cans in most computer or carpet stores.
- **Install a grounded pad under each computer.** Before you touch the computer, touch the pad, and discharge any built-up static electricity.
- **If all else fails, install humidifiers to replace the moisture in the air.** Dry air can cause static electricity.

Airborne uglies

Other environmental hazards that you need to safeguard your network's computers from are dust, smoke, and other airborne flotsam and jetsam. Never smoke tobacco or other plants (I suppose broccoli is okay) around computers and networking hardware. The tars and resins in the smoke can really gum up the works. You should also protect your network's equipment from dust, industrial oversprays, and other airborne contaminants.

You don't want to know the damage that the vaporized oil in a fried-chicken fast-food restaurant can do to computers and a proxy server. I have also seen what three years of chalk dust can do to a computer fan and motherboard. That scene was horrible, and the computer was located where children could see it. Is there no shame?

In areas that have airborne contaminants, you should install special air filters to protect the computers and connectivity devices of the network. Either do that or move the networking equipment.

Protecting Against Power Evils

Certainly you can fight back against the evils of external power somewhat. In fact, several levels of protection exist, ranging from none to too much, that you can use to protect your computer system from power problems. The level of protection depends on how much you want to spend, with costs ranging up to thousands of dollars.

At least one question, maybe two, on the Network+ test inquires about the use of UPS (uninterruptable power supply), power conditioners, and surge-suppressor devices. The exam has very few trick questions, but one question that you may want to watch for asks, "Which of these devices provide surge suppression?" The answer is that almost all these devices provide surge suppression, and that's the answer on the test, too.

Suppressing the surge

Most user workstations are plugged into a surge-suppressor power strip. These devices, which provide protective levels ranging from psychological to pretty good, are generally inexpensive and readily available. At the psychological level are the less-than-$10 power strips, which are not much more than glorified extension cords. At the pretty-good level are full surge suppressors that also include line conditioning, which weigh-in between $25 and $45.

A surge suppressor reduces power problems by absorbing spikes and surges and by smoothing out EMI noise (which is called line conditioning). High-end surge suppressors offer more protection, but some protection is always better than none. Unfortunately, how much protection you have really depends on how much you pay.

Here are some other things to look for (familiarize yourself with the units of measures — Joules, decibels, and watts — used in the following descriptions):

✔ **Energy absorption (Joules):** Surge suppressors are rated in Joules, which measures their capability to absorb energy. The higher the rating, the better the protection: 200 Joules provide basic protection, 400 give good protection, and 600 offer superior protection. You need to be familiar with Joules for the test.

✔ **Line conditioning (decibels):** A surge suppressor's line-conditioning capability is measured in decibels. The more decibels of noise reduction, the better the line conditioning.

✔ **Levels of protection (watts):** Surge suppressors have three levels of protection that indicate the maximum number of watts that you can pass through the suppressor to anything plugged into it. The standard ratings are 330 (best), 400 (better), and 500 (good).

Conditioning the line

Line conditioners filter the power stream to eliminate line noise. They have some power in reserve and smooth the power signal to keep it within normal operating levels. They absorb power spikes and fill in low-voltage conditions. Line conditioners, also called power conditioners, are usually expensive, and as a result, very few networks have true line conditioners. The less-expensive alternatives, UPS units and high-end surge suppressors, can provide the level of line conditioning needed at a much lower price.

May the flow be with you

An uninterruptable power supply (UPS) tries to live up to its name by providing a constant (uninterrupted) power stream to the computer. Under normal operating conditions, a UPS is a surge protector that can also handle brownout (low-voltage) conditions. After the power drops below a certain voltage or is cut off completely, the UPS kicks in and provides power for a certain number of minutes — or even hours in some cases.

Two types of UPS units are available: standby and in-line. All UPS units have two sets of circuits. One side is the AC circuit that, in effect, is an expensive surge suppressor. The other side is the battery and DC to AC conversion. Yes, that's right — DC to AC conversion. The batteries store a DC charge that must be converted to AC because that's what the PC expects.

The standby and in-line differ in the following ways:

✔ **The standby UPS operates normally from its AC side.** When the power drops, the standby UPS switches over to its battery (DC) backup side.

✔ **The in-line UPS operates normally from its DC or battery backup side.** The AC side is used only in the event of a problem with the battery-powered circuits.

UPS units are often confused with a standby power supply (SPS) or battery backup (which supplies power only when none is available and has no power-conditioning capabilities). This information is on the test!

Prep Test

1 A device that can supply backup power to a PC when the electricity fails as well as provide for line conditioning is called a(n)

A ○ SPS

B ○ UPS

C ○ Surge suppressor

D ○ Line conditioner

2 A device that protects a computer against power spikes is called a

A ○ UPS

B ○ Power conditioner

C ○ Surge suppressor

D ○ All of the above

3 What are the two types of uninterruptable power supplies?

A ○ Standby and interactive

B ○ In-line and out-line

C ○ Standby and in-line

D ○ In-line and interactive

4 A computer workstation doesn't function correctly when the room lights are turned on. What would you suspect to be the problem?

A ○ The lights create a low-voltage situation.

B ○ The computer's power supply is faulty.

C ○ The internal power connections are loose.

D ○ The computer's power cord is loose.

5 A network workstation located in the basement of the main building is having difficulty logging onto the network and on occasion reboots itself or drops the network connection. You investigate and find that a space heater is plugged into the same power outlet as the computer. What do you suspect to be the source of this problem?

A ○ The electrical outlet is faulty.

B ○ The heater is creating a low-voltage situation.

C ○ The capacitor in the computer's power supply is faulty.

D ○ The NIC is faulty.

6 Which of the following conditions are conducive to the creation of static electricity? (Choose all that apply.)

A ❑ Untreated carpet fibers
B ❑ Humidity levels higher than 60 percent
C ❑ Humidity levels lower than 40 percent
D ❑ Thunderstorms

7 Which of the following are measurements used with surge suppression and line conditioning? (Choose three.)

A ❑ Joules
B ❑ Watts
C ❑ Jaggers
D ❑ Decibels

8 Which of the following devices can provide power line conditioning capabilities? (Choose two.)

A ❑ SPS
B ❑ UPS
C ❑ Surge suppressor
D ❑ Plug strip

9 The power device that is often called a battery backup is the

A ○ UPS
B ○ SPS
C ○ Power conditioner
D ○ BBPS

10 Environmental elements that can pose a threat to network computers and connectivity devices are? (Choose all that apply.):

A ❑ Cigarette smoke
B ❑ Fog
C ❑ Static electricity
D ❑ Heat
E ❑ Airborne contaminants

Answers

1 *B.* A battery backup supplies only backup electricity. A surge suppressor provides line-conditioning protection as does a true line conditioner. The uninterruptable power supply (UPS) does both. *See "May the flow be with you."*

2 *C.* All of these devices provide some level of surge suppression, and I told you watch for trick questions about this. However, the best answer is a surge suppressor, which absorbs the spike and prevents it from damaging your computer. *Review "Suppressing the surge."*

3 *C.* The standby UPS (aka SPS) is like a big surge suppressor with a battery backup; the in-line UPS is a big self-charging battery that runs your computer with an emergency AC line, just in case. *Check out "May the flow be with you."*

4 *A.* Anytime a computer problem coincides with a change in the usage or addition of an electrical device or fixture, you can bet that the cause is related to that usage or addition. *Take a look at "Pop machines, heaters, and other power monsters: A pop quiz."*

5 *B.* Appliances such as heaters, refrigerators, and air conditioners produce more than enough EMI to give a computer problems if placed on the same circuit. *See "Pop machines, heaters, and other power monsters: A pop quiz."*

6 *A, C, D.* Of these conditions, only A and C are under your control. However, a good idea is not to operate your network during an electrical storm. *Review "Eliminating static electricity."*

7 *A, B, D.* Of course you know that a Jagger is not a measurement, but the Network+ test references the other units of measure (Joules, watts, and decibels). *Check out "Suppressing the surge."*

8 *B, C.* Only better surge suppressors provide line conditioning, but nearly all UPS units do. Plug strips are good for Christmas trees and associated house lights. *Take a look at "Conditioning the line."*

9 *B.* An SPS (standby power supply) provides only a battery backup with no line-conditioning services. *See "May the flow be with you."*

10 *A, B, C, D, E.* Okay, *all of the above* should have been a choice, but I wanted you to consider each choice separately. All of these things, and more, are certainly environmental threats to a network, but as the network administrator, you already knew that. *Review the entire "Protecting the Network from the Environment" section.*

Chapter 19

Network Administration

● ●

Exam Objectives

▶ Implementing configuration control procedures

▶ Using drive mapping

▶ Using printer port capturing

▶ Defining common network administration elements

● ●

*T*he overriding principle to network administration is consistency. I don't go so far as to say the *S*-word (standardization), but the network administrators' jobs are much easier if they know consistently what the configuration of a workstation is and should be.

The network administrator can and must use certain procedures, processes, commands, and records to maintain and control the configuration of the network and its workstations. The combination of tools that each network administrator uses varies with the size, complexity, and maturity of the network itself.

On the Network+ test, expect to see questions that deal with network and workstation configuration tracking, drive mapping, and working directly with printer ports. In addition, you should have a good understanding of the major network concepts and terminology that relate directly to the configuration, maintenance, and control tasks performed by the network administrator.

Don't get too hung up on the overall job of the network administrator. What you actually need to know for the test is what the words mean, the actions used to accomplish a management task, and when each is used and why. You see only about four questions on the entire test that deal with any or all of the activities involved with network administration. Having a strong network vocabulary and a solid grasp of concepts is the best way to prepare for this area of the test.

Quick Assessment

Implementing configuration control procedures

1 Group and user management tools used by Windows NT and NetWare respectively are _____ and _____.

2 Three utilities that can be used to display a workstation's configuration are _____, _____, and _____.

Using drive mapping

3 Mapping a network resource assigns a _____ to the resource so that a workstation can reference that resource directly.

4 Mapping a drive in NetWare uses the _____ command.

Using printer port capturing

5 Capturing a printer port enables _____ applications to print on network printers.

6 On a Windows system, you perform a printer port capture in the _____ properties window.

7 On a NetWare system, you use the _____ command to capture a printer port.

Defining common network administration elements

8 Full, incremental, and differential are three types of _____ used on a network.

9 Desktop settings, colors, icons, and program groups are among the information established in a user's _____.

10 The two security levels used on networks are _____ and _____.

Answers

1 *User Manager for Domains, SYSCON or NWADMIN.* See "Collecting the configuration."

2 *NetWare CONFIG, TCP/IP IPCONFIG, WINIPCFG.* Review "Collecting the configuration."

3 *Local drive letter.* Check out "Mapping a Network Drive."

4 *MAP.* Take a look at "Mapping a drive in NetWare."

5 *Legacy.* See "It's My Party, and I'll Print Where I Want To."

6 *Printer.* Review "Capturing the printer port."

7 *CAPTURE.* Check out "Capturing a NetWare printer port."

8 *Backups.* Take a look at "Ten Network Administration Terms You Should Know for the Test."

9 *Profile.* See "Ten Network Administration Terms You Should Know for the Test."

10 *User-level, share-level.* Review "Ten Network Administration Terms You Should Know for the Test."

Controlling the Configuration and Configuring the Controls

Why it never occurs to network administrators to keep records on the configurations of the network servers and workstations within their kingdom and domain is beyond me. The more that you know about a network's configuration, the easier it is to maintain, troubleshoot, and support than if you must guess each time that a problem arises just what each workstation holds.

Collecting the configuration

Although generally thought of as troubleshooting tools, a number of NOS and TCP/IP utilities enable you to collect and monitor the configuration of network servers and workstations. I cover most of these same tools in more detail in Chapter 14.

Following are some configuration tools that you can use:

✔ **Group and user tools**: Windows NT has the User Manager for Domains and NetWare has its NWADMIN (versions 4.*x* and 5) and SYSCON (versions 3.*x* and earlier). These tools enable you to display user and group access rights and permissions.

✔ **NetWare CONFIG system console command:** Although this command sounds like what you would use to configure NetWare, it actually shows you only the configuration of the system. It displays the installed LAN drivers, the server's network ID, the protocols in use, the types of packets in use, and more. If you need to know the configuration of a NetWare server, this is your tool.

✔ **TCP/IP IPCONFIG:** You use this command to display the Internet Protocol configuration of a server or workstation, including the host name, DNS (Domain Name Server) servers, node type, MAC (Media Access Control) address, DHCP (Dynamic Host Control Protocol) status, IP address, subnet mask, and default IP gateway of a network node.

✔ **Windows WINIPCFG:** Included with Windows 95, 98, and NT, this utility is the Windows equivalent of IPCONFIG. It displays a workstation's IP address, subnet mask, and default gateway. Lab 19-1 details the steps that you follow to use WINIPCFG to display a workstation's configuration data.

Lab 19-1   Displaying a Windows 95/98 Workstation's IP Configuration

1. **Click the Start button and then click Run.**

2. **Type** WINIPCFG **in the Open box and then click OK.**

   The current TCP/IP settings for the workstation appear. To view additional information, click the More Info button.

3. **If your IP address was dynamically allocated by a Dynamic Host Control Protocol (DHCP) server, you can use the Release and Renew buttons to release and renew the IP address.**

Mapping a Network Drive

When a workstation logs on to the network, its local drives are already set. More than likely, the workstation's floppy disk drive is assigned to drive A and its hard disk drive to drive C. Mapping a network resource completes this action by assigning F, H, M, or Z to the resource so that it can be readily referenced from the workstation. The mapped resource may be a server logical drive, a share folder or directory, a shared CD-ROM drive, or whatever.

If you create a drive map, a pointer to a file system location is assigned a letter, which is assigned to a directory path. For example, if you map the local drive F to the directory \\NT1\ACCTS\RECEIVE, you can access this directory on the workstation where the drive mapping was created by referring to drive F.

Lab 19-2 shows you how to map a network drive on a Windows workstation.

Lab 19-2   Mapping a Network Drive on a Windows Workstation

1. **On the Windows desktop, right-click the Network Neighborhood icon.**

2. **Choose Map Network Drive from the pop-up menu.**

   A Map Network Drive dialog box appears.

3. **In the top section of the Map Network Drive dialog box, select a drive letter; in the bottom section of the dialog box, select a path to assign to the drive letter.**

4. **Select the Reconnect at Logon check box to ensure that this drive path is mapped whenever the workstation is logged on.**

5. **Click OK.**

In Novell NetWare, you can map a drive from a DOS or Windows workstation by executing the NetWare MAP command from the command prompt, from within a login script, or from a batch file. A NetWare MAP command looks like this:

```
MAP F:=SYS:WINAPPS\POPART
```

The directory WINAPPS\POPART on the server volume SYS is mapped to the local logical F drive. If the login script of the user or the workstation includes this command, this mapping takes place each time the script is run. I guess this could be called a drive-by mapping.

It's My Party, and I'll Print Where I Want To

You can expect to see a question on capturing a printer port on the Network+ test, but explaining this concept is difficult without contrasting it to printer shares. On most networks, you can print to a network printer as long as the printer has been set up correctly as a shared resource or network printer. You can direct a print job to a network printer in one of two ways: by capturing a printer port or by choosing a network printer by its share name to use as your default printer. These are different and exclusive actions.

Okay, I'll capture the port, but why?

Most of the common application software programs and suites are designed to work with network printing services. For example, word-processing software, such as WordPerfect or MS Word, submit their print jobs directly to the print queue of the default printer or another designated printer. These applications specify what the printer needs to know to produce the document, including the fonts, page setup, number of copies, and the necessary print driver (control sequences, functions, and so on). This type of application doesn't need support from the network print utilities built into the NOS.

Some legacy applications, however, aren't designed for network printing. For these programs, the NOS includes special command-line utilities or function properties to enable them to print on network printers. In NetWare, printer ports are captured with the CAPTURE command, and in Windows NT, the printer port is captured though printer port settings. These tools set up a redirection that sends a workstation's print output to a network printer or file.

Capturing the printer port

Although it may sound like something you do in a game of *Stratego* or *Battleship*, what capturing a printer port really involves is redirecting print sent to a workstation LPT port directly to a specific network printer. In other words, the print-data stream sent to one of a computer's LPT ports is captured and redirected to a network printer or file.

Lab 19-3 illustrates how a printer port is captured in Windows.

Lab 19-3   Capturing a Windows Printer Port

1. **Click the Start button and choose Settings⇨Printers.**

2. **Right-click the icon of the local printer that you want to redirect.**

3. **Choose Properties from the pop-up menu.**

4. **On the Properties window, click the Details tab.**

5. **Click the Capture Printer Port button.**

   You should find the Capture Printer Port and End Capture buttons about two-thirds of the way down the window. The Capture Printer Port window appears.

6. **In the Capture Printer Port window, verify that the device name is in the Device text box and then select or enter the network printer path that you want to use in the Path text box.**

7. **Make sure that the Reconnect at Logon check box is selected so that the printer port capture is reconnected after the workstation is logged on.**

8. **Click all the necessary OKs to set the new settings and close the Printers window.**

Should you want to cancel the port capture, use the End Capture button mentioned in Step 5 — but you probably figured that out already.

Capturing a NetWare printer port

The NetWare CAPTURE command is a command-line utility that you use to capture a printer port for a program or application that cannot use network printer services. To print from a non-NetWare-compatible application or to print directly from the monitor screen of a workstation, the print file must be rerouted from the local LPT printer port to a file server queue.

Lab 19-4 lists the steps that you follow to add a CAPTURE command to the user login script (the equivalent of the Reconnect at Logon check box in Windows).

Lab 19-4	Capturing a Printer Port in NetWare

1. **Enter** SYSCON **on the NetWare command line.**

2. **Select User Information from the SYSCON menu.**

3. **Select the username to be affected by the CAPTURE command.**

4. **Select Login Script.**

5. **Insert the following command into the login script:**

   ```
   #CAPTURE Q=name of printer queue
   ```

6. **Exit SYSCON and save the changes.**

7. **Have the user reboot the workstation to put the CAPTURE command into effect.**

You use the ENDCAP command to cancel the CAPTURE setting, much as you use the End Capture button in Windows.

Ten Network Administration Terms You Should Know for the Test

Although I mention them throughout the book, following are 10+ network administrator terms and concepts that you should know for the Network+ test:

✔ **Backups:** You see three different types of backups on the test:

- **Full (archive) backup:** Everything is backed up, and each file's archive bit is reset to off.

- **Incremental backup:** Everything that has changed since the last full or incremental backup is backed up, and the archive bit of each backed-up file is reset off.

- **Differential backup:** Everything that has changed since the last full or incremental backup is backed up, but the archive bits aren't affected.

✔ **System and node upgrades:** You should make software and hardware upgrades carefully and cautiously. Changes to the server or nodes can directly affect the entire network's performance.

✔ **Drive mapping:** Enables a user to relate to a shared network resource or remote device as a local resource referenced by a drive letter.

✔ **Universal Naming Convention (UNC):** The convention used to name resource components, such as \\SERVER_NAME\SHARE_NAME.

✔ **Profiles:** Pre-established screen, application, and file access permissions and rights. Profiles are assigned as local (a user at a particular workstation) or as roaming (a user who may login from multiple workstations).

✔ **Login account:** Also called a *username*, this value, along with a password, identifies the user to the system.

✔ **Groups:** Used to amalgamate multiple users with the same profiles and access rights. Maintaining a group of user accounts is much easier than maintaining individual user accounts with similar rights.

✔ **Shared resources:** Network resources — such as printers, disk drives, and local directories and resources — can be shared with network users via a share name or pathname.

✔ **Password:** Used to complete the unique identification of a user. The password is the key element in network security systems.

✔ **Security level:** Two security levels are used in networks:

  • **User-level security:** Assigns access to a shared resource to any user who knows the password.

  • **Share-level security:** Gives access to a shared resource on a user-by-user assignment made by the resource's owner.

Prep Test

1 To create a shared resource on a NetWare system, you use

A ○ NetWare Explorer

B ○ NWADMIN

C ○ NDS

D ○ SYSCON

2 Which of the following tools are used on either a Windows NT or NetWare network to manage network user accounts and groups? (Choose three.)

A ❑ User Manager for Domains

B ❑ NDS

C ❑ NWADMIN

D ❑ SYSCON

3 Which of the following are types of backups commonly used on network servers and workstations? (Choose three.)

A ❑ Incremental

B ❑ Differential

C ❑ Progressive

D ❑ Full

4 The TCP/IP utility used to display the TCP/IP configuration of a Windows NT server or workstation is

A ○ NETSTAT

B ○ IPCONFIG

C ○ NBTSTAT

D ○ WINIPCFG

5 The Windows utility used to display the TCP/IP configuration of a Windows 9*x* workstation is

A ○ NBTSTAT

B ○ IPCONFIG

C ○ WINIPCFG

D ○ NetBIOS

6 Which of the following is a valid example of a UNC name on a Windows NT Server?

A ○ // SERVER/SHARE

B ○\\SERVER\SHARE

C ○ //SHARE/SERVER

D ○ \\SHARE\SERVER

7 You find the Map Network Drive option through which Windows NT desktop option?

A ○ My Computer

B ○ Control Panel

C ○ Settings⇨Printers

D ○ Network Neighborhood

8 The NetWare commands used to capture and release a printer port are

A ○ CAPTURE/RELEASE

B ○ CAPPORT/ENDCAP

C ○ CAPTURE/ENDCAP

D ○ CAPPORT/RELEASE

9 You set up a share name for a network printer and assign it a password. Which type of security is in use?

A ○ Share-level security

B ○ Network-level security.

C ○ User-level security.

D ○ Device-level security.

10 The process of assigning a local drive letter to a network resource is called

A ○ Capturing a printer port

B ○ Mapping a printer port

C ○ Mapping a drive

D ○ Creating a network share

Answers

1 *C.* You use NetWare's NWADMIN on Novell NetWare systems to create resource shares. *See "The administrator's toolbelt."*

2 *A, C, D.* You do not use NDS to manage user or group accounts, but you do use each of the other three. For the Network+ test, remember the Windows tool (User Manager for Domains) and NetWare tools (SYSCON or NWADMIN) used to create and manage users and groups. *Review "The administrator's toolbelt."*

3 *A, B, D.* Incremental backups are often used between full backups. Differential backups are used to back up files between incremental or full backups. *Check out "Ten Network Administration Terms You Should Know for the Test."*

4 *B.* You can use IPCONFIG to display the TCP/IP configuration of an *NT* workstation or server for documentation purposes. *Take a look at "Collecting the configuration."*

5 *C.* WINIPCFG is the Windows equivalent of the TCP/IP IPCONFIG command. You can use it in conjunction with IPCONFIG to display a workstation's configuration for documentation purposes. *See "Collecting the configuration."*

6 *B.* UNC names follow a prescribed convention. Windows NT uses the UNC convention, whereas NetWare uses a slightly different format. *Review "Ten Network Administration Terms You Should Know for the Test."*

7 *D.* Choosing this option displays the Map Network Drive dialog box, which is used to assign a drive letter to a network resource or pathname. *Check out "Mapping a Network Drive."*

8 *C.* You use CAPTURE to redirect to a network printer queue the print file sent to an LPT port, and use ENDCAP to cancel the port capture. *Take a look at "Capturing a NetWare printer port."*

9 *A.* On the Network+ test, you're asked to differentiate user-level and share-level security models. User-level permissions, popular in larger organizations are commonly used at the login level, and share-level at the resource level. *See "Ten Network Administration Terms You Should Know for the Test."*

10 *C.* Mapping a network drive, actually. *Review "Mapping a Network Drive."*

Part VII

Maintaining and Supporting the Network

The 5th Wave   By Rich Tennant

"It's okay. One of the routers must have gone down and we had a brief broadcast storm."

In this part . . .

A network is made up of computers and peripheral devices. From time to time, computers and peripheral devices do malfunction or breakdown. This means that a significant portion of a network technician's responsibilities involve maintaining the network and diagnosing and troubleshooting its failures.

For the Network+ exam, you must know the common maintenance and preventive maintenance procedures used to ensure the network operates efficiently and effectively. Performing vendor upgrades, creating data backups, and dealing with computer viruses are among these procedures, which this part covers.

You must also have an understanding of the procedures used to troubleshoot and diagnose network problems. This includes knowledge of how to apply a systematic approach to identifying the extent and seriousness of a network problem and the ramifications of changes made at the server or client on the whole network. You should also know the hardware and software tools that can be used to troubleshoot network problems.

Chapter 20

Maintaining the Network

· ·

Exam Objectives

▶ Developing a system maintenance policy

▶ Documenting the network

▶ Applying vendor upgrades

▶ Backing up the system

▶ Explaining the need for antivirus software on a network

· ·

*A*ll network administrators must learn to take the good with the bad and the fun stuff with the boring stuff. Nothing's better than the thrill of setting up a new network or installing a new router to create some new network segments. Or the chills you get from creating a backup domain controller or adding accounts from a trusted server. The point is that you can do some interesting things as a network administrator, but network maintenance is not one of them. Make no mistake; although it may not be a thrill a minute, the maintenance part of the network management job is every bit as important as all the fun stuff you can do. Keeping the network operating system up-to-date; applying software patches and fixes; backing up the data, files, and programs stored on the network; and protecting the system from the likes of Melissa, Ethan, and their virus pals are all extremely important tasks to the integrity, reliability, and functionality of the network.

Six percent of the Network+ exam is devoted to questions that relate to the policies and activities used to control the frequency, process, and application of network maintenance issues. You should be ready to demonstrate your understanding of the considerations, tasks, and actions that must be applied to maintain an operating network. The good news is that if you have worked with a network server, and especially the network operating system, you most likely have firsthand experience. The better news is that most of this stuff is just common sense anyway.

Even if your title is network software update and upgrade, system backup, and effective antivirus campaign supervisor, you need to review this chapter to be sure of the terminology and process used on the Network+ exam. The way you do things may not be the basis for the questions on the test.

Quick Assessment

Developing a system maintenance policy

1   Network maintenance should be performed according to a _____.

Documenting the network

2   _____ ensures a written record of the network's past and present.

Applying vendor upgrades

3   Before applying a vendor's software upgrade, you should first _____.

4   Three good sources for finding vendor product information are _____, _____, and _____.

Backing up the system

5   The type of backup that captures everything on the system and marks it as being archived is a _____ backup.

6   A _____ backup captures only those files that have changed since they were last backed up and marks those files as being archived.

7   _____ is the favorite backup media in use.

8   The three most common forms of magnetic tape media are _____, _____, and _____.

Explaining the need for antivirus software on a network

9   A virus that can hide its damage and itself so that all appears normal is a(n) _____ virus.

10 The general name of the software used to find and clean files infested with a virus is _____.

Answers

1 *Network maintenance policy.* See "Developing a Network Maintenance Policy."

2 *Documenting the network.* Review "Documenting the Network."

3 *Among other things, back up the system.* Check out "Change can be a good thing."

4 *Product documentation; vendor-related newsletters, listservs, and newsgroups; vendor Web sites.* Take a look at "Sources for vendor information."

5 *Full.* See "Deciding the backup type."

6 *Incremental.* Review "Deciding the backup type."

7 *Magnetic tape.* Check out "Choosing the backup media."

8 *DLT, DAT, QIC.* Take a look at "Choosing the backup media."

9 *Polymorphing or stealth.* See "Playing hide and seek with viruses."

10 *Antivirus.* Review "Combating viruses."

Developing a Network Maintenance Policy

You should not perform network maintenance haphazardly. Network maintenance should be the result of a planned, documented, and structured process for several reasons, most of them involving the frailties of the human part of the system. Unless you perform maintenance activities according to a plan and document them as you perform them, you can easily forget what you've done, overlook a critical step or activity, or leave little or no records should you be hit by that proverbial runaway garbage truck.

A sound maintenance program includes the following considerations:

- **Anticipated activities:** The plan should attempt to anticipate all the activities that may be needed and describe the procedure for each.

- **Data integrity:** You should develop a formal plan, outlining the process for creating and storing network server and client backups. The plan should include the procedures to be used for each different computer, data media, and storage combination.

- **Hardware and software standards:** Standardization tends to reduce the complexity of a maintenance program. In a perfect world, every client computer is exactly the same, every operating system is the same version, every cable is the same length, and so on. However, in the real world, you can standardize only to a certain extent. Whatever the standard is, it should be documented in the maintenance plan.

- **Network documentation:** Network management and network maintenance can work together if you keep an up-to-date record of the cabling, network layout, the protocols in use, installed equipment, warranties, and so on. You must keep this documentation current and reflect any and all changes made to the network.

- **Repair policies:** The plan should stipulate how to handle repairs to hardware and cabling, including those on warranty or maintenance agreements.

- **Software upgrades:** The maintenance plan should indicate how often you should apply software upgrades, patches, fixes, or releases, the level of their effect on network operations, and who is authorized to apply them.

- **System monitoring:** The plan should outline when and how frequently to perform network monitoring activities. By monitoring the system against established early warning criteria, you can head off serious problems by identifying the problems while they're still small problems.

- **Training:** Often neglected is the importance of keeping key network maintenance personnel up-to-speed on the elements of the network, such as the network and client operating systems, hardware and software developments, and correct maintenance procedures.

Documenting the Network

Gilster's Law of Network Documentation is "Write it down." You should write down virtually every fact about a network and then painstakingly update the information as the network changes. You cannot overdocument a network and its components. A well-done network documentation package consists of the following elements, among others:

- ✔ Topological maps of the entire network showing both the physical and logical locations of network components, including servers, cabling, connectivity devices, clients, and so forth.

- ✔ A detailed profile of the server that includes a list of the programs and data stored on it, how often it is backed up, and where the backups are stored.

- ✔ A detailed list of all the computer and connectivity equipment included in the network.

- ✔ Software licensing information for all the standard software supported on the network servers and clients.

- ✔ The name, address, phone number, e-mail address, Web page URL, contact name, and any other information available for each product vendor used in the network.

- ✔ A list of active and expired warranties, service agreements, maintenance contracts, and so on for network components.

- ✔ A history of all network problems, their symptoms, remedies, dates, the person to whom you spoke, the troubleshooting procedure used, and the final outcome.

- ✔ A list of the users and their accounts on each of the network segments, domains, and trusted domains. This list should also include as much information as possible, including the account policies, permissions, and rights.

If you're the administrator of a small network of 10 to 25 workstations, you can very easily remember most of this information. However, if you suffer from CRS (can't remember stuff), like me, or if your network is larger, you can quickly lose sight and possibly control of your network's information if you don't write it down. Stay away from garbage trucks and write everything down!

Applying Vendor Upgrades

A fact of network life is that the vendors from whom you purchased your hardware and software at some point choose to update, upgrade, or replace their products, making your system obsolete. If you're faced with one of these situations, you can choose to do nothing and operate under the philosophy that, if it ain't broke, don't fix it. You can choose to apply only a part of the change, fixing only the areas affecting your system. Or you can apply the entire fix, patch, plug, release, upgrade, or update to take full advantage of its promise. Regardless, your decision should be directed by the guidelines in your maintenance policy.

Change can be a good thing

In today's network world, vendors are constantly making changes to their software and hardware, and applying these changes can keep a network administrator quite busy. The guidelines of the system maintenance policy should cover whether to apply a vendor upgrade to the system; you do not need to apply every vendor upgrade to every system.

Following are some guidelines for applying changes to an existing network:

- ✔ Analyze the upgrade completely for its applicability to your network and users.

- ✔ Announce upgrades in advance and try to minimize the network's downtime.

- ✔ Develop a recovery procedure for handling any problems that occur during the application of the upgrade or in its testing.

- ✔ Back up the system before and after the upgrade.

- ✔ Test the upgraded system yourself and then test it with a small group of users before releasing the upgrade to all users.

Sources for vendor information

You can find information concerning upgrades, updates, and other vendor information in a number of places. Following are some of the most commonly used sources of vendor information:

- ✔ **Product documentation:** You know — the books, pamphlets, and printed material that came with the product. This information may also be on a CD-ROM or a diskette, but somewhere, somehow you received documentation on the product. If no documentation comes with a product, contact your supplier or the manufacturer to find out why not.

- ✔ **Vendor Web sites:** If you've ever visited the Microsoft (and who hasn't?), Novell, or Intel Web sites, you have an appreciation for the kinds of information available on a vendor's Web site. Some sites offer searchable FAQs (Frequently Asked Questions) or knowledge bases to help you solve problems yourself.

> ✔ **Vendor-related newsletters, newsgroups, or listservs:** These sources seem to have replaced the vendor-specific users' groups that were common in the past. Although getting specific information on your desktop is nice, the meetings were kind of fun.

Backing Up the System

No one disputes that you should back up your network. But how you go about it is a different issue. No one backup plan fits all situations. A network backup policy must be tailored specifically to each individual network's situation. Decisions that the local administrator must make to best serve the needs of the network and its organization include what data to back up, how frequently to back up, the type of backup to create, and where the backup media is stored.

Creating a backup plan

Creating a backup plan doesn't mean that you should create a contingency plan, although that never hurts. A backup plan includes specific instructions for each of the following considerations:

- ✔ The data that needs to be backed up and how often the backup should be done. Network system databases and user data files need to be backed up more frequently than do program or configuration files.

- ✔ The backup schedule used to create backups, including the type of backup created by each run. See "Deciding on the backup type," following this section.

- ✔ Who is responsible for creating the backup, listed by name, job, or assignment. Also make sure that this individual knows that this responsibility has been assigned to him. One way to document that fact is to have that person sign and date this part of the plan.

- ✔ A policy stating exactly where and the conditions under which backup media are stored.

- ✔ A backup log that shows the when, which, and who of each backup created.

Deciding on the backup type

Expect to see at least one question on the exam regarding the types of backups and what each one includes.

You can use the following five types of backups:

- ✔ **Full (archival) backup:** This backup type captures everything on the system and marks each file as archived. This backup includes files regardless of whether they've been changed since the last full backup.

- ✔ **Incremental backup:** This backup captures only those files that have been changed since the last time the file was backed up, and marks them as being archived.

- ✔ **Differential backup:** This backup captures those files that were changed since the last time they were backed up, but it does not mark those files as being archived. You can use this backup type between incremental backups.

- ✔ **Copy backup:** This backup type copies selected files created using a copy command or action. Files are not marked as archived.

- ✔ **Daily copy backup:** This backup method copies only those files that were changed on that day and does not mark them as being archived.

Choosing the backup media

Integral to the frequency and type of backup used is the type of backup media used. The first rule is that the backup media must be appropriate to the data that you're backing up. This means that the media should be fast enough to capture the data before the system is needed again, and it should have enough capacity to hold all the data being captured.

Virtually any storage media that can be written to can be used as a backup media. Tape is a common backup media because of its reasonable speed, high capacity, low cost, and easy storage. Other forms of media used are optical drives, Bernoulli boxes, writable CD-ROMs, and remote hard or floppy disk drives. Another possibility, which is actually an extension of the remote disk idea, is backing up data over the Internet.

For now, magnetic tape is the favorite backup media and the one that you're asked about on the exam. The most common forms of tape backup media in use are as follows:

- ✔ **DAT (Digital Audio Tape):** This tape medium is the most commonly used type. It is a 4mm tape, a little thicker but smaller than an audiocassette, that holds from 1 to 12GB of data.

- ✔ **DLT (Digital Linear Tape):** This tape media comes in a half-inch cartridge and offers storage capacities of 10 to 35GB. DLT is commonly used on medium to large-scale LANs.

✔ **QIC (Quarter-Inch Cartridge):** QIC, which originally had a width of a quarter inch, is available in two sizes, 3½-inch minicartridges (also known as Travan) and 5¼-inch data cartridges. QIC tapes hold between 40MB and 25GB, depending on size.

Protecting your backup-side

After you create a backup of your computer, server, or network resources, put that backup in a safe place. That way, it's available to you should you ever need it. Trust me — when you need it, you really need it!

Just where you store your backup media depends on which type and level of backup it is. By definition, you need to protect full backups more carefully than differential backups. One of the best places to find out where your company wants to store its backups is to ask the folks in the accounting office. Bean counters have rules and regulations for everything, and just where data backups are stored is definitely one of them. Some places, good and bad, to store backup media are as follows:

✔ **A rack in the computer room:** Good for daily copy, incremental, or differential backups; bad for full backups.

✔ **A vault in the computer room:** Good for all backups, depending on the vault's fire rating; bad for full backups taken at the end of an accounting period (monthly, quarterly, annually).

✔ **A vault not in the computer room:** Good for all backups, depending on the vault's fire rating; okay for full backups, but you can find better places.

✔ **A secured off-site location:** Good for archive backups that aren't likely to be accessed frequently; bad for daily and weekly backup types that may be needed quickly.

Viruses and Virus Protection

Viruses are nasty pieces of software that have taken on the characteristics of an infectious disease, spreading germs to infect unsuspecting and unprotected PCs. You can expect a couple questions on the exam that deal with what a virus is, how it spreads, and how it's detected.

The following characteristics define a computer virus:

✔ A virus attaches itself to another piece of programming code in memory, on a floppy disk, or on a downloaded file.

- ✔ A virus infects a system when the original program executes and also unintentionally runs the virus program code.

- ✔ A virus replicates itself and infects other programs, possibly modifying its form and manifesting other behaviors as well.

Not all viruses do catastrophic damage to a system. Many viruses are just nuisances or pranks, playing music, simulating system meltdowns, or displaying misinformation during the system boot. Viruses that are malicious can and do cause considerable damage in the form of lost data and altered program code.

Some of the reportedly nastiest viruses aren't viruses at all. Virus hoaxes spread through the rumor mill (especially on the Internet) and tell of untold horrors that will happen on the 35th anniversary of the Class of '65. (Who's old?)

Viruses and how they spread

Computer viruses are a form of electronic warfare developed solely to cause human misery. The evil, sick, and quite-talented minds that develop computer viruses would like nothing better than for your boot sectors to catch cold or for your disk drives to develop dysentery. Five major virus classes exist, each with many subclasses as the following list describes:

- ✔ **Boot sector viruses (system viruses):** These viruses target the boot program on every bootable floppy disk or hard disk. By attaching themselves to the boot sector program, the viruses are guaranteed to run whenever the computer starts up. Boot sector viruses spread mostly by jumping from disk to disk.

- ✔ **File viruses:** File viruses modify program files, such as EXE or COM files. Whenever the infected program executes, the virus also executes and does its nastiness. File viruses spread via infected floppy disks, networks, and the Internet.

- ✔ **Macro viruses:** The newest general virus class, macro viruses take advantage of the built-in macro programming languages of application programs such as Microsoft Word and Microsoft Excel. Macro languages enable users to create *macros,* scriptlike programs that automate formatting, data-entry, or frequently repeated tasks. A macro virus, most commonly found in Microsoft Word documents, can cause as much damage as other viruses and can spread by jumping from an opened document to other documents.

- ✔ **BIOS program viruses:** This is one type of the file viruses that attacks flash BIOS programs by overwriting the system BIOS program and leaving the PC unbootable.

- ✔ **Multipartite viruses:** Especially nasty affairs, multipartite viruses infect both boot sectors and program files.

Because a virus is a program, it can infect only programs. A virus can't hide where it doesn't blend into the scenery. Viruses that infect graphic files, e-mail, or text files are just myths. Hiding viruses in those places would be like trying to hide a bright red ball among bright white balls. However, viruses can be attached to text files or e-mail and transmitted or copied to a new host system.

Playing hide and seek with viruses

As virus-detection software has become more sophisticated, so have the viruses. Most antivirus software works by recognizing a predefined pattern of characters unique to individual viruses, a sort of fingerprint called its *signature.* As viruses get more devious, they include new ways to elude the virus detectors. These tricks, as a group, are called *cloaking.*

One of the most common cloaking techniques is *polymorphing.* This technique enables viruses, such as so-called stealth viruses, to change their appearance, signature, and size each time they infect a system. A stealth virus changes its binary pattern each time that it infects a new file to keep it from being identified.

Another type of polymorph virus is a *directory virus,* which hides itself by changing directory entries to point to itself rather than the files it is replacing. The affected files are not changed, and the directory virus appears normal on directory lists and in Windows Explorer lists, which helps it avoid detection.

Combating viruses

Viruses manifest themselves on a PC in a wide variety of ways, including spontaneous system reboots; system crashes; application crashes; sound card or speaker problems; distorted, misshapen, or missing video on the monitor; corrupted or missing data from disk files; disappearing disk partitions; or boot disks that don't boot.

In spite of virus developers' efforts, the best defense against virus infection is antivirus software, also called *scanners* or *inoculators.* Don't you just love all this medical talk?

Following are the general types of antivirus software in use today:

> ✔ **Scanner software:** This run-on-demand software scans the contents of the memory and the disk drive, directories, and files that the user wants to check. This type of software is the most common form of an antivirus program. Another form is memory-resident scanner software, which stays in memory, automatically checking for viruses.

✔ **Startup-scan software:** This software runs when the PC boots and does a quick scan of boot sectors and essential files to detect boot sector viruses before the PC boots up.

✔ **Inoculators:** This antivirus software looks for changes to files and boot sectors and for other evidence left behind by viruses. The inoculator takes a snapshot of clean boot sectors and then periodically compares the snapshots of the clean files to the actual files to check for changes.

Except for inoculators, which look only for the damage caused and not the virus itself, most antivirus software uses a database of virus profiles and signatures for reference. You should update this database frequently; most antivirus packages include a number of free updates.

Fighting the good fight

Protecting a network against computer viruses is a matter of using the following prudent and timely actions that detect and clean viruses on the system:

✔ Install a virus scanner/inoculator application.

✔ Perform regular scans of the system.

✔ Update the virus signature database frequently.

✔ Treat viruses as a serious and real threat to the network.

Prep Test

1 A well-developed network maintenance policy should address which of the following considerations? (Choose five.)

  A ❑ Training

  B ❑ Personnel histories

  C ❑ Repair policies

  D ❑ Standards

  E ❑ Network documentation

  F ❑ Future plans

2 The primary purpose behind documenting the network is to

  A ○ Document the work of the network administrator.

  B ○ Ensure that network activities, uses, and problems are formally recorded for analytical and historical purposes.

  C ○ Provide a turnover document for the next network administrator.

  D ○ Provide a record of network errors, situations, and maintenance actions should it be needed in a court of law.

3 Good sources for information on a vendor's products, updates, and upgrades include: (Choose three.)

  A ❑ Product documentation

  B ❑ Trade publications

  C ❑ Shopping guides

  D ❑ Vendor Web sites

  E ❑ A vendor-specific newsgroup

4 A network backup policy should address which considerations? (Choose three.)

  A ❑ The backup media appropriate for the amount of data to be archived

  B ❑ The cost of the backup media

  C ❑ How often backups are created

  D ❑ Where backup media is stored

  E ❑ Data-restoration policies

5 A network administrator takes a full system backup weekly, usually on Friday nights. Due to increased activity on the network, a daily backup also needs to be created each night. As required, a backup is also needed during the day following special large, project-oriented transaction volumes. Which two types of backups should be used for 1) the daily backup and 2) the as-required backups?

A ○ Full/copy backup

B ○ Incremental/differential

C ○ Differential/daily copy backup

D ○ Incremental/full

6 Which of the following are commonly used as backup media? (Choose three.)

A ❑ Remote hard drive

B ❑ CD-ROM

C ❑ Magnetic tape

D ❑ Printed hard copy

7 The company requires that the network administrator take a full backup of the server supporting the company's accounting and financial records and applications after the close of each accounting period. Which of the following is likely the best possible location to store these backups?

A ○ A computer room vault

B ○ An accounting office vault

C ○ A safety deposit box at a local bank

D ○ In the network administrator's garage

8 What tasks should a network administrator perform to ensure that the network is protected from computer viruses? (Choose three.)

A ❑ Install an antivirus program

B ❑ Regularly update the virus signature database

C ❑ Frequently test the system using a virus-infected file

D ❑ Regularly scan the system storage facilities for viruses

9 The type of virus that can hide from detection by masquerading as another file is a

A ○ File virus

B ○ Macro virus

C ○ Stealth virus

D ○ BIOS virus

10 Which statement is most accurate regarding the application of vendor system updates?

A ○ All vendor updates should be applied immediately after they're received.

B ○ After careful analysis, a vendor update should be installed only if it solves an existing local issue or problem.

C ○ Vendor updates should be batched and implemented together.

D ○ After careful analysis, a vendor update should be installed if it solves an existing or potential issue or problem.

Answers

1 *A, B, C, D, E.* The one not usually included is future plans. However, this
option would not be a bad inclusion if it focuses on planned expansions,
moves, or upgrades. So, *all of the above* could be the answer. *See
"Developing a Network Maintenance Policy."*

2 *B.* Although arguably the others could be the answer, the real purpose is to
provide an ongoing chronological record of the network's history for the
existing network administrator (as well as the next) to use. I hope you're
never dragged into court, and if you are, I'm not sure what role your network
documentation may play. *Review "Documenting the Network."*

3 *A, D, E.* You may find good stories and articles in trade and shopping rags
about a vendor, but they aren't the best places to get specific product-ori-
ented information. *Check out "Sources for vendor information."*

4 *A, C, D.* If your backup policy includes directives on how much to spend on
the network media or which files can or cannot be restored, I can safely say
that policy's focus is askew. *Take a look at "Creating a backup plan."*

5 *B.* The incremental backup captures all the files that have changed since the
last full or incremental backup and marks them as having been archived.
These features make the incremental backup a good choice for a daily
backup. The differential backup performs all the same actions of the incremental backup except that it doesn't mark the files as archived. The
differential backup creates a backup but leaves the file unmarked for inclusion on the incremental backup. *See "Deciding the backup type."*

6 *A, B, C.* Printing documents is, to really stretch the definition, a form of
backup, but it does not work for all types of data. *Review "Choosing the
backup media."*

7 *C.* Secured offsite storage is the best possible storage location for milestone
and end-of-period backups. You can also find archive companies that
securely store data and backups. *Check out "Protecting your backup-side."*

8 *A, B, D.* Regular updates to the virus signature database and frequent scans
of the system are key elements in a good antivirus program. *Take a look at
"Fighting the good fight."*

9 *C.* A stealth virus cloaks its signature each time that it infects a new body.
See "Playing hide and seek with viruses."

10 *D.* If you chose B, you need to remember that some vendor updates can prevent future problems that you may grow into or have not yet encountered. *Review "Change can be a good thing."*

Chapter 21

Troubleshooting the Network

● ●

Exam Objectives

▶ Using standard troubleshooting methods

▶ Determining the cause of a network problem

▶ Identifying the risks of applying upgrades to a network

▶ Isolating common network problems

● ●

*A*lthough not many network administrators would ever admit it openly, the most exciting part of their job is troubleshooting, diagnosing, and fixing network problems. After a network is designed, configured, and in place, network administrators don't have much more to do — unless the organization is constantly and rapidly growing. So, an occasional network problem adds a little spice to the network administrator's life.

The Network+ exam attempts to measure your problem-solving abilities along with your ability to isolate and fix the problem. To this end, this chapter goes over the systematic procedures that you should use to determine the source of a problem and decide and carry out the appropriate corrective action.

On the exam, expect to see three basic types of questions on troubleshooting:

✔ Content questions that ask about the steps of a systematic approach to troubleshooting and fixing network problems.

✔ Course-of-action questions that describe a situation and the steps that have been performed so far. Your task is to pick the action that is most appropriate in the situation given.

✔ Troubleshooting questions that describe the symptoms of a network problem and ask you to identify the next best network resource or element to check.

Troubleshooting (covered in this chapter and Chapter 22) is an important skill for network technicians and administrators to have, which is why 11 percent of the Network+ exam is devoted to it. If you do not have much network hands-on experience, seek out a friendly network technician and have her or him go over common network problems and the process and tools that you use to troubleshoot and fix these problems.

Quick Assessment

Using standard troubleshooting methods

1 The first four steps in the process that you use to troubleshoot network problems are: _____, _____, _____, and _____.

Determining the cause of a network problem

2 To eliminate user error as a problem source, you should first _____.

3 One way to isolate the error is to have another user use a(n) _____ to perform the same action.

4 A key consideration among environmental and physical conditions of a network is the quality and stability of the _____ source.

5 If none of the network's workstations are able to logon to the network, the first place to look is the _____.

Identifying the risks of applying upgrades to a network

6 Changes made at the _____ can impact the operation of the network.

7 You should analyze vendor upgrades to protect against _____.

8 The network's _____ is a good place to start looking for network problems.

Isolating common network problems

9 Three common problem areas to begin troubleshooting are: _____, _____, and _____.

10 On a thinnet network, replacing the network cable with a _____can isolate a workstation.

Answers

1 *Identify the problem, re-create the problem, isolate the problem, and develop a solution.* See "Step-by-step, inch-by-inch,. . . ."

2 *Politely ask the user to explain how the error occurred.* Review "Identifying the user's problem."

3 *Equivalent workstation.* Check out "Identifying the user's problem."

4 *Power.* Take a look at "So, if it isn't the user, it must be. . . . "

5 *Server.* See "So, if it isn't the user, it must be. . . ."

6 *Workstation.* Review "The Side Effects of Applying Vendor Updates and Making Repairs."

7 *Impacts on the network.* Check out "Errors at the network level."

8 *Cabling (cable plant).* Take a look at "Common Sources of Network Errors."

9 *Cabling, performance, and power issues.* See "Common Sources of Network Errors."

10 *Terminator.* Review "Isolating Common Network Problems."

Using a Systematic Approach to Network Problems

How often have you invested a lot of your time and the company's money to apply a solution to a network problem, only to find out that solution doesn't solve the original problem? So, then what do you do? You try another solution hoping it solves the problem. Of course, this approach is all theoretical. You would never actually resolve a problem this way, would you? Of course not!

However, as hard as it may be to believe, some network technicians use this all-too-common, solution-based approach to network problem solving. Many network solutions are available that I am eager to apply to my network, if only the right problem will just come along. My dilemma is that I don't approach network troubleshooting and problem-solving from a solution-oriented point of view. I use a problem-oriented systematic approach to finding and fixing network problems, which is lucky for me because the Network+ exam includes questions on this type of problem-solving approach.

Step-by-step, inch-by-inch, . . .

The Network+ exam blueprint identifies an eight-step systematic approach for troubleshooting network problems:

1. **Identify the problem.**

2. **Re-create the problem.**

3. **Isolate the source of the problem.**

4. **Develop a solution.**

5. **Implement the correction.**

6. **Test.**

7. **Document the problem and the solution.**

8. **Give feedback.**

The following sections briefly explain each of these steps. You should review them to understand how each step fits into the overall process.

Identifying the problem

Identifying the problem is by far the most important step in the process. If you don't know what problem you're solving, you are operating completely in the dark and have to solve the problem by trial and error. This step is also where your knowledge of networking, in general, and your network, specifically, is most valuable. This process step is the most daunting to new network technicians, and how they handle the task reflects the true value of their training and experience.

The product of this step is a clear statement of what the problem is and how it manifests itself. If a network user reports the problem, then be sure that you understand the what, when, how, and why of the problem as seen by the user. If network monitoring utilities report the problem, be sure that you know the nature and location of the problem.

Write it down! Using a formal problem-report form is an excellent idea for several reasons. By writing down the problem, you create a log of the actions that you take, good or bad, which you can refer to later, should the problem happen again. Using a form also allows you to document recurring problems.

Re-creating the problem

In the networking world, don't believe anything you hear. Believe only what you see with your own eyes and then still be somewhat dubious. If you can't re-create a problem as described, solving it is difficult.

You should try several times to re-create a problem. You may need to use different locations, times of the day, network activity loads, and so on, to get the problem to repeat. Unless you know that the problem is a user-training issue or the like, you should document the problem and the ways in which you attempted to re-create it, should it ever be reported again.

If you are able to re-create the problem as reported, you have the input that you need to begin determining the contributing causes of the problem.

Isolating the cause

After you reliably re-create the problem, you should be able to pinpoint the network elements involved and which ones may be causing the trouble. This process step is complex because each element reacts to other network elements and situations in a variety of ways.

With any problem, usually a number of possible causes exists. Try to identify as many possibilities as you can and then rank them in order of the likeliness that they're the root cause of the problem. At this point, you should begin using the troubleshooting tools appropriate for each possible cause to verify and isolate the cause. I suggest starting with what you believe is the most likely cause and then work your way down your ranking. After you precisely identify the cause, you can move on to developing a remedy.

Developing a solution

After you know exactly what the problem is, you can decide what changes you need to make to resolve it. I recommend that before you start making changes, you first write down the steps to fix the problem, including any new or replacement software or hardware that must be installed. Then review the steps one more time before starting.

I realize that this process sounds very formal and time-consuming for what could very well be a simple fix, such as setting user access permissions. But even the simplest problem may hold a wealth of information at a later date when the *real* problem emerges. For a problem that involves damaged hardware or poorly operating software, the process that you use to solve a problem may be much more complicated.

Implementing the correction

When applying your solution, proceed cautiously and systematically. Make only one change at a time, and verify that the change brings about the result you expected. It is not unusual for another underlying problem to surface when you're applying changes to fix what you thought was the problem.

Testing

You should test the correction or change at all levels of the system or network. If the change directly impacts only the software on a client workstation, you must test the software on the client and test the client as a part of the network.

Never assume that just because an action occurs infrequently or never at all, it won't happen the minute following the completion of your test. Test for everything that conceivably can be affected and then test again.

Documenting the problem and the solution

All the way through the troubleshooting and correction processes, you should write down exactly what is going on. If you document as you go, then this task won't loom quite as large after you complete your testing. Document every problem, large or small, and exactly what you did to fix it. Most problems do happen again, and your troubleshooting documentation may save you, or your replacement, some time and trouble.

Giving feedback

Inform the affected parties about the problem that you identified and just what you did to fix it. Believe it or not, telling these parties — users, coworkers, vendors, or the readers of your newsgroup — as much as you can about how you were able to solve a particular problem eases the burden for everyone. You must use some judgment as to which problems to share with whom. Some problems may be so routine that they aren't worth sharing.

Finding the Source of a Problem

Network users report a significant number of network troubles. The range of problems that users report is directly related to the range of network and computer knowledge and experience of the users themselves. Complaints and questions like "The network is slow today," "I can't logon to the server," or "Is the network down?" are commonplace, and I'm sure that you recognize them. These questions, though seemingly easy to remedy, may be the catalyst to a major system fix that you weren't aware was needed.

The obvious first place to look for the source of a problem is with the person reporting it. You know the saying about the skunk smelling its own scent first. This process is like that, and you need to proceed politely because in effect you're telling the skunk that it stinks. The first tool to pull out of your bag is your interpersonal skills.

Eliminating user errors: The impossible dream

Your first action is to eliminate any user errors as the cause of the problem. As I'm sure you're aware, most reported problems are user errors, or what I call user-training problems. Politely ask the user what he or she was doing when the error happened and to retrace the steps used (keystrokes and mouse actions). If the user is nearby, visit the user personally. However, as is becoming commonplace, the user may be quite remotely located. If this is the case, you should do the following:

1. **Ask another user on an equivalent workstation to perform the same action.**

2. **Ask another user to perform the same action on the original user's workstation.**

3. **Verify that the users performing the task are using the appropriate or the most efficient procedure.**

4. Determine whether the users are using the appropriate versions of hardware and software required for the action being performed.

Simply restarting the Windows computer can solve many user problems. Even before you begin your troubleshooting process, you may want to have the user reboot his or her computer.

If it isn't the user, it must be . . .

For the Network+ test, you need to know the various network elements that may cause a network problem and how each element manifests itself. Some of the more common contributors to network problems are

- ✔ **Account names and passwords:** Not all logon problems are system problems. Users may simply forget their account usernames or passwords. Although much less likely to occur, the network administrator may also enter the username and password incorrectly. In either case, the users aren't able to log into their network accounts.

- ✔ **Faulty network media:** If network media (cabling) is installed correctly, it usually doesn't suddenly go bad. More likely, improper installation of connectors and connectivity devices — such as hubs, repeaters, and patch panels — can cause intermittent problems that later manifest as a connection failure to a single workstation, workgroup, or network segment.

- ✔ **Network configuration:** Another reason that connections to network resources, e-mail, or the Internet may have problems is that the configuration may have changed. Network configurations don't change by themselves, but they can be inadvertently changed by other administrative changes. Configuration areas that can affect network operations are DNS (Domain Name System), WINS (Windows Internet Name Service), and host file designations. If they become disabled or their IP addresses change, their services can be interrupted.

- ✔ **Network servers:** The network's servers can potentially cause a wide variety of problems on the network. If the network's shared resources are no longer available, or users cannot logon, or e-mail or Internet access suddenly stops, the problem most likely is on a network server or one of its connections.

- ✔ **Physical conditions:** The physical environment includes such environmental conditions as heat, cold, humidity (or the lack of it), or dust. The outside environment can also affect network operations — for example, thunderstorms, humidity levels, and other outside weather or natural phenomena, such as earthquakes, tornadoes, and so on. The quality and stability of the power source is another consideration. Physical conditions can directly impact the operation of the network, especially if they change rapidly. Of the conditions listed, power is most likely where the problem will manifest itself.

> ✔ **Viruses:** If a user's workstation or a server cannot suddenly boot up, or if files are becoming corrupted, a virus is likely the cause, and immediate action is required.

Using troubleshooting tools to isolate network problems

Chapter 22 covers troubleshooting tools in more detail, but here is a brief overview of the different categories of network tools that help you isolate a network problem:

> ✔ **Network monitors:** These software packages track and report all or a certain portion of a network's traffic. Network monitors track network traffic by packet types, errors, or traffic to and from a certain computer.
>
> ✔ **NOS event and alert logs:** Whereas each of the three preceding categories are physical devices, this category is data-based and software-oriented. Most network operating systems (NOSs) maintain log files in which they record system events and alerts set by the administrator. You use reporting tools to display the log file contents for analysis purposes.
>
> ✔ **Physical media testers:** This category of tools includes digital voltmeters (DVM), time-domain reflectometers (TDR), oscilloscopes, and advanced cable testers. These devices help you find and isolate problems at the physical level of the network.
>
> ✔ **Protocol analyzers:** This category of network troubleshooting devices, which are also called network analyzers, enables you to evaluate the overall condition of the network by monitoring all network traffic. Protocol analyzers are commonly used to determine problems in network layer 3 (OSI Reference Model Network layer — see Chapter 10) operations.

Vendors, technical groups, and users provide a wide variety of information and advice on the Internet and World Wide Web that may save you troubleshooting time and effort. Before tackling a new and difficult troubleshooting project, you may want to check the Web for related information.

The Side Effects of Applying Vendor Updates and Making Repairs

Unfortunately, an operating network can be much like a house of cards — making even the simplest change can upset the network's operations. Most of the changes to a network are made at the workstation, as users change their hardware and software needs. Each workstation change can have adverse effects on the network and the workstation.

Errors at the workstation level

You can expect to see at least one question on the Network+ test that deals with errors introduced into a network by changes made at a workstation. Changes at the workstation level can introduce four types of network problems:

- ✔ **Changes to the logon procedure.** New software may cause changes to the boot or logon procedures used at the workstation. In this case, you should make the user aware of the changes and train that person to connect to the network successfully.

- ✔ **The network client software is missing a key element.** Installing new application software in the Windows environment can mean that older or newer versions of network-related software can be installed over any versions that are already on the system. .DLL files, which are shared by many Windows-based programs, are common victims in software installations. In the process of the installation, they can be overlaid by older or incompatible .DLL files.

- ✔ **Unable to connect to the network.** A new network interface card (NIC) that is not properly configured or is incompatible with the network media can prevent the workstation from connecting to the network. Also, if the user's network account name or password are configured incorrectly, the user will have difficulty connecting.

- ✔ **Workstation does not boot.** New hardware installed incorrectly may prevent the workstation from booting. In some network situations, this problem can affect other users relying on shared resources that are on or connected to the workstation.

Errors at the network level

As discussed in Chapter 20, you should carefully analyze vendor updates to network hardware and software before applying them to your network. However, after you decide to make the changes, you must be alert to possible impacts to the network and its workstations. You should thoroughly test all network updates and upgrades before releasing them for network operations — particularly if you're installing new layer 3 (Network) equipment, such as a router, firewall, switch, or the like.

A few of the problems that may arise from changes made at the server or network level are

- ✔ **Loss of Internet access:** The network is not properly configured to see a new router, firewall, switch, DNS, or other Internet access device. Network users will likely report this problem.

✔ **User cannot logon:** Required network services aren't starting up or the connection to the user is linking end to end. A new NIC in the server or a new connectivity device, such as a hub or switch, is not properly configured or connected.

✔ **Missing segments:** If several users from a newly created network segment are reporting problems, more than likely a configuration or addressing problem is in either the router or bridge creating the segment or on the server.

Remember that a segment is a subset of a network created by the insertion of a router or bridge. Another way to view a segment is that it, by itself, does not contain a router or bridge. You're likely to be asked to identify a segment on the test by choosing it from a diagram. Just look for a group of workstations separated from the server by a router or bridge.

Common Sources of Network Errors

Experience is probably the best tool that you have to recognize common network errors. Eventually, as you gain experience with a network, you're able to recognize common errors and know their solutions without performing many, if any, tests. For example, when a group of users, all of whom are connected to a certain hub, report a loss of network connectivity, you may recognize that the hub needs to be reset. Because you've been religiously writing these things down, you know the problem is now happening quite frequently.

When network errors occur, these common troubleshooting areas are good places to start your investigation:

✔ **Cabling (also called the cable plant):** This is always a good place to start looking for problems. Cable troubleshooting should include the organization of the cabling, especially around hubs and other connectivity devices. That big wad of cable just thrown around the device may be the problem.

✔ **Performance issues:** You can easily solve performance issues — such as excessive traffic, cabling failures, and poorly operating hubs, routers, or switches — after you identify them. Excessive traffic may require segmentation of the network, and you can reconfigure bad devices and replace bad cable.

✔ **Power:** You should protect network hardware from faulty power with a UPS (uninterruptable power supply). This device ensures that essential network devices have an adequate source of power at all times. Power-related problems are often difficult to isolate, because they show up as hardware operation problems.

Isolating Common Network Problems

Solving a problem that shows up on two workstations is far easier than solving one that occurs randomly across 100 network workstations and in different segments. By isolating the problem to its source, most of the network can continue to operate while you're testing.

Here are some common methods used to isolate network problems:

- ✔ **Same connection, different workstation test:** If a different computer doesn't have the problem when it's attached to the original workstation's cable, then the problem is in the original workstation. Otherwise, the problem is in the network.

- ✔ **Same workstation, different connection test:** If the problem reoccurs when the original workstation is connected to a different line, then the problem is in the workstation. Otherwise, the problem is in the original connection.

- ✔ **Replacing components test:** If the problem is thought to be in the connectivity of the workstation, begin replacing the components that are most likely causing the problem, including the NIC, patch cords, patch panel connection, hubs, and so on. After you resolve the problem, then independently test the component that is isolated as the cause.

- ✔ **The terminator test:** On Thinnet coax networks (10Base2), you can use terminators to isolate a workstation by removing the network cable from one side of its BNC-T connector and replacing the cable with a terminator. If the network problem goes away, you now know the source of the problem.

Prep Test

1 To isolate a workstation on a 10Base2 network, you should

A ○ Reboot the computers on the workstation's segment.

B ○ Remove all the network terminators.

C ○ Turn off all the workstations except the one being isolated.

D ○ Replace one of the workstation's cable connections with a terminator.

2 After a recent reorganization in which many people moved their computers to new offices, a workstation is not functioning properly. The network is a 10BaseT Ethernet network with workgroups arranged in hubs. Which of the following is likely the cause of the problem? (Choose two.)

A ❑ The hub is faulty.

B ❑ The NIC is using the wrong drivers.

C ❑ A cable has been damaged.

D ❑ The workstation is not connected to the network.

3 What is often the easiest way to correct a problem on a user's workstation?

A ○ Reboot the computer.

B ○ Reinstall the operating system.

C ○ Reconfigure the workstation's hardware settings.

D ○ Create a new user profile.

4 Which areas of the network are good places to start your network troubleshooting?

A ○ Eliminate user error on the workstation.

B ○ Check the network cable.

C ○ Check power sources.

D ○ All of the above.

5 Which of the following are included in the eight steps of the troubleshooting approach described in the chapter? (Choose four.)

A ❑ Train the user.

B ❑ Re-create the problem.

C ❑ Develop a solution.

D ❑ Identify the problem.

E ❑ Reset the system.

F ❑ Install new cabling.

G ❑ Isolate the source of the problem.

6 A user contacts you to report an application error on his workstation. Which of the following could you use to isolate the user's workstation problem?

A ○ Ask the user to restart his or her computer.

B ○ Ask another user to perform the same action on the original user's computer.

C ○ Ask another user to perform a related action on an equivalent workstation.

D ○ Ask the user to reinstall the NIC in the workstation.

7 Which of the following are common contributors to network problems? (Choose five.)

A ❑ Physical or environmental conditions

B ❑ Network media

C ❑ Workstations that aren't logged into the network

D ❑ Network servers

E ❑ Computer viruses

F ❑ User account names and passwords

G ❑ ISP configuration

8 Which of the following are common troubleshooting devices and resources? (Choose all that apply.)

A ❑ DVM

B ❑ Network monitoring software

C ❑ Protocol analyzers

D ❑ NOS event logs

9 After installing a new version of a word processing application, the NOS client fails to start up, giving the error, "Bad or Missing .DLL file." What has likely caused this error?

A ○ The Windows client was not restarted.

B ○ The new software has installed an incompatible version of the missing file.

C ○ The NOS client is corrupted.

D ○ The NIC is faulty.

10 When you install a router or a bridge into the network structure, the groups of workstations on either side of the new device are called

A ○ Sectors

B ○ Subnets

C ○ Segments

D ○ Domains

Answers

D. If the problem goes away after terminating a workstation by replacing its upstream cable connection with a terminator, the source of the network problem becomes isolated. *See "Isolating Common Network Problems."*

2 *C and D.* If the network and the workstation functioned together before the move, and unless severe damage was introduced, the likely causes are that the workstation is not connected, or if it is connected, that the cabling was damaged in the move. *Review "Common Sources of Network Errors."*

3 *A.* Restarting the user's workstation clears up a vast majority of workstation errors, including many network connection errors. *Check out "Errors at the workstation level."*

4 *D.* Not necessarily in the order given, these three areas are good starting points for troubleshooting network problems. *Take a look at "Common Sources of Network Errors."*

5 *D, B, G, C.* I know, you weren't asked to put them in order, but I thought I would to reinforce the steps and their sequence. Remember, *IRID* the network of problems! *See "Step-by-step, inch-by-inch, . . ."*

6 *B.* Restarting the computer is more of a way to resolve problems than a way to isolate problems. In order to determine the scope of a problem, you must use the same actions on all workstations. I don't think that asking the user to open the system unit to install a NIC card is a part of problem isolation, either. *Review "Without users, this would be a good job."*

7 *A, B, D, E, F.* Logged-off workstations should not present a network problem, and hopefully, your ISP (Internet service provider) is beyond your internal network. *Check out "If it isn't the user, it must be. . . ."*

8 *A, B, C, D.* I should have included an *all of the above* choice. You can use each of these tools to troubleshoot, diagnose, and analyze a network and its performance. *Take a look at "Using troubleshooting tools to isolate network problems."*

9 *B.* This question, or one very close to it, is on the Network+ exam. When installing new software, you must be alert to possible network or workstation impacts. *See "Errors at the workstation level."*

Troubleshooting the Network

10 *C.* This is an important concept to network troubleshooting. Often, you can isolate the problem on a network segment. *Review "Errors at the network level."*

Chapter 22

Network Troubleshooting Tools

● ●

Exam Objectives

▶ Explaining physical and logical indicators

▶ Describing commonly used troubleshooting hardware

▶ Identifying common troubleshooting situations

▶ Finding troubleshooting resources

● ●

*D*epending on your outlook and what part of the network administration job you like, troubleshooting network problems is either what you love or what you hate about networks. No network administrators have mixed feelings about this job; everyone has an opinion one way or the other. Those who enjoy troubleshooting claim it's an art, and those who don't enjoy it claim they spend too much time worrying about trivial matters. The enjoyment of solving the puzzle of why a workstation, server, or entire network is malfunctioning — especially when the solution is exactly right — is why some network administrators do the job — or is it the money?

Regardless of how you feel about it, troubleshooting is a fact of networking life, and you must do it all too often. Networks usually combine a wide variety of hardware and software technologies and vendors to create an environment just right for conflicts. Have you ever noticed that networks have a strange habit of breaking down just when a user wants to perform or access something very important? It very well could be a conspiracy.

Troubleshooting network problems is such a large and important part of the network administrator's job that the Network+ test allocates 11 percent (around seven questions) of the entire test to this one area, making it one of the top four areas of the exam. The procedures outlined in Chapter 21 and the tools and resources described in this chapter provide you with all the troubleshooting-related information that you need to know for the test.

Quick Assessment

Explaining physical and logical indicators

1 Many network devices, including NICs, hubs, and others, have _____ that indicate a connection is working.

2 Workstations display _____ to indicate errors, such as when a user enters an erroneous password or username.

3 System actions, events, alerts, and errors are recorded in a _____.

4 A(n) _____ is any device that restricts a network from operating at optimal levels.

5 You can use _____ tools to monitor and report on a variety of system resources.

Describing commonly used troubleshooting hardware

6 A _____ measures a cable's continuity.

7 A _____ test checks whether a NIC can communicate with a network and whether cable and interfaces are working.

Identifying common troubleshooting situations

8 Two types of boot failures are: _____ and _____.

9 You can correct most workstation errors by simply _____ the workstation.

Finding troubleshooting resources

10 _____ and _____ are excellent sources for troubleshooting resources and documentation.

Answers

1   *Link lights.* See "I see the light!"

2   *Error messages.* Review "Speak to me!"

3   *Log file.* Take a look at "Logs, alerts, events, and other records."

4   *Bottleneck.* Check out "Performance art."

5   *Performance monitoring.* See "Performance monitoring."

6   *DVM (digital voltmeter).* Review "The Troubleshooting Toolkit."

7   *Loopback.* Check out "The Troubleshooting Toolkit."

8   *System startup, virus-related failures.* Take a look at "Common Troubleshooting Situations."

9   *Restarting.* See "Common Troubleshooting Situations."

10   *Subscription services, telephone support, bulletin boards, magazines.* Review "Finding Troubleshooting Resources."

Looking for Physical and Logical Indicators

In any network troubleshooting situation, physical or logical indicators are always present to help you figure out what's happening (or not happening, as the case may be). In westerns or jungle movies, the native guides can always determine the day and time that a person walked by a bush — along with that person's shoe and hat size and date of birth — by looking at bent and broken twigs. If you know where to look and what to look for, you can find some bent twigs on the network to help you determine a problem's cause. I don't mean that literally. If you actually do have twigs in your network, you really need to do some housekeeping. However, it does give a whole new meaning to the term *cable plant,* doesn't it?

I see the light!

Some of the more telling indicators available to you on the network are the little link lights, usually green or amber, on the network connectivity devices, such as NICs (network interface cards), hubs, switches, and so on. Link lights indicate when a connection is working from one point to another. Most network devices have link lights in one form or another.

The link lights on a NIC indicate that it is seeing a signal from an upstream device, such as a router, switch, hub, or even the NIC in a server. If a workstation user is unable to connect to the network by logging in and the link light on the NIC is not on, this is your first clue that something is amiss physically. In much the same way that you would look for the power light on a PC to see if it's on (not a bad thing to check as well), the link lights let you know whether the connection is on.

Speak to me!

Other physical indicators that help you troubleshoot a network problem are error code or message displays. The workstation operating system may display a message that indicates that the user is unable to logon because the domain server is unavailable to verify the username and password. This message is a surefire clue that a connection problem exists or that the domain controller or server for the workstation is not operating correctly, if at all.

Some higher-end network devices, such as routers, switches, or bridges, also have error displays to indicate a fault. More commonly, these devices have only an alarm light to indicate a problem, but some have little green screens, like copiers have, to display error codes and messages. Of course, you must have the manual memorized or at least very handy to know what the code means. In most cases, you can bet that if an error light or a code is displayed, you have a problem.

Logs, alerts, events, and other records

When network, workstation, or server problems occur, in most cases they're recorded as logical indicators in a log file. Most network operating systems, including Windows NT and NetWare, create and constantly update system actions, events, alerts, and errors to log files. The three general types of log files are as follows:

- ✔ **Application log files:** Contain events, messages, and errors posted by network applications and services
- ✔ **Security log files:** Contain security-related events and alerts generated by administrator-enabled auditing services of the NOS
- ✔ **System log files:** Contain messages, events, and errors posted by the NOS internal services and drivers

If you don't actually use them, generating endless log files wastes both system resources and a wealth of information about the network's performance. Windows NT has a special tool, the Event Viewer, which enables you to (what else?) view log file events. The Windows NT Event Viewer has a built-in filter to help you select events from a particular time, date, workstation, device, segment, domain, and so on from any of the log files.

Performance art

I'm sure that you know the term *bottleneck* and that it generally means a constricting point. A network bottleneck is any device that restricts the network from operating at optimal performance levels. Every system has a bottleneck or two. The art of performance-tuning a network is finding and eliminating bottlenecks. However, technically when you find and eliminate one bottleneck, another one appears instantly. Bottlenecks create network administrator job security.

Eliminating a bottleneck may require more memory, a faster hard disk, faster NICs, more processors, or the like. However, after you eliminate the more serious bottlenecks on a network, you can still find some performance areas on a network that you can improve or fine-tune.

You can improve performance on many areas of the network by improving or implementing the following:

✔ **Disk caching:** This feature reduces the amount of disk I/O traffic on the system. Frequently accessed data is stored in physical memory, eliminating unnecessary I/O activity.

✔ **Multiprocessors:** Upgrading the server to multiple microprocessors enables the NOS to take advantage of multiprocessing capabilities.

✔ **Physical memory:** Network operating systems that use smaller physical memory page sizes tend to reduce the problem of memory fragmentation and increase the amount of memory available to applications.

✔ **Virtual memory:** You distribute virtual memory pagefiles across several logical disk drives to increase the overall memory available to the server. Although this process does increase memory, it can create another kind of bottleneck.

Performance monitoring

An integral step of performance tuning is performance monitoring, which tracks the usage of resources by network components and applications. Performance monitoring is an excellent tool for determining just where bottlenecks and utilization problems are present on a system. After you identify them, you can improve or eliminate these problems.

You can use tools, such as Windows NT's Performance Monitor, to monitor and report a variety of system resources, including:

✔ Bottlenecks in CPU, memory, disk I/O, or network I/O activities

✔ Utilization trends on certain devices for different periods of time

✔ The impact of system configuration or upgrade changes

✔ System real-time performance

The Troubleshooting Toolkit

For all you A+'ers who are wondering when I'm going to talk about tools — tools that you hold in your hands or wear on a tool belt — with apologies to Tim Allen, It's Tool Time! Network troubleshooting hardware tools cover a wide range of uses and functions, ranging from voltage testers to devices that diagnose a network's overall health.

Here are some tools mentioned on the Network+ test:

✓ **Cable testers:** A cable tester not only determines if any breaks are in a cable, but also tells you everything about the cable, including performance data, such as frame counts, packet collisions, broadcast storms, and more.

✓ **Crossover cable:** This network cable crosses the transmit and receive wires and eliminates the need for a hub when connecting two computers. Crossover cables enable you to test the computer in a peer-to-peer fashion off the network. You also use them to connect hubs and switches using MID-X connections.

✓ **Digital voltmeter (DVM):** A DVM measures a cable's continuity and determines if any breaks are in the cable. It can also indicate if a coaxial cable has been crushed and if its sheathing is in contact with the copper core wire.

✓ **Hardware loopback plug:** A loopback test checks to see whether a NIC can communicate with the network and whether the cable and interfaces are working. It works very similarly to the way a PING works over the network by sending out an echo signal and then treating the incoming echo as an incoming signal.

✓ **Protocol analyzers:** The most advanced tool in the troubleshooting toolbelt is the protocol analyzer. Protocol analyzers monitor network traffic in real time, capturing network packets and decoding them to track network performance and determine the cause of network problems and bottlenecks. Protocol analyzers commonly include a TDR as well. Popular protocol analyzers include Hewlett-Packard's Internet Advisor, Network Associates' Sniffer, and the Network Communications Corp's Network Probe.

✓ **Time-domain reflectometer (TDR):** You use this tool specifically to determine whether a cable has a break or short in it. A TDR has some advantages over a DVM if you use it for this purpose. For one, a TDR can measure the distance from itself to a detected break. If you study the name of this device, it tells you how this is done: It measures the time that it takes the signal to reflect back and then computes the distance based on the cable type.

✓ **Tone generator and tone locator (fox and hound):** These two devices are compact, handheld instruments. The tone generator generates a tracer tone down a wire that can be heard by an inductive amplifier (the tone locator) to locate the wire. If you've ever tried to locate a single wire in the bundle of spaghetti usually found in the floor or ceiling, you'll appreciate this set of tools.

Common Troubleshooting Situations

The number of potential network problems probably outnumbers the number of actual networks, but after the first ten or so problems, they're generally variations of a previous problem area. Here are some troubleshooting situations that you should be familiar with for the Network+ exam:

- ✔ **Installation problems:** If server or client software is installed improperly, it can cause unpredictable errors that may be hard to replicate, which is always a pain. When problems occur on a network server or client workstation immediately after you install new software, guess where you should look first?

- ✔ **Boot failures:** The range of problems that show up as boot failures is too long to list here. The Network+ exam asks about two particular kinds of boot failures: system startup and virus-related failures. A corrupted disk, bad video driver, or even a stuck key on the keyboard can cause a system startup problem. These are not usually network problems but must be overcome to get the user connected. The virus-related failure may be caused by a corrupted master boot record or other essential system resources.

- ✔ **Cabling:** The vast majority of network problems, and headaches, happen on the OSI model's Physical layer. The problems are in the NIC, cabling, or connectors. A problem in the Physical layer must be first isolated to a particular computer or network segment. One way to eliminate the computer (including its NIC) as a suspect is to plug a different computer, like a notebook, onto the cable and see if you can login and transfer files. If you can't login, then the problem is the cable. If you can login, then the original computer is the problem.

- ✔ **Power:** Expect to see some questions on the Network+ exam that relate to network power problems. Even with surge suppressors and UPSs in use, network clients may face other power-related problems. For example, if a workstation works fine during the day when the lights are out but performs badly at night when the lights are on, you should suspect that the voltage on the computer's line is dropping too low for proper operation.

- ✔ **Hardware changes:** Just like adding new software, if a workstation or a network fails immediately after you add new hardware devices to the network, it is very likely that the network body is rejecting its new organ. However, some faults may take a while to show up. When a problem occurs, your lineup of suspects should always include the last hardware change made to the network.

✔ **Software updates:** As I discuss in Chapter 21, vendor updates, upgrades, or patches that are intended to solve current or future problems can and do cause system problems at times. If a system update or patch is applied, you should test the system each step of the way and verify that the changes work. You may need to restore a backup if you can't fix the problem easily.

You can resolve most network-related problems on a workstation or client computer by merely restarting the workstation and having the user logon to the network.

Finding Troubleshooting Resources

You can find resources to help you troubleshoot a network in a variety of places. Some software, online services, subscription services, and printed documents in digital and analog forms give you up-to-the-minute help on troubleshooting techniques, tools, and answers to frequently asked questions (FAQs).

Here are some of the more helpful sources of troubleshooting information:

✔ **Telephone technical support:** Generally a fee-based service, telephone technical support is often the best source to get specific answers to a particular problem — if you have the time and patience. Some services are subscription-based with annual, quarterly, or monthly fees, and others are toll-based telephone services.

✔ **Microsoft TechNet:** A subscription service that provides information on technical networking issues for both Windows systems and non-Windows systems. Some TechNet information is available online, but the majority of it is supplied on monthly CD-ROMs. The CDs contain information on products, technical support data, software drivers, and even tutorials that show you how to troubleshoot common problems. Novell has a similar product, called the Novell Support Connection CD.

✔ **TSANet (Technical Support Alliance Network):** Hardware and software vendors — such as 3Com, Intel, Novell, and Compaq — have joined together to form an alliance to "support their mutual customers' success." You can find TSANet at www.tsanet.org.

✔ **Technical support bulletin boards:** Many bulletin boards are dedicated to technical support of networks, such as the Microsoft Download Library (MSDL). You usually access these services via a dial-up line or through a newsgroup.

✔ **E-zines and magazines:** More technical-topic trade print and online (e-zine) magazines are available every day. You can find a wealth of information at such sites. Some of the more interesting and informative are

- CMPNet (www.cmpnet.com)
- Ezine (www.ezine.com)
- PC Guide (www.pcguide.com)
- TechWeb (www.techweb.com)
- ZDNet (www.zdnet.com)

Prep Test

1 A particular workstation has been giving you fits. It seems to work just fine early in the day when the room lights are off, but later in the day, when the room lights are on, it has trouble connecting to the network or holding a connection after it's established. What do you think is the problem?

A ○ The NIC should be replaced.

B ○ The room is cabled incorrectly.

C ○ Low-voltage power.

D ○ User error.

2 Which of the following are indicators that a workstation is connecting to the network and functioning properly? (Choose three.)

A ❑ Link light on the NIC

B ❑ User login successful

C ❑ Username account in domain username database

D ❑ File transfer between workstation and server

3 What type of test can you perform to determine if a NIC is working properly?

A ○ PING

B ○ TRACERT

C ○ LOOPBACK

D ○ ICMP

4 Which of the following are types of network system log files? (Choose three.)

A ❑ Master event log file

B ❑ System log file

C ❑ Application log file

D ❑ Security log file

5 Any device that restricts the network from operating at its optimal levels is a

A ○ Fault

B ○ Bottleneck

C ○ Alert

D ○ System event

6 The troubleshooting tool that is used to directly connect computers without using a hub is a

A ○ Switch

B ○ Crossover cable

C ○ Bridge

D ○ Protocol analyzer

7 Which device checks to see whether a NIC can communicate with a network and whether the cables and interfaces of a workstation are working?

A ○ Hardware loopback

B ○ PING

C ○ Tone generator

D ○ TDR

8 NIC, cabling, and connectors operate on which layer of the OSI model?

A ○ Physical

B ○ Data Link

C ○ Network

D ○ Transport

9 Which of the following are good sources of technical information for the hardware and software of a network? (Choose all that apply.)

A ❑ Telephone support

B ❑ Vendor CD-ROM

C ❑ Trade magazines

D ❑ Online support

10 After installing new software on three workstations and installing antivirus software on the network server, the three workstations cannot connect to the server. Where would you begin your search for the problem?

A ○ Check the software on the workstation.

B ○ Check the software on the server.

C ○ Reboot the workstations.

D ○ Restart the server.

Answers

C. If a computer's performance coincides with an environmental situation — such as power on or off, heaters in use, the pop machine coming on, and so on — most likely the problem is in the environmental factors and not the computer. *See "Common Troubleshooting Situations."*

2 *A, B, D.* A username should always be in the domain user database, if valid. Link lights that are on indicate that the connection is established. Logging on and transferring data are surefire ways to tell that a connection is good. *Review "Common Troubleshooting Situations."*

3 *C.* A loopback test sends out a signal and then receives it to test the send and receive functions of a connection. *Check out "Common Troubleshooting Situations."*

4 *B, C, D.* If a master event log file exists, it is not considered a standard log file type. *Take a look at "Logs, alerts, events, and other records."*

5 *B.* Bottlenecks restrict the flow or usage of network resources. *See "Performance art."*

6 *B.* You use a crossover cable to interconnect hubs in their link (MID-X) ports. *Review "The Troubleshooting Toolkit."*

7 *A.* You will encounter questions on the Network+ exam that differentiate loopback tests from hardware loopback devices. Lookback tests are performed by hardware loopback devices, so be careful that you know what's being asked on any loopback questions. *Check out "The Troubleshooting Toolkit."*

8 *A.* This question may seem out of place at the end of a chapter on troubleshooting, but you'll be asked this question in the context of troubleshooting and device failures. *Take a look at "Common Troubleshooting Situations."*

9 *A, B, C, D.* Putting your qualitative judgment and experience aside, each of these resources can be a good source of technical troubleshooting information. *See "Finding Troubleshooting Resources."*

10 *B.* Because the three workstations have two things in common (the server software installation and the local computer software installs), start with the one that may eliminate the largest problem. If the server is the problem, you fix all three workstations at once. *Review "Common Troubleshooting Situations."*

Part VIII
The Part of Tens

The 5th Wave   By Rich Tennant

NETWORK+ EXAM

"I'm not sure you're taking this exam seriously enough. When asked to give a description of a 'Repeater', you wrote the recipe for a large bean burrito."

In this part . . .

After you have scheduled a time to take the test, you can begin preparing for the test in earnest. This part includes some great places to get study guides, test demonstrations, and other information to help you prepare. I don't believe that you can see too many different styles of test preparatory materials, but I would use caution on which ones you buy. Some are definitely better than others. Visit the Web sites, try out the demonstrations, and use the tools that best work for you.

When your test day finally arrives, I have included a list of things you should think about or do before, during, and after the test. The Network+ test is administered online and you cannot use study materials, notes, or anything besides good old brainpower to take the test. The test is not tricky. It is an honest measurement of your knowledge and understanding. So, remain calm. If you have carefully prepared yourself, you'll do just fine.

Chapter 23

Ten Test Day Tips

Get Me to the Test on Time

When you schedule your exam, you'll first be asked where you want to take the test. If you're uncertain, the friendly, helpful Sylvan Prometric counselor (more on this later) will help you choose the location closest to your home or find the most exotic location that you'd like to visit. The only reason that I mention the location is to let you know that the operating days and hours of your test location are the only limits on when you can choose to take the test. Taking the Network+ test or any Sylvan Prometric exam is not like taking the SAT, GMAT, or GRE tests where you're given a time and date to show up, or else. You're free to pick the time and date that works best for you.

I took the Network+ exam at a community college about an hour away from my home that was only open Monday through Thursday, 8:00 a.m. to 2:30 p.m. My other nearby choice was a site about three hours away that was open all day and into the evening, as well as Saturdays. So, if your first choice of a testing center doesn't meet your time needs, look for another place that does.

Make sure that you get to the testing center at least a half hour before your test time, or perhaps earlier if you want to do some last-minute cramming. The last thing that you want or need is to rush to make the test time (that you set yourself, remember) and feel agitated when you begin the test. Get there early, find a quiet place, relax, have a cup of coffee, tea, Postum, or whatever helps you relax, and go over the *Network+ Certification For Dummies* Cheat Sheet (included in the front of this book) as well as your notes.

Be sure to contact the site directly to check whether it requires you to check into the testing center or another office for a parking permit. If you do, be sure to add additional time for this task when calculating your arrival time.

Review Your Notes One Last Time

In the time right before you check in, review the things guaranteed to be on the test: IP address classes, TCP/IP protocols, OSI model layers, network cabling, NICs, and connectivity devices, and all the information marked by the Instant Answer icons throughout this book. In most cases, these items all have a list or sequence of things. Right before the test, review any of your cheat phrases (salami pizza and so on) and other reminders. You may not benefit by cramming for conceptual topics, but a last-minute cram with lists and sequences can help you focus on the test.

Check In on Time

A few minutes before your scheduled test time, check in with the test administrator. Be sure that you have the two pieces of identification that you were asked to bring. Because you need only one picture ID, your driver's license, passport, or work badge (if it also has your signature on it) should work. You also need a second identification that has your full name on it. A credit card, library card, or the like should do fine.

Because the Network+ exam is a closed-book test, you can't carry your notes or books with you into the test area, so surrender them without whimpering. Don't play tug-of-war with your notes; keep yourself relaxed and focused on the test. Remember that this test is something that you wanted to do and that it is a good thing. One thing to keep in mind is that even if you do fail, you will have at least seen the test once and will definitely know what to study for next time. In addition, the Network+ exam report tells you exactly how you did in each area and what each area covers. So, regardless of the result, the test should be a positive experience. I know, this is easy for me to say; it isn't my $185.

Do a Brain Dump, But Do It on the Plastic

You aren't allowed to bring in any paper at all. In most test centers, you're given sheets of plastic and a grease pen, a dry-erase board and a dry-erase pen, or even one or two sheets of paper and a pencil. You use these items for scribbling notes during the test. You must turn them in after the test. Ask for or take as much as you think you'll need.

After you are situated at your assigned station and have received your basic instructions, unload your lists by writing them down on the board, plastic, or paper. Write down as much of the lists and sequences and special relationships, such as the OSI model layers, that you can remember. You can then refer to your notes during the exam without getting flustered about whether you're remembering something correctly.

Do the Tutorial!

At the beginning of the test session, you're offered a tutorial on the different types of questions, illustrations, response types, and the Sylvan Prometrics testing system. Do yourself a favor and go through the tutorial. No matter how many times you've taken the driver's test on the testing machine, or even if you are a Sylvan Prometrics veteran, this testing experience is likely very different, and much better, than any you've experienced before. Don't think that if you've seen one online test, you've seen them all. Take the time to casually move through the tutorial. Your time doesn't begin until you finish the tutorial and actually start the test. Use the tutorial as a way to relax; adjust your chair, keyboard, and mouse and get ready for the exam.

Ready, Steady, Go

When you're ready to begin, take a deep breath, clear your head (or at least try), and start the exam. You have 90 minutes to answer the 65 questions on the exam. The distribution of questions on the test should be very close to what's shown in Table 23-1.

Table 23-1	Network+ Question Distribution by Section
Section Topic	*Number of Questions*
Basic knowledge	12
Physical layer	4
Data Link layer	3
Network layer	3
Transport layer	3
TCP/IP fundamentals	11
TCP/IP suite: Utilities	7
Remote connectivity	3
Security	4
Implementing the installation of the network	4
Maintaining and supporting the network	4
Troubleshooting the network	7

Take your time, but occasionally check the time remaining (it appears in the upper-right corner of the display). Even if you aren't a particularly fast test-taker, you should have plenty of time as long as you stay on track.

Mark Questions You Want to Think About

The Sylvan Prometric test software allows you to mark a question with a check box in the upper-left corner of the screen so that you can review it again later. You should also make a note on your plastic as to why you have marked this question, as in the following examples:

✔ 33. Is it A or D? First impression is D.

✔ 41. B or D?

✔ 61. Isn't this asked a different way earlier in the test?

Avoid the temptation to mark every question. You don't really need to mark a question to review it later, but the software lets you step through only the marked questions if you choose.

Answer Every Question

Some people recommend that you read through an entire test before you begin answering questions. Don't waste your time reading the entire Network+ exam before starting. Instead, answer all the questions that you're sure of and mark the ones that you're not. If you're the least bit hesitant on a question, choose your best choice and then mark it.

If you forget to answer a question or if you don't give all the answers on a multiple-answer question, the testing software indicates that these questions are incomplete. You have the opportunity to go back and answer them, but remember that you only have the 90 minutes. Reviewing your answers must still be done in the alloted test time.

Watch Out for Questions with Multiple Right Answers

If you go through the tutorial, you find out that questions with a single right answer use a radio button for the answer, and questions with multiple correct answers use check boxes. In addition, if a question has three answers, you're reminded of this in the lower-left corner of the screen. So, if the answer choices for a question have boxes instead of round buttons and the answer reminder says "Provide three answers," or words to that effect, those are good signs that the question needs three answers. Gone are the questions that leave it up to you to decide how many answers a question needs.

No Hootin' and Hollerin', Please

The good, and sometimes bad, part of taking a Sylvan Prometric interactive online test is that you get your results immediately. As soon as you finish the test, not only do you know whether you passed or failed, but you also receive a printed report that tells you how well you did in each section. Of course, if you pass, you don't really care about which areas you can improve — until later. However, if you fail, this information is the positive part of an otherwise disappointing time and can be helpful for next time.

When you do receive your passing test score, celebrating boisterously at your terminal is considered bad manners. However, when you receive that happy news, take along my congratulations and those of the entire _Network+ Certification For Dummies_ team for a job well done.

Chapter 24

Ten Really Great Web Sites for Study Aids

• •

In This Chapter

▶ Network+ exam study materials on the Web

▶ Other resources that you can use to prepare for the Network+ exam

• •

*V*ariety is one of the keys to preparing for the Network+ exam. By using a number of different study tools and aids, you see many ways of asking the same question. This approach to studying helps you prepare for whatever wording and approach the Network+ test uses.

A number of Web sites simulate the test content and format fairly accurately. Some are free; some are slightly more. The free sites are certainly worth the cost; the others — *caveat emptor*. You need to consider how much you want to spend on study aids to prepare yourself for a $185 test. Of course, if you don't pass, the cost of the test begins to multiply. Be cautious when buying study aids and look for the bargains that are out there.

The Web sites and other resources listed in this chapter are sites that you'll find helpful without having to spend a fortune. Please understand that all of these sites exist at the time that I write this book. If any of these sites have disappeared, just search for others. Remember that searching for *Network+* gets you nowhere; instead, search for *Networkplus* or *network certification*. (You have to weed through the CNE and MCSE stuff.)

By the way, www.networkplus.com is *not* a Network+ materials site.

CompTIA.org

www.comptia.org/networkplus/index.htm

This site should be your first stop when preparing for the Network+ exam. This site is the proverbial *horse's mouth* for the Network+ test. Although it may not be the best-looking, best-organized, or fastest site on the Web, it does provide answers to just about any question that you may have about taking the test.

The CompTIA site also displays a series of commercial training company banner ads if you're looking for preparation courses, materials, or practice tests.

AFSMI.org

```
www.amsi.org/networkplus/
```

The Association For Services Management International (AFSMI) markets the Network+ exam internationally (outside of the United States). Its Web site provides a lot of background information on CompTIA, Sylvan Prometrics, and the exams. This site was still under construction at the time this book was printed. Assuming AFSMI lives up to their quality standard used on earlier sites, this one should be great. However, you may need to wait for it.

NetworkPlusCertify.com and DaliDesign.com

```
www.networkpluscertify.com
```

Dali Design (as in Hello dali) has created a product called PREP! for Network+, which is an excellent study and test-prep aid. A sample test with about 40 questions is available for downloading.

The full PREP! for Network+ contains over 400 total questions that Dali Design has taken from "actual Network+ Certification test experiences," so all the test topics are included. If you like the sample test, the price for the full test engine is very reasonable.

CramSession.com

```
www.cramsession.com/cramsession/aplus/network/
```

Of the exam-related sites, this Web site has perhaps the best organization and information. It is perfect for that last-minute cram before the test.

As you get closer to exam day, use this site to finely hone your memory banks for the test. You may also find it useful to outline the areas that you need to study when you first get started.

SelfTest.co.uk

`www.stsware.com/networkplus.htm`

This British site offers probably the best freebie test demo on the Web. In fact, its practice test, of all the practice tests available on the Web, is probably the one most like the real thing.

You can download a sample Network+ test demo and a few other certification tests as well. The idea is that if you like the practice tests, you can buy the full-blown test simulators. If you can afford it, buying these simulators may not be such a bad idea.

Marcraft International (MIC-INC.com)

`www.mic-inc.com/Nplus`

Of the free downloadable practice tests, this one is probably the most challenging. The questions are written in such a way that you must think about why an answer is correct as well as why the other answers may be wrong. Marcraft's full-blown practice-test study aid is reasonably priced, and if you haven't already shot your bankroll on other study tools, it's worth buying.

By all means, try out each of the demos available before buying one. You may actually find one for free that does the job for you. If you plan to use only interactive practice tests (not the best idea in my opinion), then the Marcraft product is a good choice.

GTSPartners.com

`www.networkplus.net`

If you're interested in finding an instructor-lead class, GTSPartners.com may be the site for you. The site also has a training partner that offers online classes.

ComputerPrep.com

www.computerprep.com/products/netplus.htm

Another training company that produces high-quality training materials is ComputerPrep, Inc. It offers a full package to prepare you for certification, which includes a student guide, hands-on exercises, and a CD-ROM containing an interactive self-test.

PCGuide.com

www.pcguide.com/

The PC Guide is not a Network+ site specifically, but it is without a doubt the most comprehensive site on PC hardware on the Web. Even if you don't use this site to round out your studies for the Network+ exam, you should probably bookmark it for later reference.

The honorable thing to do would be to purchase the site's content in CD-ROM form to encourage the site's author to continue maintaining this excellent Web site.

amazon.com, barnesandnoble.com, and borders.com

www.amazon.com
www.barnesandnoble.com
www.borders.com

Why, you ask, are booksellers on the list of Network+ sites? Well, whether you use Amazon.com, Barnes and Noble, Borders, or another online bookstore, these sites provide you with a list of the latest Network+ exam guides, cram books, and question banks available in print. The test simulators are good, especially if you buy some of the complete test banks, but a study guide in print form is a good way to study when you're away from the PC, like on an airplane, in the bath, or out on a date. (This is important stuff!)

Visit these sites and search for *networkplus*.

Other Resources You Should Consider

Perhaps the best of the resources are my favorite books from my favorite publisher (IDG Books Worldwide, Inc.), not to mention some of my favorite authors:

- *Networking For Dummies,* 3rd Edition, by Doug Lowe
- *Upgrading & Fixing Networks For Dummies,* by Bill Camarda
- *Windows NT Networking For Dummies,* by Ed (Mr. Networking) Tittel, Mary Madden, and Earl Follis
- *Networking with NetWare For Dummies,* 4th Edition, by Ed (He's the Man) Tittel, James E. Gaskin, and Earl Follis
- *Windows NT Server 4 For Dummies,* by Ed (Guess Who) Tittel
- *Novell's Encyclopedia of Networking,* by Kevin Shafer

In spite of the fact that this list is a shameless plug, these books are an entertaining and informative way to brush up on your networking knowledge. You need to have some fun while studying, and at least this way you'll have an excuse for that smile on your face.

Part IX
Appendixes

The 5th Wave   By Rich Tennant

"You know, this was a situation question on my Network+ exam, but I always thought it was just hypothetical."

In this part . . .

This part contains sample questions for each section of the Network+ exam to help you prepare for the test. I have tried to give you about the same number and type of questions as you'll find on the actual exam. For many reasons (memory being foremost), I am prevented from just giving you the exact questions you find on the test. The questions you see on your test are likely very different from those that I saw when I took the test, although they cover the same material. Use my sample questions to measure the areas in which you need to study more. If you do fairly well on these questions, then you are probably reaching your peak.

This part also explains the tools included on the CD-ROM. These tools help you prepare for the test, including a test engine that generates practice tests for you in a variety of combinations.

Appendix A

Sample Test

• •

*H*ere are sample questions from all of the sections of the Network+ examination. The Network+ test has 65 questions spread over 12 test topic sections, and I have provided you with the same number and ratio of questions that you find on the actual test.

These questions are not intended to represent the exact questions you find on the Network+ exam. Instead, the questions are examples of the topics and question formats you should expect to see on the actual test. Practice with these questions, and if you do well, you are probably just about ready to take the Network+ exam.

There is one type of question I am unable to reproduce for you here in the book. On at least one question, you're asked to use the mouse and a crosshair marker to mark a particular feature or item in a diagram. For example, you may be asked to choose a particular network topology from a group of diagrams, or you may be asked to indicate a certain type of network segment or device on a network layout diagram. So, study all the diagrams you can find and be sure you can identify all the features depicted.

The following questions are samples of what you may find on the Network+ examination in each of the exam sections.

Basic Knowledge

1 Connecting to a network server running Novell NetWare from a Windows 9*x* client requires which client protocol?

A ○ NDS Services for Windows

B ○ Client Service for NetWare

C ○ File and Print Services for NetWare

D ○ Microsoft TCP/IP for Windows

2 A workstation that is a part of a 10BaseT Ethernet network is located in a remote part of the building. It is connected into a passive hub located 15 meters away. The hub is connected into a patch panel by a 5-meter long patch cord. The patch panel terminates an 85-meter run of Cat 5 cabling whose other end terminates into a switch near the server. On occasion, the workstation is experiencing data loss and also loses its network connection.

Proposed solution: It is proposed that a 100BaseT card be installed in the workstation.

Required objectives: To eliminate the workstation-based data and network connection problems.

Optional objectives: To provide a higher bandwidth to the workstation.

A ○ The proposed solution achieves both the required and optional objectives.

B ○ The proposed solution achieves only the required objective.

C ○ The proposed solution achieves only the optional objective.

D ○ The proposed solution achieves none of the required and optional objectives.

3 The device used to connect network nodes to a token ring network is a

A ○ Hub

B ○ Bridge

C ○ MAU

D ○ Ring bridge

4 Which of the following describes the mesh topology?

A ○ Each node is directly connected to a central concentrating device.

B ○ Every node is redundantly connected to every other node.

C ○ Network nodes are arranged in a looping pattern.

D ○ Network nodes are connected directly to the network backbone.

5 Disk mirroring is support on which RAID level?

A ○ RAID0

B ○ RAID1

C ○ RAID3

D ○ RAID5

6 Which 100BaseT standard implements 100Mbps networking using two-pair Cat 5 UTP?

A ○ 100BaseT4

B ○ 100BaseFX

C ○ 100BaseVG-AnyLAN

D ○ 100BaseTX

7 Which network connectivity device operates on both the Data Link and the Network layers of the OSI Reference Model?

A ○ Router

B ○ Brouter

C ○ Catalyst switch

D ○ Bridge

8 Which of the following devices regenerate a network signal before passing it on? (Choose two.)

A ❑ Repeater

B ❑ Passive Hub

C ❑ Active Hub

D ❑ Patch Panel

9 A network bridge operates on which OSI Reference Model layer?

A ○ Physical

B ○ Data Link

C ○ Network

D ○ Transport

10 Which of the following are characteristics of 10BaseT network media? (Choose two.)

A ❑ 185-meter segment length

B ❑ 100-meter segment length

C ❑ RJ-45 connectors

D ❑ BNC-T connectors

E ❑ 500-meter segment length

11 Ethernet networks use which access method?

A ○ CSMA/CA

B ○ CSMA/CD

C ○ Ethernet SNAP

D ○ Demand Priority

12 Network segments are created on a network through the use of which of the following devices? (Choose two.)

A ❑ Hub

B ❑ Router

C ❑ Bridge

D ❑ Gateway

Physical Layer

13 Which of the following can be used to configure a network interface card (NIC)? (Choose three.)

A ❑ Jumpers

B ❑ DIP switches

C ❑ Server-based software

D ❑ Plug-and-play

14 Loopback testing is commonly used to test the function of a

A ○ File server

B ○ Print server

C ○ NIC

D ○ Hub

15 A workstation has difficulty communicating on the network whenever the sound card is in use. What is the likely problem?

A ○ The NIC is faulty.

B ○ The sound card and NIC have the same IRQ setting.

C ○ The sound card has an electrical short.

D ○ The problem is unrelated to the hardware.

16 After connecting a workstation to the network by installing a NIC, the workstation is unable to connect to the network. The NIC is connected to the network cable and testing indicates the cable is fine, but internal loopback testing on the NIC fails to run. What should be your next course of action?

A ○ Replace the NIC.
B ○ Replace the cable connector.
C ○ Run an external loopback test.
D ○ Install the NIC's device driver on the workstation.

Data Link Layer

17 The Data Link layer consists of two sublayers: (Choose two.)

A ❑ MAC sublayer
B ❑ LLC sublayer
C ❑ DMA sublayer
D ❑ ECC sublayer

18 What Data Link device is used to filter network traffic and interconnect LANs and LAN segments?

A ○ Router
B ○ Hub
C ○ Bridge
D ○ MAU

19 Which IEEE 802 standard defines the error- and flow-control actions of the LLC sublayer?

A ○ 802.1
B ○ 802.2
C ○ 802.5
D ○ 802.10

Network Layer

20 Which of the following actions occur on the Network layer?

A ○ Error control
B ○ Flow control
C ○ Connection-oriented session control
D ○ Routing

21 Which of the following are characteristics of a brouter?

A ❑ Serves as a bridge to non-routable protocols
B ❑ Serves as a router to routable protocols
C ❑ Serves as a bridge on networks without routers
D ❑ Serves as a router on networks without bridges

22 Which of the following protocols are routable? (Choose two.)

A ❑ TCP

B ❑ IP

C ❑ IPX

D ❑ NetBEUI

Transport Layer

23 Which of the following protocols are connection-oriented protocols? (Choose two.)

A ❑ IP

B ❑ TCP

C ❑ UDP

D ❑ SPX

24 Which of the following Windows names conforms to the UNC standard?

A ○ \\SERVER_NAME\SHARE_NAME

B ○ \\SHARE_NAME\SERVER_NAME

C ○ //SHARE_NAME\PATH

D ○ //SERVER_NAME/PATH

25 A protocol that is reliable, although slower than other protocols, that guarantees the delivery of data packets is

A ○ Connectionless

B ○ Connection-oriented

C ○ Routable

D ○ Nonroutable

TCP/IP Fundamentals

26 The routable device that provides a network node with the ability to communicate with computers on other subnets or networks is referred to as the node's

A ○ Subnet mask

B ○ DNS

C ○ Default gateway

D ○ Server

27 An e-mail message sent from `www.dummies.com` to `www.bigstateu.edu` will follow which DNS path?

   A ○ `.com,` then `www.bigstateu`

   B ○ `www.dummies,` then `.edu`

   C ○ `www.dummies.,` then `.com`

   D ○ `.edu,` then `www.bigstateu`

28 The default subnet mask used for a Class C network is

   A ○ 255.0.0.0

   B ○ 255.255.0.0

   C ○ 255.255.255.0

   D ○ 255.255.255.255

29 Which of the following is a valid Class B IP address?

   A ○ 100.20.200.1

   B ○ 10.0.100.1

   C ○ 200.204.100.6

   D ○ 127.0.0.1

30 The IP address 10.0.100.2 is most likely a

   A ○ Server

   B ○ Router

   C ○ Intranet node

   D ○ Firewall

31 The well-known port used to transfer documents using the HTTP protocol is

   A ○ Port 20

   B ○ Port 80

   C ○ Port 25

   D ○ Port 137

32 Which of the following are TCP/IP protocols? (Choose three.)

   A ❑ UDP

   B ❑ ICMP

   C ❑ SMTP

   D ❑ WINIPCFG

   E ❑ DNS

   F ❑ WINS

33 The service used on a Windows system to resolve IP addresses to NetBIOS addresses is

A ○ WINS

B ○ DNS

C ○ HOSTS

D ○ DHCP

34 The TCP/IP protocol used to transfer e-mail across the network is

A ○ SNMP

B ○ SMTP

C ○ POP3

D ○ IMAP

35 A LAN has more than 200 users who all access essentially the same URLs on the Web. What device can the network administrator install that may have the affect of speeding up Web page access for the users?

A ○ Web server

B ○ Gateway

C ○ IP proxy

D ○ Larger hard disk drive

36 The e-mail service that retains user e-mail on the server is

A ○ POP3

B ○ IMAP

C ○ SMTP

D ○ FTP

TCP/IP Suite: Utilities

37 Which of the following TCP/IP utilities can be used to display MAC addresses on a Windows client? (Choose two.)

A ❑ NBTSTAT

B ❑ IPCONFIG

C ❑ PING

D ❑ TRACERT

38 Which TCP/IP utility can be used to verify that an IP address is valid?

A ○ TRACERT

B ○ PING

C ○ IPCONFIG

D ○ NBTSTAT

39 Which TCP/IP utility displays information on each of the hops crossed to reach an IP address?

A ○ TRACERT

B ○ PING

C ○ IPCONFIG

D ○ NBTSTAT

40 You wish to renew the DHCP lease on your Windows workstation. Which TCP/IP utility should you use?

A ○ NBTSTAT

B ○ NETSTAT

C ○ IPCONFIG

D ○ WINIPCFG

41 The TCP/IP utility used to display and modify the IP to MAC address translation table is

A ○ WINIPCFG

B ○ NETSTAT

C ○ ARP

D ○ RIP

42 Yuri is having trouble connecting to some Web sites. Because no other users are reporting problems and you have not experienced any trouble connecting to the Web, you decide the problem must either be his workstation or the URL he is trying to contact. Which of the following utilities may be helpful in tracking down the problem? (Choose three.)

A ❑ Web browser

B ❑ PING

C ❑ TRACERT

D ❑ ARP

E ❑ NBTSTAT

43 The TCP/IP protocol used by a UNIX system to transfer a file across the Internet is

A ○ HTTP

B ○ PPTP

C ○ SLIP

D ○ FTP

Remote Connectivity

44 To create a VPN over a TCP/IP network, which protocol is used?

A ○ PPP

B ○ SLIP

C ○ CSLIP

D ○ PPTP

45 The dial-up networking protocol that supports TCP/IP, NetBEUI, and IPX/SPX data packets over a communications link is

A ○ PPP

B ○ SLIP

C ○ CSLIP

D ○ PPTP

46 The technical name for the standard telephone system is

A ○ ISDN

B ○ PRI

C ○ PSTN

D ○ PVC

Security

47 The security mode that assigns access to shared resources based on the permissions assigned to a user account is

A ○ User-level security

B ○ Share-level security

C ○ Resource-level security

D ○ Managed security access

48 The security mode that grants access to shared resources based on the rights and permissions assigned to the resource is

A ○ User-level security

B ○ Share-level security

C ○ Resource-level security

D ○ Managed security access

49 A well-developed password program requires the following: (Choose three.)

A ❑ Users must cycle through 8 passwords before repeating a password.

B ❑ Passwords should be simple, easily remembered, common words.

C ❑ Passwords should include numbers or special characters.

D ❑ Passwords should be more than four characters in length.

E ❑ A central file of all passwords should be maintained by the administrator.

50 What of the following are functions of a network firewall? (Choose two.)

A ❑ Restricts outside access to the internal network

B ❑ Records remote user access to internal resources

C ❑ Provides document-caching services

D ❑ Restricts internal user access to external resources

Implementing the Installation of the Network

51 A user calls to report that she is unable to logon to the network. She claims she has tried to logon from a number of workstations with no success. You get her account and password and logon successfully on the first try. What is likely the problem?

A ○ The user does not have the correct permissions.

B ○ The user is misspelling her user account name.

C ○ The user has been deleted from her department's group.

D ○ No trust relationship exists for the user's subnet.

52 Which of the following should be gathered before beginning a network implementation? (Choose three.)

A ❑ Administrative and test accounts and passwords

B ❑ Network IP addresses and configurations

C ❑ The MAC address of all connected devices

D ❑ All relevant operating procedures

53 A group of network workstations have begun to have intermittent problems every afternoon. From your initial troubleshooting you find that the room lights are being turned on around 1:00 p.m. each afternoon and are not used in the morning hours. What do you suppose is the source of the problem?

A ○ A low voltage situation on the power lines

B ○ A high voltage situation on the power lines

C ○ Not enough information to form a judgment

D ○ The room lights have an electrical short

54 External SCSI devices use which of the following connectors? (Choose two.)

A ❑ Centronics 50-pin

B ❑ 50-pin ribbon cable

C ❑ DB25-pin female

D ❑ DB25-pin male

Maintaining and Supporting the Network

55 Which of the following are good sources for documentation regarding a vendor's patches, fixes, and upgrades? (Choose three.)

A ❑ Vendor's website

B ❑ Release CD-ROM

C ❑ Technical support telephone service

D ❑ Trade magazines

56 Which type of backup copies all files changed since the last full backup without resetting their archive status?

A ○ Incremental backup

B ○ Differential backup

C ○ File Copy backup

D ○ Archival backup

57 Users throughout the network are complaining about missing files, and some workstations now cannot boot up. After you fix the immediate problems, what do you suppose you should consider doing?

A ○ Re-installing all client operating systems

B ○ Installing server and client antivirus software

C ○ Instigating procedures that back up user workstations to the server's hard disk

D ○ No action necessary; the problems are routine network situations

58 Recently your nightly backup DLT tapes are beginning to have data read and write errors. You have had these tapes for over a year without problems until just recently. What action do you suppose you should take to eliminate the tape errors?

A ○ Purchase new tapes.

B ○ Purchase and install a DAT tape drive.

C ○ Clean the tape drive read/write head.

D ○ Change the storage location of the tapes.

Troubleshooting the Network

59 A user calls to report that she cannot logon to the network. You check with other users in the same segment and find that they cannot logon as well. A check with users in a different, but nearby, segment finds that they are not experiencing any problems. What should you do next?

    A ○ Continue checking other network segments to determine the scope of the problem.

    B ○ Reset the router on which the reporting segment is attached.

    C ○ Reset each of the workstations having difficulty.

    D ○ Reset the server to restore service to the problem segment.

60 A user reports that they cannot access an application on the application server. Before you take any other actions, what should you do?

    A ○ Have the user try to access the application from a different workstation.

    B ○ Have another user in the same subnet try to access the application from their workstation.

    C ○ Try to access the application yourself.

    D ○ Verify the command or process the user is using to launch the application.

61 A workstation monitor is not functioning. You have verified that it is plugged in, switched on, and attached to the proper port on the system unit. What would you do next?

    A ○ Plug another monitor on the original system.

    B ○ Plug the monitor into another computer.

    C ○ Place a service call to the manufacturer.

    D ○ Replace the video card and re-install the device driver.

62 Which of the following would you use to help determine if the NIC in a workstation is functioning? (Choose two.)

    A ❑ PING 127.0.0.1

    B ❑ A hardware loopback plug

    C ❑ Software diagnostics available for the NIC

    D ❑ An internal loopback routine

63 Whenever the soda pop vending machine's compressor motor comes on, a portion of the network begins having intermittent problems. What do you suppose the source of the problem is?

    A ○ Low voltage

    B ○ High voltage

    C ○ EMI

    D ○ ESD

64 Recently, the accounting department reorganized its floor plan. In the process, several workstations and their cabling were moved to new places in the room. On one workstation, the existing cabling was left attached to the NIC while the computer was moved. This workstation now cannot see the network. You have tested the NIC with both external and internal loopbacks and the workstation's configuration is fine. What possibility do you suspect to be the problem?

A ○ When the equipment was moved, the hard disk was damaged.

B ○ The workstation's DHCP lease has expired.

C ○ When the equipment was moved, the cabling was damaged.

D ○ The electricity in the new location is faulty.

65 A server that uses the IPX/SPX protocol is unable to communicate with other segments of the network. What could be the problem? (Choose two.)

A ❏ IPX/SPX protocol is not installed.

B ❏ TCP/IP clients are not installed properly.

C ❏ The frame type is incorrect.

D ❏ The default gateway setting is incorrect.

Answers

1 B. Windows includes a number of different protocols that allow it to connect to other network operating systems and servers. *See Chapter 5.*

2 D. Installing a 100BaseT NIC does not address any of the issues, especially if the network is only a 10BaseT system. The 105-meter total distance is the problem. Regardless, the objectives are not addressed. *See Chapters 2 and 6.*

3 C. A Multistation Access Unit (MAU or MSAU) is used to connect workstations to token ring networks. You may see this question on the test. If there is a drawing, check to see if they are connected in a loop. *See Chapter 6.*

4 B. The Internet is the ultimate mesh network. *See Chapter 4.*

5 B. RAID1 also is also associated with disk duplexing. *See Chapter 2.*

6 D. 100BaseT4 and 100BaseVG-AnyLAN use four pairs of UTP wire and 100BaseFX uses fiber-optic cable. *See Chapter 6.*

7 B. The brouter operates on the Data Link layer as a bridge to non-routable protocols and on the Network layer as a router for routable protocols. *See Chapters 3 and 9.*

8 A, C. That's all a repeater does, but an active hub also interconnects multiple workstations and devices. *See Chapters 2 and 6.*

9 B. These devices are also referred to as Data Link bridges. *See Chapter 9.*

10 B, C. 10Base2 has a 185-meter segment length limit and uses BNC-T connectors. 10Base5 has a 500-meter segment length limit. *See Chapter 6.*

11 B. Carrier Sense Multiple Access/Collision Detection (CSMA/CD) is defined in IEEE 802.3. *See Chapter 9.*

12 B, C. Routers and bridges are used to create subnetworks and network segments that reduce the amount of traffic on the network as a whole. *See Chapter 3.*

13 A, B, D. Another way is with installation software that comes with the NIC. *See Chapters 3 and 8.*

14 C. Loopback plugs (external loopback) and software loopback (internal loop-back) are used to create an echo process that sends out a signal that is looped back to the sending device. *See Chapter 22.*

15 B. Often plug-and-play or installation software will create IRQ and I/O address conflicts. *See Chapter 8.*

16 D. The second step of installing a NIC is to install the device driver. *See Chapter 8.*

17 A, B. These two sublayers carry out the functions of the Data Link layer. *See Chapter 9.*

18 C. A bridge does not have the ability to route packets beyond the local net-work, but it can filter packets to the network segment to which they are addressed. *See Chapter 9.*

19 B. IEEE 802.2 defines error- and flow-control procedures for the LLC and MAC sublayers. *See Chapter 9.*

20 D. The other actions listed occur on either the Data Link or Transport layers. *See Chapter 10.*

21 A, B. Brouters operate on two OSI layers: the Data Link and the Network. *See Chapter 10.*

22 B, C. TCP is the Transport protocol of TCP/IP and, just in case you haven't heard, NetBEUI is non-routable. *See Chapter 10.*

23 B, D. IP and UDP are both connectionless protocols. *See Chapter 11.*

24 D. Don't be fooled if the UNC examples use a pathname instead of a share-name. In fact, the UNC name could include both in the form of //SERVER_NAME/PATH/SHARE_NAME. *See Chapter 11.*

25 B. Slower because the overhead involved in controlling and managing the connection. *See Chapter 11.*

26 C. The default gateway is typically the IP address of the router used to access beyond the local network. *See Chapter 13.*

27 C. The DNS search moves from the local network to the root domain and then on to the root domain (.edu) and on to the remote network. *See Chapter 12.*

28 *C.* Typically the subnet attempts to filter out the NETID. Most Class CHOSTIDs are identified in the fourth octet. *See Chapter 13.*

29 *A.* B represents an internal address behind a firewall, C is a Class C address, and D is the special address reserved for loopback testing. *See Chapter 13.*

30 *C.* These addresses are reserved for networks that do not connect to the Internet (non-routed) or those located behind a firewall. *See Chapter 13.*

31 *B.* Port 20 is used for FTP data, port 25 is used for SMTP, and port 137 is used for NetBIOS. *See Chapter 13.*

32 *A, B, C.* The remaining are proprietary protocols (WINIPCFG and WINS) or are services rather than protocols (DNS). *See Chapter 13.*

33 *A.* DNS is used to resolve domain names to IP addresses; HOSTS is a Windows function that is used to resolve host names to IP addresses; and DHCP is used to assign and manage dynamic host IP addresses. *See Chapter 13.*

34 *B.* Watch those acronyms. SNMP is used to manage networked devices, and POP3 and IMAP are used to manage e-mail mailboxes. SMTP is the simple mail transport protocol. *See Chapter 13.*

35 *C.* An IP proxy, or proxy server, among other services will cache frequently accessed Web documents to reduce the amount of traffic being routed out of the network. *See Chapter 13.*

36 *B.* POP3 downloads a mailbox's contents to the client; IMAP retains the mailbox contents on the server. *See Chapter 13.*

37 *A, B.* NBTSTAT is used to display the NetBIOS name cache and IPCONFIG displays the Internet Protocol configuration for a workstation. *See Chapter 14.*

38 *B.* PING transmits an echo request to the IP address which, if it is a valid address, will be returned. *See Chapter 14.*

39 *A.* TRACERT lists the information on each router (hop) its packet passes over on its way to the IP address target. *See Chapter 14.*

40 *C.* The Windows NT utility IPCONFIG can be used to renew DHCP leases. *See Chapter 14.*

41 *C.* ARP, a Microsoft utility, can be used to edit or view the address resolution protocol cache file. *See Chapter 14.*

42 *A, B, C.* These tools each will connect to an IP address or URL in different ways. The browser will attempt to transfer the file at the URL, PING verifies its IP address is valid, and TRACERT verifies the route used to it. *See Chapter 14.*

43 *D.* FTP is the universal file transfer protocol in TCP/IP. *See Chapter 14.*

44 *D.* The Point-to-Point Tunneling Protocol (PPTP) creates a virtual private network over TCP/IP. *See Chapter 15.*

45 *A.* The primary reason for PPP emergence over SLIP is its ability to support other protocols. *See Chapter 15.*

46 *C.* The Public Switch Telephone Network, or POTS (plain old telephone system) is the everyday telephone system we all know and love. *See Chapter 15.*

47 *A.* You have more permission options using user-level security because access is controlled by the settings in each individual login account. *See Chapter 16.*

48 *B.* Access to a shared device is granted by setting rights and permissions on the sharename created for the device. *See Chapter 16.*

49 *A, C, D.* Passwords should not be filed or use common words. *See Chapter 16.*

50 *A, D.* A firewall keeps out the bad guys and keeps the good guys from going bad places. *See Chapter 16.*

51 *B.* If you can logon with a user account and password, they should be able to. *See Chapter 17.*

52 *A, B, D.* Usually the MAC addresses will be logged by the Data Link layer functions on the network. *See Chapter 17.*

53 *A.* It seems likely that the fact the problem and the lights come on at the same time is hardly a coincidence. *See Chapter 18.*

54 *A, C.* Be sure you know which is being asked: internal (50-pin ribbon cable) versus external SCSI connectors. *See Chapter 17.*

55 *A, B.* Technical phone support can be expensive and trade magazines, while good for learning about upcoming upgrades, rarely contain the detail needed. *See Chapter 20.*

56 *B.* An incremental backup copies all of the files that have changed since the last time each file was backed up and changes the archive settings. Copy backups only make a copy, and the archival backup is another name for a full backup. *See Chapter 20.*

57 *B.* Unexplainable or reproducible errors are often a telltale sign of virus infection. *See Chapter 20.*

58 *C.* The tape media rarely wears out and most of the time the mechanical parts are the problem. *See Chapter 19.*

59 *A.* The problem source and scope should be completely determined before you begin solving it. *See Chapter 21.*

60 *D.* Before you go off on lengthy troubleshooting processes, check the obvious. Maybe they are spelling the name wrong or using the wrong icon. *See Chapter 21.*

61 *B.* First, verify that the monitor is good, and then verify that the video card is good, and so on. *See Chapter 21.*

62 *B, C.* Okay, we can argue about using a PING command or internal loopback, but usually if the NIC is working, an external loopback and some diagnostics are a good first effort. *See Chapter 21.*

63 *C.* Perhaps even low voltage, but compressor motors are notorious for EMI (electromagnetic interference). The real solution is to take the workstations off of the same circuit as the pop machine. *See Chapter 18.*

64 *C.* When all else fails, it very well could be the cabling, which could have been crimped or cut during the move. *See Chapter 18.*

65 *A, C.* Novell NetWare supports several different frame types. If the IPX/SPX clients are installed, chances are the frame type is incompatible. *See Chapters 5 and 21.*

Appendix B

About the CD

. . . .

On the CD-ROM:

▶ Sample questions and test engine demos from some of the top names in test preparation materials

▶ Some great links I recommend for Network+ test information, study aids, and sample questions

▶ The great QuickLearn game: Outpost to make test preparation fun

▶ The Dummies Certification test engine with lots of sample Network+ questions

. . . .

System Requirements

Make sure that your computer meets the minimum system requirements shown in the following list. If your computer doesn't meet most of these requirements, you may have problems using the contents of the CD.

- ✔ A PC with a 486 or faster processor.

- ✔ Microsoft Windows 95 or later.

- ✔ At least 16MB of total RAM installed on your computer.

- ✔ At least 32MB of available hard drive space to install all the software on this CD. (You need less space if you don't install every program.)

- ✔ A CD-ROM drive — double-speed (2x) or faster.

- ✔ A sound card for PCs.

- ✔ A monitor capable of displaying at least 256 colors or grayscale.

- ✔ A modem with a speed of at least 14,400 bps.

If you need more information on the basics, check out *Networking For Dummies* by Doug Lowe; *Upgrading & Fixing Networks For Dummies* by Bill Camarda; *Windows NT Networking For Dummies* by Ed Tittel, Mary Madden, and Earl Follis; *Networking with NetWare For Dummies* by Ed Tittel, James E. Gaskin, and Earl Follis; *Windows NT Server 4 For Dummies* by Ed Tittel; or *Novell's Encyclopedia of Networking* by Kevin Shafer. (All published by IDG Books Worldwide, Inc.)

Using the CD with Microsoft Windows

Note: To play the QuickLearn game, you must have a Windows 95 or Windows 98 computer — it will not run on Windows NT. You must also have Microsoft DirectX 5.0 or a later version installed. If you do not have DirectX, you can download it at `www.microsoft.com/directx/resources/dx5end.htm`.

Using the CD with Microsoft Windows

To install the items from the CD to your hard drive, follow these steps:

1. **Insert the CD into your computer's CD-ROM drive.**

2. **Click Start⇨Run.**

3. **In the dialog box that appears, type** D:\SETUP.EXE.

4. **Click OK.**

   A License Agreement window appears.

5. **Read through the license agreement, and then click the Accept button if you want to use the CD. After you click Accept, you'll never be bothered by the License Agreement window again.**

   The CD interface Welcome screen appears. The interface is a little program that shows you what's on the CD and coordinates installing the programs and running the demos. The interface basically enables you to click a button or two to make things happen.

6. **Click anywhere on the Welcome screen to enter the interface.**

   The next screen lists categories for the software on the CD.

7. **To view the items within a category, just click the category's name.**

   A list of programs in the category appears.

8. **For more information about a program, click the program's name.**

   Be sure to read the information that appears. Sometimes a program has its own system requirements or requires you to do a few tricks on your computer before you can install or run the program, and this screen tells you what you may need to do, if necessary.

9. **If you don't want to install the program, click the Go Back button to return to the previous screen.**

   You can always return to the previous screen by clicking the Go Back button. This feature enables you to browse the different categories and products and decide what you want to install.

10. **To install a program, click the appropriate Install button.**

    The CD interface drops to the background while the CD installs the program you chose.

11. **To install other items, repeat Steps 7 through 10.**

12. **When you finish installing programs, click the Quit button to close the interface.**

    You can eject the CD now. Carefully place it back in the plastic jacket of the book for safekeeping.

In order to run some of the programs on the *Network+ Certification For Dummies* CD, you need to leave the CD in the CD-ROM drive.

What You'll Find on the CD

The following is a summary of the software included on this CD.

Dummies test prep tools

This CD contains questions related to Network+ Certification. The questions are similar to those you can expect to find on the exams. We've also included some questions on Network+ topics that may or not be on the current tests or even covered in the book, but they are things that you should know to perform your job.

QuickLearn Game

The QuickLearn Game is the *...For Dummies* way of making studying for the Certification exam fun. Well, okay, less painful. OutPost is a DirectX, high-resolution, fast-paced arcade game.

Answer questions to defuse dimensional disrupters and save the universe from a rift in space-time. Missing a few questions on the real exam almost never results in a rip in the fabric of the universe, so just think how easy it will be when you get there!

Practice Test

The Practice Test is designed to help you get comfortable with the Network+ testing situation and pinpoint your strengths and weaknesses on the topic. You can accept the default setting of 60 questions in 60 minutes, or you can customize the settings. You can pick the number of questions, the amount of time, and even decide which objectives you want to focus on.

After you answer the questions, the Practice test gives you plenty of feedback. You can find out which questions you got right or wrong and get statistics on how you did, broken down by objective. Then you can review the questions — all of them, all the ones you missed, all the ones you marked, or a combination of the ones you marked and the ones you missed.

Self-Assessment Test

The Self-Assessment test is designed to simulate the actual Network+ testing situation. You must answer 60 questions in 60 minutes. After you answer all the questions, you find out your score and whether you pass or fail — but that's all the feedback you get. If you can pass the Self-Assessment test fairly easily, you're probably ready to tackle the real thing.

Links Page

I've also created a Links Page, a handy starting place for accessing the huge amounts of information about the Network+ tests on the Internet. You can find the page, Links.htm, at the root of the CD.

Commercial demos

Network+ ExamPrep Exam Simulator, from Super Software, Inc.

This demo, designed to help you prepare for the Network+ certification exam, gives you five practice questions — just enough to get a taste. Get lots more by ordering the software.

Network+ SelfTest PEP, from Self Test Software

Self Test provides 40 more questions in this practice test demo. Visit www.stsware.com for more information about the full product.

If You've Got Problems (Of the CD Kind)

I tried my best to compile programs that work on most computers with the minimum system requirements. Alas, your computer may be somewhat different, and some programs may not work properly for some reason.

The two most likely culprits are that you don't have enough memory (RAM) for the programs you want to use, or that you have other programs running that are affecting installation or running of a program. If you get error messages such as Not enough memory or Setup cannot continue, try one or more of the following procedures and then try using the software again:

🗸 **Turn off any antivirus software monitor that you may have running on your computer.** Installers sometimes mimic virus activity and may make your computer incorrectly believe that it is being infected by a virus.

🗸 **Close all running programs.** The more programs you're running, the less memory is available to other programs. Installers also typically update files and programs; if you keep other programs running, installation may not work properly.

🗸 **In Windows, close the CD interface and run demos or installations directly from Windows Explorer.** The interface itself can tie up system memory or even conflict with certain kinds of interactive demos. Use Windows Explorer to browse the files on the CD and launch installers or demos.

🗸 **Add more RAM to your computer.** This is, admittedly, a drastic and somewhat expensive step. However, if you have a Windows 95 PC, adding more memory can really help the speed of your computer and enable more programs to run at the same time.

If you still have trouble installing the items from the CD, please call the IDG Books Worldwide Customer Service phone number: 800-762-2974 (outside the U.S.: 317-596-5430).

Index

• Q •

QuickLearn Game
  system requirements for playing, 412
  test prep tool on the CD, 413

• R •

radio frequency interference (RFI),
    effect on network cable, 105
RAID (Redundant Array of Independent
    Disks), 53–54
RAID level 0, minimum number of disk
    drives needed for, 53
RAID level 1, minimum number of disk
    drives needed for, 53–54
RAID level 5, minimum number of disk
    drives needed for, 53–54
RAID level 10, 53
READ, NetWare security rights, 86
Read-only property, in NetWare and
    Windows NT, 83
Read-write property, in NetWare, 83
real-time clock, IRQ assignment, 147
redirectors, 97
Redundant Array of Independent Disks
    (RAID), levels and number of disk
    drives required for, 53–54
registered ports, 230
registration, for Network+ exam, 20–21
Remote Access Services, for Windows
    NT security services, 89
remote connectivity
  percentage of exam questions about,
    13, 255
  and protocols, 255–270
  study plan for exam, 25
remote printer, Windows NT, 91
remote procedure call (RPC), remote file
    access with, 96
repair policies, as part of network
    maintenance policy, 332

repeaters
  as network connectivity devices,
    149–150
  operation of at Physical layer, 129
  as Physical layer connectivity devices,
    46–47
resource sharing, on networks, 62–63
RG-8 cable, 108
RG-11 cable, 108
RG-58 cable, 108
RG-59 cable, 108
ribbon cable, 45
ring network topology, 67–68, 69
RIP (Routing Information Protocol)
  routing algorithm, 176
  TCP/IP suite protocol, 134
  Windows NT routing services provided
    by, 90
RIP (IPX), as part of IntraNetWare
    software bundle, 88
riser cable, 45
RJ-11 plug, for connecting modems, 260
RJ-45 connector, 298
  for UTP cable, 52, 112
routable protocols, 49
  versus nonroutable protocols, 177
ROUTE, TCP/IP utility, 203
ROUTE command, displaying routing
    information with, 244, 245
routers, 49
  advantages of, 173
  versus bridges, 173
  as Network layer connectivity devices,
    46, 172
  as primary Network layer devices, 130
  providing multiple paths through
    network segments with, 172
  routing tables, 174–175
routing, process of on the Network
    layer, 169
routing algorithms, used by routers to
    calculate routes, 176

From PCs
to Personal Finance,
We Make it Fun and Easy!

ISBN 0-7645-0435-5
$19.99 US/$28.99 CAN

ISBN 0-7645-5013-6
$19.99 US/$26.99 CAN

**For more information,
or to order, please
call 800.762.2974.**

**www.idgbooks.com
www.dummies.com**

Dummies Books™
Bestsellers on Every Topic!

TECHNOLOGY TITLES

INTERNET

America Online® For Dummies®, 5th Edition	John Kaufeld	0-7645-0502-5	$19.99 US/$26.99 CA
E-Mail For Dummies®, 2nd Edition	John R. Levine, Carol Baroudi, Margaret Levine Young, & Arnold Reinhold	0-7645-0131-3	$24.99 US/$34.99 CA
Genealogy Online For Dummies®	Matthew L. Helm & April Leah Helm	0-7645-0377-4	$24.99 US/$35.99 CA
Internet Directory For Dummies®, 2nd Edition	Brad Hill	0-7645-0436-3	$24.99 US/$35.99 CA
The Internet For Dummies®, 6th Edition	John R. Levine, Carol Baroudi, & Margaret Levine Young	0-7645-0506-8	$19.99 US/$28.99 CA
Investing Online For Dummies®, 2nd Edition	Kathleen Sindell, Ph.D.	0-7645-0509-2	$24.99 US/$35.99 CA
World Wide Web Searching For Dummies®, 2nd Edition	Brad Hill	0-7645-0264-6	$24.99 US/$34.99 CA

OPERATING SYSTEMS

DOS For Dummies®, 3rd Edition	Dan Gookin	0-7645-0361-8	$19.99 US/$28.99 CA
LINUX® For Dummies®, 2nd Edition	John Hall, Craig Witherspoon, & Coletta Witherspoon	0-7645-0421-5	$24.99 US/$35.99 CA
Mac® OS 8 For Dummies®	Bob LeVitus	0-7645-0271-9	$19.99 US/$26.99 CA
Small Business Windows® 98 For Dummies®	Stephen Nelson	0-7645-0425-8	$24.99 US/$35.99 CA
UNIX® For Dummies®, 4th Edition	John R. Levine & Margaret Levine Young	0-7645-0419-3	$19.99 US/$28.99 CA
Windows® 95 For Dummies®, 2nd Edition	Andy Rathbone	0-7645-0180-1	$19.99 US/$26.99 CA
Windows® 98 For Dummies®	Andy Rathbone	0-7645-0261-1	$19.99 US/$28.99 CA

PC/GENERAL COMPUTING

Buying a Computer For Dummies®	Dan Gookin	0-7645-0313-8	$19.99 US/$28.99 CA
Illustrated Computer Dictionary For Dummies®, 3rd Edition	Dan Gookin & Sandra Hardin Gookin	0-7645-0143-7	$19.99 US/$26.99 CA
Modems For Dummies®, 3rd Edition	Tina Rathbone	0-7645-0069-4	$19.99 US/$26.99 CA
Small Business Computing For Dummies®	Brian Underdahl	0-7645-0287-5	$24.99 US/$35.99 CA
Upgrading & Fixing PCs For Dummies®, 4th Edition	Andy Rathbone	0-7645-0418-5	$19.99 US/$28.99CA

GENERAL INTEREST TITLES

FOOD & BEVERAGE/ENTERTAINING

Entertaining For Dummies®	Suzanne Williamson with Linda Smith	0-7645-5027-6	$19.99 US/$26.99 CA
Gourmet Cooking For Dummies®	Charlie Trotter	0-7645-5029-2	$19.99 US/$26.99 CA
Grilling For Dummies®	Marie Rama & John Mariani	0-7645-5076-4	$19.99 US/$26.99 CA
Italian Cooking For Dummies®	Cesare Casella & Jack Bishop	0-7645-5098-5	$19.99 US/$26.99 CA
Wine For Dummies®, 2nd Edition	Ed McCarthy & Mary Ewing-Mulligan	0-7645-5114-0	$19.99 US/$26.99 CA

SPORTS

Baseball For Dummies®	Joe Morgan with Richard Lally	0-7645-5085-3	$19.99 US/$26.99 CA
Fly Fishing For Dummies®	Peter Kaminsky	0-7645-5073-X	$19.99 US/$26.99 CA
Football For Dummies®	Howie Long with John Czarnecki	0-7645-5054-5	$19.99 US/$26.99 CA
Hockey For Dummies®	John Davidson with John Steinbreder	0-7645-5045-4	$19.99 US/$26.99 CA
Tennis For Dummies®	Patrick McEnroe with Peter Bodo	0-7645-5087-X	$19.99 US/$26.99 CA

HOME & GARDEN

Decks & Patios For Dummies®	Robert J. Beckstrom & National Gardening Association	0-7645-5075-6	$16.99 US/$24.99 CA
Flowering Bulbs For Dummies®	Judy Glattstein & National Gardening Association	0-7645-5103-5	$16.99 US/$24.99 CA
Home Improvement For Dummies®	Gene & Katie Hamilton & the Editors of HouseNet, Inc.	0-7645-5005-5	$19.99 US/$26.99 CA
Lawn Care For Dummies®	Lance Walheim & National Gardening Association	0-7645-5077-2	$16.99 US/$24.99 CA

IDG
BOOKS
WORLDWIDE

For more information, or to order, call (800)762-2974

BESTS
BOOK

Dummies Books™
Bestsellers on Every Topic!

TECHNOLOGY TITLES

SUITES

Microsoft® Office 2000 For Windows® For Dummies®	Wallace Wang & Roger C. Parker	0-7645-0452-5	$19.99 US/$28.99 CAN
Microsoft® Office 2000 For Windows® For Dummies®, Quick Reference	Doug Lowe & Bjoern Hartsfvang	0-7645-0453-3	$12.99 US/$19.99 CAN
Microsoft® Office 4 For Windows® For Dummies®	Roger C. Parker	1-56884-183-3	$19.95 US/$26.95 CAN
Microsoft® Office 97 For Windows® For Dummies®	Wallace Wang & Roger C. Parker	0-7645-0050-3	$19.99 US/$26.99 CAN
Microsoft® Office 97 For Windows® For Dummies®, Quick Reference	Doug Lowe	0-7645-0062-7	$12.99 US/$17.99 CAN
Microsoft® Office 98 For Macs® For Dummies®	Tom Negrino	0-7645-0229-8	$19.99 US/$28.99 CAN

WORD PROCESSING

Word 2000 For Windows® For Dummies®, Quick Reference	Peter Weverka	0-7645-0449-5	$12.99 US/$19.99 CAN
Corel® WordPerfect® 8 For Windows® For Dummies®	Margaret Levine Young, David Kay, & Jordan Young	0-7645-0186-0	$19.99 US/$26.99 CAN
Word 2000 For Windows® For Dummies®	Dan Gookin	0-7645-0448-7	$19.99 US/$28.99 CAN
Word For Windows® 95 For Dummies®	Dan Gookin	1-56884-932-X	$19.99 US/$26.99 CAN
Word 97 For Windows® For Dummies®	Dan Gookin	0-7645-0052-X	$19.99 US/$26.99 CAN
WordPerfect® 6.1 For Windows® For Dummies®, Quick Reference, 2nd Edition	Margaret Levine Young & David Kay	1-56884-966-4	$9.99 US/$12.99 CAN
WordPerfect® 7 For Windows® 95 For Dummies®	Margaret Levine Young & David Kay	1-56884-949-4	$19.99 US/$26.99 CAN
Word Pro® for Windows® 95 For Dummies®	Jim Meade	1-56884-232-5	$19.99 US/$26.99 CAN

SPREADSHEET/FINANCE/PROJECT MANAGEMENT

Excel For Windows® 95 For Dummies®	Greg Harvey	1-56884-930-3	$19.99 US/$26.99 CAN
Excel 2000 For Windows® For Dummies®	Greg Harvey	0-7645-0446-0	$19.99 US/$28.99 CAN
Excel 2000 For Windows® For Dummies® Quick Reference	John Walkenbach	0-7645-0447-9	$12.99 US/$19.99 CAN
Microsoft® Money 98 For Dummies®	Peter Weverka	0-7645-0295-6	$24.99 US/$34.99 CAN
Microsoft® Money 99 For Dummies®	Peter Weverka	0-7645-0433-9	$19.99 US/$28.99 CAN
Microsoft® Project 98 For Dummies®	Martin Doucette	0-7645-0321-9	$24.99 US/$34.99 CAN
MORE Excel 97 For Windows® For Dummies®	Greg Harvey	0-7645-0138-0	$22.99 US/$32.99 CAN
Quicken® 98 For Windows® For Dummies®	Stephen L. Nelson	0-7645-0243-3	$19.99 US/$26.99 CAN

GENERAL INTEREST TITLES

EDUCATION & TEST PREPARATION

The ACT For Dummies®	Suzee Vlk	1-56884-387-9	$14.99 US/$21.99 CAN
College Financial Aid For Dummies®	Dr. Herm Davis & Joyce Lain Kennedy	0-7645-5049-7	$19.99 US/$26.99 CAN
College Planning For Dummies®, 2nd Edition	Pat Ordovensky	0-7645-5048-9	$19.99 US/$26.99 CAN
Everyday Math For Dummies®	Charles Seiter, Ph.D.	1-56884-248-1	$14.99 US/$22.99 CAN
The GMAT® For Dummies®, 3rd Edition	Suzee Vlk	0-7645-5082-9	$16.99 US/$24.99 CAN
The GRE® For Dummies®, 3rd Edition	Suzee Vlk	0-7645-5083-7	$16.99 US/$24.99 CAN
Politics For Dummies®	Ann DeLaney	1-56884-381-X	$19.99 US/$26.99 CAN
The SAT I For Dummies®, 3rd Edition	Suzee Vlk	0-7645-5044-6	$14.99 US/$21.99 CAN

CAREERS

Cover Letters For Dummies®	Joyce Lain Kennedy	1-56884-395-X	$12.99 US/$17.99 CAN
Cool Careers For Dummies®	Marty Nemko, Paul Edwards, & Sarah Edwards	0-7645-5095-0	$16.99 US/$24.99 CAN
Job Hunting For Dummies®	Max Messmer	1-56884-388-7	$16.99 US/$24.99 CAN
Job Interviews For Dummies®	Joyce Lain Kennedy	1-56884-859-5	$12.99 US/$17.99 CAN
Resumes For Dummies®, 2nd Edition	Joyce Lain Kennedy	0-7645-5113-2	$12.99 US/$17.99 CAN

For more information, or to order, call (800)762-2974

BESTSELLING BOOK SERIES

Dummies Books™
Bestsellers on Every Topic!

TECHNOLOGY TITLES

WEB DESIGN & PUBLISHING

Title	Author	ISBN	Price
Creating Web Pages For Dummies®, 4th Edition	Bud Smith & Arthur Bebak	0-7645-0504-1	$24.99 US/$34.99 CA
FrontPage® 98 For Dummies®	Asha Dornfest	0-7645-0270-0	$24.99 US/$34.99 CA
HTML 4 For Dummies®	Ed Tittel & Stephen Nelson James	0-7645-0331-6	$29.99 US/$42.99 CA
Java™ For Dummies®, 2nd Edition	Aaron E. Walsh	0-7645-0140-2	$24.99 US/$34.99 CA
PageMill™ 2 For Dummies®	Deke McClelland & John San Filippo	0-7645-0028-7	$24.99 US/$34.99 CA

DESKTOP PUBLISHING GRAPHICS/MULTIMEDIA

CorelDRAW™ 8 For Dummies®	Deke McClelland	0-7645-0317-0	$19.99 US/$26.99 CA
Desktop Publishing and Design For Dummies®	Roger C. Parker	1-56884-234-1	$19.99 US/$26.99 CA
Digital Photography For Dummies®, 2nd Edition	Julie Adair King	0-7645-0431-2	$19.99 US/$28.99 CA
Microsoft® Publisher 97 For Dummies®	Barry Sosinsky, Christopher Benz & Jim McCarter	0-7645-0148-8	$19.99 US/$26.99 CA
Microsoft® Publisher 98 For Dummies®	Jim McCarter	0-7645-0395-2	$19.99 US/$28.99 CA

MACINTOSH

Macs® For Dummies®, 6th Edition	David Pogue	0-7645-0398-7	$19.99 US/$28.99 CA
Macs® For Teachers™, 3rd Edition	Michelle Robinette	0-7645-0226-3	$24.99 US/$34.99 CA
The iMac For Dummies	David Pogue	0-7645-0495-9	$19.99 US/$26.99 CA

GENERAL INTEREST TITLES

BUSINESS & PERSONAL FINANCE

Accounting For Dummies®	John A. Tracy, CPA	0-7645-5014-4	$19.99 US/$26.99 CA
Business Plans For Dummies®	Paul Tiffany, Ph.D. & Steven D. Peterson, Ph.D.	1-56884-868-4	$19.99 US/$26.99 CA
Consulting For Dummies®	Bob Nelson & Peter Economy	0-7645-5034-9	$19.99 US/$26.99 CA
Customer Service For Dummies®	Karen Leland & Keith Bailey	1-56884-391-7	$19.99 US/$26.99 CA
Home Buying For Dummies®	Eric Tyson, MBA & Ray Brown	1-56884-385-2	$16.99 US/$24.99 CA
House Selling For Dummies®	Eric Tyson, MBA & Ray Brown	0-7645-5038-1	$16.99 US/$24.99 CA
Investing For Dummies®	Eric Tyson, MBA	1-56884-393-3	$19.99 US/$26.99 CA
Law For Dummies®	John Ventura	1-56884-860-9	$19.99 US/$26.99 CA
Managing For Dummies®	Bob Nelson & Peter Economy	1-56884-858-7	$19.99 US/$26.99 CA
Marketing For Dummies®	Alexander Hiam	1-56884-699-1	$19.99 US/$26.99 CA
Mutual Funds For Dummies®, 2nd Edition	Eric Tyson, MBA	0-7645-5112-4	$19.99 US/$26.99 CA
Negotiating For Dummies®	Michael C. Donaldson & Mimi Donaldson	1-56884-867-6	$19.99 US/$26.99 CA
Personal Finance For Dummies®, 2nd Edition	Eric Tyson, MBA	0-7645-5013-6	$19.99 US/$26.99 CA
Personal Finance For Dummies® For Canadians	Eric Tyson, MBA & Tony Martin	1-56884-378-X	$18.99 US/$24.99 CA
Sales Closing For Dummies®	Tom Hopkins	0-7645-5063-2	$14.99 US/$21.99 CA
Sales Prospecting For Dummies®	Tom Hopkins	0-7645-5066-7	$14.99 US/$21.99 CA
Selling For Dummies®	Tom Hopkins	1-56884-389-5	$16.99 US/$24.99 CA
Small Business For Dummies®	Eric Tyson, MBA & Jim Schell	0-7645-5094-2	$19.99 US/$26.99 CA
Small Business Kit For Dummies®	Richard D. Harroch	0-7645-5093-4	$24.99 US/$34.99 CA
Successful Presentations For Dummies®	Malcolm Kushner	1-56884-392-5	$16.99 US/$24.99 CA
Time Management For Dummies®	Jeffrey J. Mayer	1-56884-360-7	$16.99 US/$24.99 CA

AUTOMOTIVE

Title	Author	ISBN	Price
Auto Repair For Dummies®	Deanna Sclar	0-7645-5089-6	$19.99 US/$26.99 CA
Buying A Car For Dummies®	Deanna Sclar	0-7645-5091-8	$16.99 US/$24.99 CA
Car Care For Dummies®: The Glove Compartment Guide	Deanna Sclar	0-7645-5090-X	$9.99 US/$13.99 CAN

IDG BOOKS WORLDWIDE

For more information, or to order,
call (800)762-2974

Dummies Books™
Bestsellers on Every Topic!

TECHNOLOGY TITLES

ATABASE

ccess 2000 For Windows® For Dummies®	John Kaufeld	0-7645-0444-4	$19.99 US/$28.99 CAN
ccess 97 For Windows® For Dummies®	John Kaufeld	0-7645-0048-1	$19.99 US/$26.99 CAN
pproach® 97 For Windows® For Dummies®	Deborah S. Ray & Eric J. Ray	0-7645-0001-5	$19.99 US/$26.99 CAN
rystal Reports 7 For Dummies®	Douglas J. Wolf	0-7645-0548-3	$24.99 US/$34.99 CAN
ata Warehousing For Dummies®	Alan R. Simon	0-7645-0170-4	$24.99 US/$34.99 CAN
ileMaker® Pro 4 For Dummies®	Tom Maremaa	0-7645-0210-7	$19.99 US/$26.99 CAN
tranet & Web Databases For Dummies®	Paul Litwin	0-7645-0221-2	$29.99 US/$42.99 CAN

ETWORKING

uilding An Intranet For Dummies®	John Fronckowiak	0-7645-0276-X	$29.99 US/$42.99 CAN
c: Mail™ For Dummies®	Victor R. Garza	0-7645-0055-4	$19.99 US/$26.99 CAN
lient/Server Computing For Dummies®, 2nd Edition	Doug Lowe	0-7645-0066-X	$24.99 US/$34.99 CAN
otus Notes® Release 4 For Dummies®	Stephen Londergan & Pat Freeland	1-56884-934-6	$19.99 US/$26.99 CAN
etworking For Dummies®, 4th Edition	Doug Lowe	0-7645-0498-3	$19.99 US/$28.99 CAN
pgrading & Fixing Networks For Dummies®	Bill Camarda	0-7645-0347-2	$29.99 US/$42.99 CAN
indows NT® Networking For Dummies®	Ed Tittel, Mary Madden, & Earl Follis	0-7645-0015-5	$24.99 US/$34.99 CAN

GENERAL INTEREST TITLES

HE ARTS

lues For Dummies®	Lonnie Brooks, Cub Koda, & Wayne Baker Brooks	0-7645-5080-2	$24.99 US/$34.99 CAN
lassical Music For Dummies®	David Pogue & Scott Speck	0-7645-5009-8	$24.99 US/$34.99 CAN
uitar For Dummies®	Mark Phillips & Jon Chappell of Cherry Lane Music	0-7645-5106-X	$24.99 US/$34.99 CAN
azz For Dummies®	Dirk Sutro	0-7645-5081-0	$24.99 US/$34.99 CAN
pera For Dummies®	David Pogue & Scott Speck	0-7645-5010-1	$24.99 US/$34.99 CAN
iano For Dummies®	Blake Neely of Cherry Lane Music	0-7645-5105-1	$24.99 US/$34.99 CAN

EALTH & FITNESS

eauty Secrets For Dummies®	Stephanie Seymour	0-7645-5078-0	$19.99 US/$26.99 CAN
itness For Dummies®	Suzanne Schlosberg & Liz Neporent, M.A.	1-56884-866-8	$19.99 US/$26.99 CAN
utrition For Dummies®	Carol Ann Rinzler	0-7645-5032-2	$19.99 US/$26.99 CAN
ex For Dummies®	Dr. Ruth K. Westheimer	1-56884-384-4	$16.99 US/$24.99 CAN
eight Training For Dummies®	Liz Neporent, M.A. & Suzanne Schlosberg	0-7645-5036-5	$19.99 US/$26.99 CAN

FESTYLE/SELF-HELP

ating For Dummies®	Dr. Joy Browne	0-7645-5072-1	$19.99 US/$26.99 CAN
arenting For Dummies®	Sandra H. Gookin	1-56884-383-6	$16.99 US/$24.99 CAN
uccess For Dummies®	Zig Ziglar	0-7645-5061-6	$19.99 US/$26.99 CAN
eddings For Dummies®	Marcy Blum & Laura Fisher Kaiser	0-7645-5055-1	$19.99 US/$26.99 CAN

G
OKS
WIDE

For more information, or to order,
call (800)762-2974

BESTSELLING
BOOK SERIES

IDG Books Worldwide, Inc., End-User License Agreement

READ THIS. You should carefully read these terms and conditions before opening the software packet(s) included with this book ("Book"). This is a license agreement ("Agreement") between you and IDG Books Worldwide, Inc. ("IDGB"). By opening the accompanying software packet(s), you acknowledge that you have read and accept the following terms and conditions. If you do not agree and do not want to be bound by such terms and conditions, promptly return the Book and the unopened software packet(s) to the place you obtained them for a full refund.

1. **License Grant.** IDGB grants to you (either an individual or entity) a nonexclusive license to use one copy of the enclosed software program(s) (collectively, the "Software") solely for your own personal or business purposes on a single computer (whether a standard computer or a workstation component of a multiuser network). The Software is in use on a computer when it is loaded into temporary memory (RAM) or installed into permanent memory (hard disk, CD-ROM, or other storage device). IDGB reserves all rights not expressly granted herein.

2. **Ownership.** IDGB is the owner of all right, title, and interest, including copyright, in and to the compilation of the Software recorded on the disk(s) or CD-ROM ("Software Media"). Copyright to the individual programs recorded on the Software Media is owned by the author or other authorized copyright owner of each program. Ownership of the Software and all proprietary rights relating thereto remain with IDGB and its licensers.

3. **Restrictions on Use and Transfer.**

    (a) You may only (i) make one copy of the Software for backup or archival purposes, or (ii) transfer the Software to a single hard disk, provided that you keep the original for backup or archival purposes. You may not (i) rent or lease the Software, (ii) copy or reproduce the Software through a LAN or other network system or through any computer subscriber system or bulletin-board system, or (iii) modify, adapt, or create derivative works based on the Software.

    (b) You may not reverse engineer, decompile, or disassemble the Software. You may transfer the Software and user documentation on a permanent basis, provided that the transferee agrees to accept the terms and conditions of this Agreement and you retain no copies. If the Software is an update or has been updated, any transfer must include the most recent update and all prior versions.

4. **Restrictions on Use of Individual Programs.** You must follow the individual requirements and restrictions detailed for each individual program in the "About the CD" appendix of this Book. These limitations are also contained in the individual license agreements recorded on the Software Media. These limitations may include a requirement that after using the program for a specified period of time, the user must pay a registration fee or discontinue use. By opening the Software packet(s), you will be agreeing to abide by the licenses and restrictions for these individual programs that are detailed in the "About the CD" appendix and on the Software Media. None of the material on this Software Media or listed in this Book may ever be redistributed, in original or modified form, for commercial purposes.

5. **Limited Warranty.**

   (a) IDGB warrants that the Software and Software Media are free from defects in materials and workmanship under normal use for a period of sixty (60) days from the date of purchase of this Book. If IDGB receives notification within the warranty period of defects in materials or workmanship, IDGB will replace the defective Software Media.

   (b) **IDGB AND THE AUTHOR OF THE BOOK DISCLAIM ALL OTHER WARRANTIES, EXPRESS OR IMPLIED, INCLUDING WITHOUT LIMITATION IMPLIED WARRANTIES OF MERCHANTABILITY AND FITNESS FOR A PARTICULAR PURPOSE, WITH RESPECT TO THE SOFTWARE, THE PROGRAMS, THE SOURCE CODE CONTAINED THEREIN, AND/OR THE TECHNIQUES DESCRIBED IN THIS BOOK. IDGB DOES NOT WARRANT THAT THE FUNCTIONS CONTAINED IN THE SOFTWARE WILL MEET YOUR REQUIREMENTS OR THAT THE OPERATION OF THE SOFTWARE WILL BE ERROR FREE.**

   (c) This limited warranty gives you specific legal rights, and you may have other rights that vary from jurisdiction to jurisdiction.

6. **Remedies.**

   (a) IDGB's entire liability and your exclusive remedy for defects in materials and workmanship shall be limited to replacement of the Software Media, which may be returned to IDGB with a copy of your receipt at the following address: Software Media Fulfillment Department, Attn.: *Network+ Certification For Dummies*, IDG Books Worldwide, Inc., 7260 Shadeland Station, Ste. 100, Indianapolis, IN 46256, or call 800-762-2974. Please allow three to four weeks for delivery. This Limited Warranty is void if failure of the Software Media has resulted from accident, abuse, or misapplication. Any replacement Software Media will be warranted for the remainder of the original warranty period or thirty (30) days, whichever is longer.

   (b) In no event shall IDGB or the author be liable for any damages whatsoever (including without limitation damages for loss of business profits, business interruption, loss of business information, or any other pecuniary loss) arising from the use of or inability to use the Book or the Software, even if IDGB has been advised of the possibility of such damages.

   (c) Because some jurisdictions do not allow the exclusion or limitation of liability for consequential or incidental damages, the above limitation or exclusion may not apply to you.

7. **U.S. Government Restricted Rights.** Use, duplication, or disclosure of the Software by the U.S. Government is subject to restrictions stated in paragraph (c)(1)(ii) of the Rights in Technical Data and Computer Software clause of DFARS 252.227-7013, and in subparagraphs (a) through (d) of the Commercial Computer–Restricted Rights clause at FAR 52.227-19, and in similar clauses in the NASA FAR supplement, when applicable.

8. **General.** This Agreement constitutes the entire understanding of the parties and revokes and supersedes all prior agreements, oral or written, between them and may not be modified or amended except in a writing signed by both parties hereto that specifically refers to this Agreement. This Agreement shall take precedence over any other documents that may be in conflict herewith. If any one or more provisions contained in this Agreement are held by any court or tribunal to be invalid, illegal, or otherwise unenforceable, each and every other provision shall remain in full force and effect.

Installation Instructions

To install the items from the CD to your hard drive, follow these steps.

1. **Insert the CD into your computer's CD-ROM drive.**

2. **Click Start⇨Run.**

3. **In the dialog box that appears, type D:\SETUP.EXE.**

4. **Click OK.**

   A License Agreement window opens.

5. **Read through the license agreement, and then click the Accept button. if you want to use the CD.**

6. **Click anywhere on the Welcome screen that appears to enter the interface.**

   The next screen lists categories for the software on the CD.

7. **To view the items within a category, just click the category's name.**

   A list of programs in the category appears.

8. **For more information about a program, click the program's name.**

9. **If you don't want to install the program, click the Go Back button to return to the previous screen.**

10. **To install a program, click the appropriate Install button.**

    The CD interface drops to the background while the CD installs the program you chose.

11. **To install other items, repeat Steps 7 through 10.**

12. **When you finish installing programs, click the Quit button to close the interface.**

IDG BOOKS WORLDWIDE. BOOK REGISTRATION

We want to hear from you!

Visit **http://my2cents.dummies.com** to register this book and tell us how you liked it!

- ✔ Get entered in our monthly prize giveaway.
- ✔ Give us feedback about this book — tell us what you like best, what you like least, or maybe what you'd like to ask the author and us to change!
- ✔ Let us know any other ...*For Dummies*® topics that interest you.

Your feedback helps us determine what books to publish, tells us what coverage to add as we revise our books, and lets us know whether we're meeting your needs as a ...*For Dummies* reader. You're our most valuable resource, and what you have to say is important to us!

Not on the Web yet? It's easy to get started with *Dummies 101*®: *The Internet For Windows*® *98* or *The Internet For Dummies*® 6th Edition, at local retailers everywhere.

Or let us know what you think by sending us a letter at the following address:

...*For Dummies* Book Registration
Dummies Press
7260 Shadeland Station, Suite 100
Indianapolis, IN 46256-3945
Fax 317-596-5498

BESTSELLING BOOK SERIES FROM IDG